Working Knowledge

Working

How Organizations Manage What They Know

Knowledge

THOMAS H. DAVENPORT   LAURENCE PRUSAK

HARVARD BUSINESS SCHOOL PRESS   *Boston, Massachusetts*

Published by the Harvard Business School Press in hardcover, 1998; in paperback, 2000

The Library of Congress has catalogued the hardcover edition of this title as follows:

Davenport, Thomas H., 1954–
    Working knowledge : how organizations manage what they know / Thomas H. Davenport,
    Laurence Prusak.
        p. cm.
    Includes bibliographical references and index.
    ISBN 0-87584-655-6 (alk. paper)
    1. Organizational learning. 2. Information resources management. 3. Industrial manage-
ment. I. Prusak, Laurence. II. Title.
HD58.82.D38   1998
658.4'03—dc21   97-10781
                                                                                 CIP

ISBN 1-57851-301-4 (pbk)

The paper used in this publication meets the requirements of the American National Standard
for Permanence of Paper for Publications and Documents in Libraries and Archives Z39.48-
1992.

The title of this book is not related to the registered trademark WORKING KNOWLEDGE.

346098

Contents

Preface to the Paperback Edition   vii

Acknowledgments   xvi

Introduction   xviii

1   What Do We Talk about When We Talk about Knowledge?   1

2   The Promise and Challenge of Knowledge Markets   25

3   Knowledge Generation   52

4   Knowledge Codification and Coordination   68

5   Knowledge Transfer   88

6   Knowledge Roles and Skills   107

7   Technologies for Knowledge Management   123

8   Knowledge Management Projects in Practice   144

9   The Pragmatics of Knowledge Management   162

Notes   179

Index   189

Other Books by Thomas H. Davenport and
Laurence Prusak   198

About the Authors   199

Preface to the Paperback Edition

W H E N   W E published the hardcover edition of *Working Knowledge* in 1998, we had no idea where the concept of knowledge management was in its life cycle within organizations. As it turned out, the idea was still in its infancy. In retrospect, we can see that the steps taken by the firms we described in the first edition were the easy ones—the walking before the running. These beginning steps were and still are necessary, but now that some organizations have mastered walking, the challenge of running looms.

What is also clear to us from this vantage point is how far the knowledge management movement has come. By now most managers have heard of it, and many have become advocates and practitioners. More and more companies have instituted knowledge repositories, supporting such diverse types of knowledge as best practices, lessons learned, product development knowledge, customer knowledge, human resource management knowledge, methods-based knowledge, and so forth. Groupware and intranet-based technologies have become standard knowledge infrastructures. A new set of professional job titles—the knowledge manager, the knowledge coordinator, the knowledge-network facilitator—affirms the widespread legitimacy that knowledge management has earned in the corporate world, as does the formation of its own professional association. Some organizations, including our own employers, now have hundreds of knowledge managers in place.

Other signs of the broad acceptance of knowledge management abound. There are several magazines, journals, and newsletters devoted to the field. Almost every leading consulting firm provides some sort of knowledge management service for clients. Prominent business schools offer courses and programs on the topic. Many mainstream vendors of information technology tout the applications of their particular tools to the management of knowledge. Even during a period of considerable technological ferment—including the Year 2000 conversion and the rise of electronic commerce—knowledge management continues to thrive at some of the world's largest software and hardware firms. By all accounts, knowledge management is well on its way to becoming an essential feature of advanced business culture.

Benefits of the Knowledge Management Concept

In addition to fostering many initiatives in firms, the knowledge management movement can be credited with another substantial achievement: getting the business world to focus on something other than data. As we noted in the hardcover edition, knowledge management initiatives almost always include some mix of information and knowledge, and it's not always easy to disentangle the two. But almost every organization can now distinguish between knowledge and data, and we've observed several instances in which someone in an organization tried to include data in a knowledge repository and was rebuffed. Perhaps never again will an executive feel that all forms of information are being well-managed without considering whether that information is being transformed into knowledge.

In place of this fixation on data has arisen a focus on human interaction. Whether they choose to call them communities of interest, communities of practice, or knowledge networks, many firms have encouraged the formation of social groups within their organizations to help stimulate knowledge flows. In the firms that have been most aggressive at community-building (including Andersen Consulting, DaimlerChrysler, Ernst & Young, IBM, Intel, USAA, the World Bank, Xerox, and many more), the communities have begun to constitute a critical, if somewhat tacit, dimension of organizational structure, reinforcing group cohesion not only through electronic communications across geographical boundaries but also by a renewed emphasis on face-to-face socialization. While we discussed the significance of these knowledge communities in the hardcover edition, we have been amazed at how extensively they have proliferated.

Perhaps the best news about the rise of knowledge management is that it has helped business leaders realize that technology doesn't hold all the answers. The emerging mindset within the vast majority of the firms we've observed is that successful knowledge management must entail cultural and organizational change as well as technological innovation. This was not generally a perspective that marked traditional management approaches to data and information. While not all organizations that have adopted knowledge management have made substantial headway in their push toward more knowledge-friendly cultures and behaviors, they are at least aware of the roadblocks and are attempting to steer in the right direction. It would not be a paltry legacy for knowledge management to have made individuals and organizations mindful of the social and human factors that influence all forms of information management, not just the pursuit of knowledge.

The Challenges Ahead

Impressive as this progress has been, we feel it's important to reiterate that it represents only the first phase of knowledge management's potential impact on organizational dynamics. The steps most companies have taken thus far could be accomplished without substantial change in how the organization does business. But firms that have reached the initial plateau of knowledge management now realize that using knowledge for long-term business advantage requires change in many core aspects of the business. In the first phase, the emphasis typically centers on the knowledge management project, which we described in Chapter 8 of *Working Knowledge.* Indeed, almost every firm we researched for the book had one or more projects underway. Projects are a good way to get started with knowledge management, but they are by definition peripheral to the rest of the business. Projects "bottle up" knowledge and treat it as something separate. What firms must do in the second phase of knowledge management is to integrate it with familiar aspects of the business: strategy, process, culture, behavior.

Linking Knowledge to Business Strategy

For the most mature knowledge-managing organizations today, the challenge that lies ahead is forging this link between knowledge management and fundamental business strategy. Business academics and economists have long stressed the internal role knowledge plays in business strategy and organizational performance. Nonetheless, these findings have only rarely made their way into practice. Although most knowledge management projects do improve the efficiency or effectiveness of individual departments or business processes, these results generally give CEOs and stockholders little to get excited about. By and large, the firms that have implemented highly strategic knowledge applications are those already in the business of selling knowledge, such as consulting firms, software developers, and print or Internet content publishers. As yet, there are few companies in other business sectors leveraging knowledge management in ways that really matter to long-term success.

For some organizations, the most viable model may be to *make* knowledge the product. Existing products and services can be redefined as knowledge assets, or augmented with knowledge of how they are used. This is the approach taken by James Wolfensohn at the World Bank. Shortly after his appointment as CEO, Wolfensohn announced in 1996 that the bank's mission, previously predicated on lending money to developing nations, would shift. Henceforth the bank would become "the knowledge bank" and would dispense development-oriented knowledge on the same level of importance as the money it loaned. For the last several years the World Bank has been putting in place the underlying strategies, processes, and behaviors to make "the knowledge bank" a reality.

How can knowledge management be linked to strategy when knowledge isn't the product? What this type of firm needs is not a knowledge management strategy, but a business strategy supported by knowledge. Assuming your company has a well-defined strategy, the objective is to determine how the more effective use of knowledge can support or enhance it. If your company is driven by the introduction of new products and services, then your strongest knowledge management efforts should probably be devoted to managing research or product development knowledge. If marketing is the function that drives your success, then you should be thinking about how to manage pricing knowledge, promotion knowledge, and product location knowledge, or how to turn customer data into customer knowledge. If your firm depends on the success of relatively autonomous franchises, you should try to facilitate franchise-based innovations and the exchange of knowledge among franchisees. We have found that it's not terribly difficult to envision ways of using knowledge more effectively in business strategy. The difficulty, of course, is in making the changes to strategic programs and adopting the necessary behaviors throughout your organization.

Linking Knowledge to Work Processes

As the knowledge management movement continues to evolve, it's clear that real success won't come from simply grafting knowledge activities onto existing work processes. Everyone today is already too busy; we don't have time to add knowledge management on top of our jobs. Expecting knowledge workers to peruse repositories of lessons and experiences in their spare time, or to share their own learnings at leisure, is highly unrealistic. Therefore, the knowledge management process has to be "baked" into key knowledge work processes. How companies create, gather, store, share, and apply knowledge must blend well with how market researchers, scientists, consultants, engineers, and managers work on a daily basis.

One measure that holds promise is to redesign the knowledge work processes from scratch, or at least to fine-tune them incrementally by examining how they might better channel the flow of knowledge. While knowledge workers may view their work in unstructured terms, it is possible to view knowledge work as a somewhat structured process that can be designed and improved. From what we've observed, many companies have yet to explore this avenue. In U.S. and European firms, knowledge work processes have not been commonly addressed in business-process reengineering or quality programs; administrative or operational processes have tended to be the primary focus of those movements. It is perhaps just as well that this has been the case, because top-down reengineering of knowledge work is not likely to be successful. Knowledge workers care too much about their autonomy and initiative to be handed process designs created by someone else. The emphasis in knowledge work-process redesign should rather be on participation by the relevant knowledge workers and on longer-term observation by designers, so that invisible knowledge activities can be understood and put in context. Knowledge work-process designers should also focus on eliminating non-value-adding activity; otherwise, knowledge workers will not have time to perform desired knowledge management activities. This is also a useful way of demonstrating the value of knowledge process redesign to knowledge workers.

Another important step is to build explicit linkages between knowledge management and the knowledge work process it is designed to support. The linkages must specify how knowledge should be imported to and exported from the process, when and how in the process this knowledge should be used, and what difference it should make in the outcome. Such linkages might take several forms (all of which happen to start with "p"), including:

- *People* whose job it is to transfer knowledge to and from front-line knowledge work processes at the core of the organization

- *Project management* approaches that at each phase of a process review what has been learned and what needs to be learned next

- *Prototypes* of knowledge work processes in which knowledge creation and use is maximized as a design objective

- *Process designs* that specify how knowledge is to be used at different points in the flow of work

- *Programming* in computers that automatically supplies the right form of knowledge

For an example, take what General Motors has been trying to do for several years. One of its most critical knowledge work processes is new car development. GM managers have been working to specify the role of knowledge in the development process—when, for example, it makes sense to pull in some focus group knowledge, and when it makes sense to assess and record what a development team has learned. GM has sought to institute these procedures primarily through process design, looking for junctures in the development process that clearly identify specific knowledge activities. In addition, at least in some divisions of GM, programming in computer-aided design systems determines certain aspects of new car designs based on the firm's best engineering knowledge, such as the relationship between the length and width of a chassis, or what parts already exist within the company to accomplish the design objective. GM also has designated staff positions for knowledge managers, primarily in the marketing and engineering organizations. As is usually the case, the method of linkage is probably less important than making the links explicit.

Linking Knowledge to Culture

In retrospect, one of the most obvious omissions in the hardcover edition is a separate chapter on knowledge-oriented cultures. While we do touch on ideas concerning culture at various points in the book, many important questions remain about how an organization can best create a culture that values the creation, sharing, and use of knowledge. Naturally, bringing about a change of this scope is a long-term, multi-faceted undertaking, and we're not aware of any organization that has been wholly successful at changing its entire culture in this fashion. Still, some of the measures that hold promise aren't difficult to understand, as we see them in such knowledge-oriented institutions as universities and research institutes. They include:

- Incentive structures that reward people in part on the basis of their knowledge contributions

- Senior executives that set an example of knowledge behaviors (by, among other things, reading books and talking about them!)

- Evaluating decisions and decisionmaking on the basis of the knowledge used to arrive at them

- Celebrating and rewarding people for sharing knowledge and using "stolen" or borrowed knowledge (with proper attribution, of course)

- Hiring new workers partly on the basis of their potential for knowledge behaviors

- Giving workers and managers some "slack" for knowledge creation, sharing, use, and general reflection

- Educating all employees on the attributes of knowledge-based business and knowledge management

Can knowledge-friendly cultures go too far? Of course. Like the student who can't stop doing research before writing a paper, organizations can spend too much time acquiring knowledge, and not enough using it. They need a mixture of thinking and acting, learning and doing. The "analysis paralysis" or "over-intellectualizing" syndrome is well-known in American businesses. However, most U.S. firms are a long way from having this problem, and err in the less knowledgeable direction.

Linking Knowledge to Behavior

One of the heartening things we have recently observed is the increased interest in knowledge management among human resource managers. We interpret this as a sign that organizations are realizing the vital connection between knowledge-oriented behavior and overall employee performance. As we have said, the field needs to begin linking the day-to-day behaviors of knowers with the knowledge they employ—or could have employed. Too many knowledge projects focus only on "stocking the shelves" with knowledge, with little regard for why or how users might be motivated to draw on a piece of knowledge in their work routines. Indeed, we still know very little about the favorable circumstances that stimulate people in organizations to create, share, or apply knowledge. Our first step should be to observe key knowledge workers in different business environments to learn more about their knowledge behaviors. How do they individually reconcile the need to balance learning and doing? How much time do the most effective workers spend accessing knowledge resources, and how do they go about it? Are intellectually curious workers born that way (or at least have acquired this temperament before they enter our organizations as workers), or can they be cultivated? Until we understand better the factors that drive knowledge behaviors, we won't have effective knowledge environments.

One key factor that our knowledge management approaches must begin to take into account is information and knowledge overload. We can already see indications that the central problem of knowledge management in the years ahead will be "managing the flow of knowledge through and around the critical bottleneck of personal attention and learning capacity," as one forward-looking Hewlett-Packard manager put it. Unless we link our efforts to manage knowledge to programs designed to maximize individual attention and minimize distraction, we'll never succeed in realizing the true potential of knowledge management.

Thus, one of the primary battlegrounds in the future knowledge campaign will be the management of attention: understanding how it is allocated by individuals and organizations, knowing how to capture it more effectively, and using technology both to acquire and protect it. Attention is the currency of the information economy, and is already the scarcest resource in many organizations. In addition to devoting more thinking to knowledge and knowledge management, in the future all organizations will need to focus their attention on attention.

Linking Knowledge to the Physical Business Environment

A final unexplored dimension of knowledge management is its relation to physical space in the workplace, which we have come to believe can be a pivotal factor in knowledge creation and transfer. Organizational theorists still know relatively little about how the physical environment affects knowledge and its management. However, there is reason to suspect a strong causal relationship. Recall, for example, MIT professor Thomas Allen's "thirty meter rule"—that two scientists or engineers whose desks are more than thirty meters apart have a communication frequency of almost zero. This research took place before the widespread use of the Internet and corporate e-mail, although we have reason to believe that face-to-face communication breeds more—and higher-quality—electronic communication.

In an era when many companies have felt compelled to condense office space to trim budgets, we're concerned that the knowledge-related implications of workplace environments are getting short shrift. Can knowledge workers do a good job of knowledge creation in a cubicle with overheard conversations and ambient noise? Can knowledge be effectively transferred in a "hoteling" office where each day one has a new set of neighbors, and places to store paper-based knowledge are unavailable? Many citizens of the corporate world complain to us that their office environments stifle their ability to work with knowledge. We don't know yet whether space and office design are truly inhibiting knowledge management, but we feel that academics, architects, corporate space planners, and executives should all devote more consideration and creative thought to the issue.

Summary

While we fully expect that knowledge management will branch out in new directions, the key messages presented in *Working Knowledge* have clearly held up over time. Certainly all of the topics discussed in the book are still pertinent today, and even the relevance of the technology-oriented content has largely withstood the introduction of many new knowledge-oriented technologies. We would hardly want to call the book "timeless," but little that we wrote a few years ago seems to have become dated.

And while knowledge management itself has been called faddish in some quarters, we do maintain that the movement is here to stay. There is little doubt that knowledge is one of any organization's most important resources, or that knowledge workers' roles will grow in importance in the years ahead. Why would an organization believe that knowledge and knowledge workers are important, yet not advocate active management of knowledge itself?

Our model for the future of knowledge management is the quality movement. Both concepts began similarly as managerial enthusiasms given extensive coverage by the business press and gurus. And just as quality precepts became embedded in many firms' cultures and daily operating procedures, we believe the best outcome for the knowledge management movement will be a similar embeddedness. Knowledge management should become part of everything an organization does, and be part of everyone's job. If companies are successful in managing knowledge, they may even forget that they are doing it.

Acknowledgments

LIKE ALL good knowledge products, this one was not produced in a vacuum. We are particularly grateful to the pioneers of knowledge management, who gave us access to their progress and problems in the field. Many of these firms were sponsors of a multiclient research program, "Mastering the Knowledge of the Organization," or its predecessor program, "Mastering the Information Environment." We thank these firms and the specific managers with whom we worked for supporting the research financially, making their firms available as research sites, and being a critical audience for our half-baked ideas.

These programs were created under the auspices of The Center for Business Innovation, where both of us spent several years as researchers. Several Center researchers and affiliates were participants in the knowledge research, and their efforts pervade the book. These include Mike Beers, Dave DeLong, Liam Fahey, Al Jacobson, Linda Kalver, Dave Klein, Chris Marshall, Rudy Ruggles, and Patricia Seeman. Amy Fiore and Julia Kirby administered and marketed the programs, respectively. Two Center directors, Bud Mathaisel and Chris Meyer, were very supportive.

Don Cohen, in his Center capacity and otherwise, deserves particular recognition. He served as editor, researcher, encourager, and friend, and the book would not have been written without him.

Several other consulting firms and individuals at them supported our work during the couple of years this project took. They include Jim Cortada, Joe Movizzo, Scott Oldach, David Smith, and Scott Smith at IBM Consulting Group; Peter Fuchs, Jeanne Harris, and Barry Patmore at Andersen Consulting; and Brook Manville at McKinsey. Pete Tierney and others at Inference Corporation were very helpful in the area of knowledge management software. Andy Michuda and Ron Helgeson from Teltech Resource Network were free with their ideas about knowledge management.

Others whose knowledge of knowledge management contributed to the book include Vince Barabba, Leif Edvinsson, John Henderson, Abbie

Lundberg, Britton Monasco, Tom Stewart, and several anonymous reviewers for the Harvard Business School Press.

At the press, we worked with several editors, but Carol Franco got us started and Kirsten Sandberg got us finished. We're appreciative of their interest, persistence, and feedback.

It's possible that we could have written the book without our families, but what would be the point? We gratefully thank, and dedicate this tome to, Brenda, Kim, and Ben Prusak, and Jodi, Hayes, and Chase Davenport.

An investment in knowledge
pays the best interest.
—Benjamin Franklin

Introduction

W H Y   A L L   this sudden interest in knowledge? Numerous conferences and hundreds of articles in scholarly and business journals have tried to get a handle on this elusive subject. The growth of knowledge consulting and much buzzing and bustling within firms signal a growing conviction that knowing about knowledge is critical to business success—and possibly to business survival.

One of the aims of this book is to explain this new emphasis on an age-old subject, one that occupied Plato and Aristotle, and a host of philosophers after their time. Like Molière's *bourgeois gentilhomme,* who delighted in discovering that he had been speaking prose all his life, managers have recently realized that they have relied on knowledge throughout their careers. Even before the days of "core competencies," "the learning organization," "expert systems," and "strategy focus," good managers valued the experience and know-how of employees—that is, their knowledge. Recently, though, many firms have come to understand that they require more than a casual (and even unconscious) approach to corporate knowledge if they are to succeed in today's and tomorrow's economies.

This understanding accords with a renewed emphasis among strategists and economists on ideas associated with a competency-based or resource-based theory of the firm.[1] Traditional economics looked at the firm mainly as a "black box" and examined the resources going in, the products coming out, and the markets in which the firm participated. Today, theorists of many disciplines are turning their attention to one of the essential dynamics inside the box: the knowledge embedded in routines and practices that the firm transforms into valuable products and services.[2]

Multiple factors have led to the current "knowledge boom." This convergence of causes is one reason that thinking clearly about knowledge has become so important so quickly. The perception and the reality of a new global competitiveness is one driving force. Rapid change and increasing competition for the dollars, marks, and yen of increasingly sophisticated consumers have led firms to seek a sustainable advantage that distinguishes them in their business environments.

Of course, this search has its negative side. Theories, fads, nostrums, and "silver bullets" have been served up to American business as all-purpose solutions to the often intractable and subtle difficulties of managing competitively. Some of these offerings have been incrementally quite valuable. The quality movement, for instance, has produced undeniable benefits and has become part of the fabric of doing business. But many highly touted management concepts have failed to keep their promises.[3] Disappointment with them has led firms to look for something more basic, something irreducible and vital to performance, productivity, and innovation. As a result, the management community has come to realize that what an organization and its employees *know* is at the heart of how the organization functions. Although the knowledge "movement" will undoubtedly spawn its own fads and buzzwords, knowledge itself is worthy of attention because it tells firms how to do things and how they might do them better.

The trend toward leaner organizations has also contributed to heightened interest in knowledge, on the principle that you really understand the value of something once it is gone. Experienced aerospace engineers encouraged to leave during downsizing periods took valuable knowledge out the door with them and, in some cases, had to be rehired so that essential work could continue. Some "expendable" middle managers proved by their absence to have been key knowledge coordinators and synthesizers; the loss to their firms went well beyond what their official job descriptions would suggest. A specific example of this corporate amnesia can be found at Ford, where new car developers wanted to replicate the success of the original Taurus design team. But no one remembered, or had recorded, what was so special about that effort. A similar experience occurred at International Harvester when Russian officials approached the company about building a new truck factory. They contacted Harvester because it had built a plant in Russia twenty years earlier. Alas, there wasn't a single soul still in the organization who knew anything about the previous project. Having made costly errors by disregarding the importance of knowledge, many firms are now struggling to gain a better understanding of what they know, what they need to know, and what to do about it.

Some of these organizations mistakenly assumed that technology could replace the skill and judgment of an experienced human worker. An important element of this book is a discussion of the relationship between knowledge and technology. The assumption that technology can replace human knowledge or create its equivalent has proven false time and again. Developments in technology, on the other hand, are among the positive factors fueling interest in knowledge and its management. For example, networked computing provides new ways for individuals to exchange information and knowledge within and outside their organizations. Technologies such as Lotus Notes and the World Wide Web have made certain forms of structured knowledge easier to collect, store in repositories, and distribute to desktops. The recent dramatic rise in Internet and intranet use is one manifestation of the expanding role of electronic technology in communication and knowledge seeking. Firms are becoming aware both of the potential of this technology to enhance knowledge work and of the fact that the potential can be realized only if they understand more about how knowledge is actually developed and shared.

Our primary aim in this book is to develop a preliminary understanding of what knowledge *is* within organizations. How does it look and sound in daily life and work? How is it different from data and information? Who has it? Where is it? Who uses it? What do we talk about when we talk about knowledge? Our second concern is what to do about knowledge. What key cultural and behavioral issues must we address to make use of it? What are the best ways to use technology in knowledge work? What are specific knowledge roles and skills? What does a successful knowledge project look like and how do you know if it has been successful? What measures and milestones can we use to evaluate it? Our answers to these questions provide at least the beginning of a response to the essential question asked about knowledge in organizations: What do I *do* Monday morning to help make our organization's use of knowledge more effective, efficient, productive, and innovative? Our aim, finally, is to provide a general perspective on how firms work that will give managers a means of decisively improving performance.

The findings we present in this book evolved from extensive discussions with corporate managers about how knowledge functions in organizations. Several years ago, when we began a research program on new approaches to information management, we brought together executives from about twenty-five client companies, including Hewlett-Packard, IBM, AT&T, and American Airlines. We asked them what they most needed to know that they didn't currently know, and how we could best help them know it. To our surprise, almost all of those smart managers from successful firms admitted, "We have no real idea how to manage value-added information and knowledge in our companies." Now, these were very sophisticated organizations. Quite a few of them were among the high-tech firms that had helped launch the information revolution; they are the great institutions of the "Information Age." But they were admitting that they didn't have any effective methods and approaches for managing and understanding how to better use information themselves. So for a couple of years we focused our research on information: why it isn't managed well, what managing information actually means, and what kinds of specific improvements our clients could make in how they obtained and used it.[4]

As we worked with these firms and came to understand reasonably well how information worked (and didn't work) within them, it became apparent that what our clients wanted as much as anything else were *insights*. They were looking for best practices, new ideas, creative synergies, and breakthrough processes that information cannot supply, regardless of how well it is managed. These kinds of results, we became convinced, could come only from making effective use of knowledge. In addition, it was clear that much of the knowledge they needed already existed within their organizations but was not accessible or available when required. Hewlett-Packard CEO Lew Platt once said (echoing a former head of HP Labs), "If HP knew what HP knows, we would be three times as profitable," expressing a belief in the potential value of knowledge shared by many other corporate executives. Of course, knowledge was being used and exchanged in these companies, as it is in all firms. What we eventually came to think of as "knowledge markets," with knowledge buyers, sellers, and brokers, operate in every organization. However, they simply don't operate very efficiently. Unrecognized, disorganized, local, often discouraged rather than fostered by company culture, these knowledge markets are deeply imperfect mechanisms for generating and exchanging insights. The need to study how knowledge is managed, mismanaged, and unmanaged in organizations became evident to us.

Eventually, knowledge became the new focus of our research and discussions (actually returned to focus; we'd studied it in graduate school in terms of "intellectual history" and "the sociology of knowledge"). We knew intuitively that knowledge is centrally important in most organizations. Economist Sidney Winter describes business firms as "organizations that know how to do things."[5] A company truly is a collection of people organized to produce something, whether it be goods, services, or some combination of the two. Their ability to produce depends on what they currently know and on the knowledge that has become embedded in the routines and machinery of production. The material assets of a firm are of limited worth unless people know what to do with them. If "knowing how to do things" defines what a firm is, then knowledge actually *is* the company in an important sense. Understanding the role of knowledge in organizations may help answer the question of why some firms are consistently successful. When people, technology, products, and the business environment change over time, what is left? What is the residual, as economists ask? What creates the *continuity* that allows particular firms to thrive over time? We strongly believe that the way firms generate and pass on knowledge is an essential part of that continuity. We're sure that future studies of organizational knowledge will make an important contribution to understanding the sources of long-term success.

At the time when we were turning our attention to knowledge, Tom Stewart in a 1994 *Fortune* magazine article warned companies to focus less on what they *own* and more on what they *know:* their intellectual capital. Since then, Peter Drucker has identified knowledge as the new basis of competition in postcapitalist society and Stanford economist Paul Romer has called knowledge the only unlimited resource, the one asset that grows with use. In 1995 two Japanese academics, Ikujiro Nonaka and Hirotaka Takeuchi, published *The Knowledge-Creating Company,* a groundbreaking study of knowledge generation and use in Japanese firms. That same year Dorothy Leonard-Barton wrote a finely detailed study of the role of knowledge in manufacturing firms, *Wellsprings of Knowledge.* Several other books exhorting managers to manage knowledge—without focusing much on how to do so—have appeared in the marketplace.[6] Firms such as Dow Chemical and Skandia and consultants such as McKinsey, Ernst & Young, and IBM Consulting have appointed "chief knowledge officers" and "directors of intellectual capital" to oversee the knowledge resources of their firms. They point to savings, improvements, and productivity increases that result from managing knowledge. Stories like these have become more and more common:

- At Hoffmann-LaRoche, the Swiss pharmaceutical firm, a knowledge management initiative in 1993–1994 reformed the process of developing new drug applications, the voluminous, complex documents that must be submitted to the Federal Drug Administration and European regulatory authorities before any new drug can be approved and brought to market. In significant measure because of the initiative, applications and approval for several new products now take many months less than the usual time to complete, at a savings of $1 million per day.

- In 1996 teams of leading heart surgeons from five New England medical centers observed one another's operating-room practices and exchanged ideas about their most effective techniques in a collaborative learning experiment. The result: a 24 percent drop in their overall mortality rate for coronary bypass surgery, or seventy-four fewer deaths than predicted.

- At Hewlett-Packard and many other high-tech firms, the amount of product knowledge required to effectively use and support complex computer products has exploded over the past several years. Customers with problems must be talked through to a solution that may involve interactions between hardware, software, and communications products, all of which change constantly. HP had difficulty finding enough good technical people to provide good customer support. So in 1995 the company implemented a knowledge management tool called "case-based reasoning" to capture technical support knowledge and make it available to personnel around the world. Results have been unequivocal and dramatic: average call times have been reduced by two-thirds, cost per call has fallen by 50 percent, and the company has been able to hire fewer technical support agents because of the help they receive from the system.

These are only a few of the many examples of knowledge management that we will describe in this book. The companies whose knowledge management efforts we profile are listed below. In addition, we include several anonymous examples drawn from firms that did not wish to be identified.

More and more, business leaders and consultants talk about knowledge as *the* chief asset of organizations and the key to a sustainable competitive advantage. "Knowledge workers," "the knowledge-creating company," "knowledge capital," and "leveraging knowledge" have become familiar phrases. Knowledge conferences and seminars are springing up everywhere. There is tremendous excitement about the potential benefits of knowledge initiatives in the corporate world.

We believe the excitement is justified. The core message of this book is that the only sustainable advantage a firm has comes from what it collectively knows, how efficiently it uses what it knows, and how readily it acquires and uses new knowledge.

Organization Examples Described in This Book

Andersen Consulting	McDonnell Douglas
Boeing	McKinsey & Company
British Petroleum	Microsoft
Buckman Laboratories	Mobil Oil
Chaparral Steel	Monsanto
Chase Manhattan Bank	National Semiconductor
Chrysler	NYNEX
Coca-Cola	Owens-Corning
CSIRO	Sandia National Laboratories
Dai-Ichi Pharmaceuticals	Sematech
Dow Chemical	Senco Products
Ernst & Young	Sequent Computer
Ford	Skandia
General Motors	Teltech
Hewlett-Packard	Texas Instruments
Hoeschst-Celanese	3M
Hoffmann-LaRoche	Time Life
Hughes Space and Communications	U.S. Army
IBM	Young & Rubicam
IDEO	

In the end, the location of the new economy
    is not in the technology, be it the microchip
        or the global
    telecommunications network.
        It is in the human mind.
        —Alan Webber[1]

1

What Do We Talk about When We Talk about Knowledge?

K N O W L E D G E is neither data nor information, though it is related to both, and the differences between these terms are often a matter of degree. We start with those more familiar terms both because they *are* more familiar and because we can understand knowledge best with reference to them. Confusion about what data, information, and knowledge are—how they differ, what those words *mean*—has resulted in enormous expenditures on technology initiatives that rarely deliver what the firms spending the money needed or thought they were getting. Often firms don't understand what they need until they invest heavily in a system that fails to provide it.

However basic it may sound, then, it is still important to emphasize that data, information, and knowledge are not interchangeable concepts. Organizational success and failure can often depend on knowing which of them you need, which you have, and what you can and can't do with each. Understanding what those three things are and how you get from one to another is essential to doing knowledge work successfully. So we believe it's best to begin with a brief comparison of the three terms and the factors involved in transforming data into information and information into knowledge.

A Working Definition of Knowledge

A word of qualification before we proceed with our definitions. We're aware that some researchers identify more than the three entities of data,

1

information, and knowledge—going on, for example, to describe wisdom, insight, resolve, action, and so forth. Since we've noticed that firms have enough difficulty distinguishing among three related concepts, however, we're not inclined to address more. For practical purposes, we'll lump higher-order concepts such as wisdom and insight into knowledge.[2] And things like "resolve" and "action," while desirably pointing to the need to do something with knowledge, we'd put into a different category of "things you do with knowledge" rather than a variation on knowledge itself. With that caution, let's proceed to some definitions.

Data

Data is a set of discrete, objective facts about events.[3] In an organizational context, data is most usefully described as structured records of transactions. When a customer goes to a gas station and fills the tank of his car, that transaction can be partly described by data: when he made the purchase; how many gallons he bought; how much he paid. The data tells nothing about why he went to that service station and not another one, and can't predict how likely he is to come back. In and of themselves, such facts say nothing about whether the service station is well or badly run, whether it is failing or thriving. Peter Drucker once said that information is "data endowed with relevance and purpose," which of course suggests that data by itself has little relevance or purpose.

Modern organizations usually store data in some sort of technology system. It is entered into the system by departments such as finance, accounting, and marketing. Until recently it has been managed by central information systems departments that respond to requests for data from management and other parts of the company. The current trend is for data to be somewhat less centralized and available on demand from desktop PCs, but the basic structure of what it is and how we store and use it remains the same.

Quantitatively, companies evaluate data management in terms of cost, speed, and capacity: How much does it cost to capture or retrieve a piece of data? How quickly can we get it into the system or call it up? How much will the system hold? Qualitative measurements are timeliness, relevance, and clarity: Do we have access to it *when* we need it? Is it *what* we need? Can we make sense out of it?

All organizations need data and some industries are heavily dependent on it. Banks, insurance companies, utilities, and government agencies such as the IRS and the Social Security Administration are obvious examples. Record keeping is at the heart of these "data cultures" and effective data management is essential to their success. Efficiently keeping track of millions of transactions is their business. But for many companies—even some data cultures—more data is not always better than less. Firms sometimes pile up data because it is factual and therefore creates an illusion of scientific accuracy. Gather enough data, the argument goes, and objectively correct decisions will automatically suggest themselves. This is false on two counts. First, too much data can make it harder to identify and make sense of the data that matters. Second, and most fundamentally, there is no inherent meaning in data. Data describes only a part of what happened; it provides no judgment or interpretation and no sustainable basis of action. While the raw material of decision making may include data, it cannot tell you what to do. Data says nothing about its own importance or irrelevance. But data is important to organizations—largely, of course, because it is essential raw material for the creation of information.

Information

Like many researchers who have studied information, we will describe it as a *message,* usually in the form of a document or an audible or visible communication. As with any message, it has a sender and a receiver. Information is meant to change the way the receiver perceives something, to have an impact on his judgment and behavior. It must inform; it's data that makes a difference. The word "inform" originally meant "to give shape to" and information is meant to shape the person who gets it, to make some difference in his outlook or insight. Strict-

Think of information as data that makes a difference.

ly speaking, then, it follows that the receiver, not the sender, decides whether the message he gets is really information—that is, if it truly informs him. A memo full of unconnected ramblings may be considered "information" by the writer but judged to be noise by the recipient. The only message it may communicate successfully is an unintended one about the quality of the sender's intelligence or judgment.

Information moves around organizations through hard and soft networks. A hard network has a visible and definite infrastructure: wires, delivery vans, satellite dishes, post offices, addresses, electronic mailboxes. The messages these networks deliver include e-mail, traditional or "snail" mail, delivery-service packages, and Internet transmissions. A soft network is less formal and visible. It is ad hoc. Someone's handing you a note or a copy of an article marked "FYI" is an example of information transmission via soft network.

Quantitative measures of information management tend to include connectivity and transactions: How many e-mail accounts or Lotus Notes users do we have? How many messages do we send in a given period? Qualitative measures measure informativeness and usefulness: Did the message give me some new insight? Does it help me make sense of a situation and contribute to a decision or the solution to a problem?

Unlike data, information has meaning—the "relevance and purpose" of Drucker's definition above. Not only does it potentially shape the receiver, it *has* a shape: it is organized to some purpose. Data becomes information when its creator adds meaning. We transform data into information by adding value in various ways. Let's consider several important methods, all beginning with the letter *C*:

- *Contextualized*: we know for what purpose the data was gathered
- *Categorized*: we know the units of analysis or key components of the data
- *Calculated*: the data may have been analyzed mathematically or statistically
- *Corrected*: errors have been removed from the data
- *Condensed*: the data may have been summarized in a more concise form

Note that computers can help to add these values and transform data into information, but they can rarely help with context, and humans must usually help with categorization, calculation, and condensing. A problem we will deal with throughout this book is the confusion of information—or knowledge—with the technology that delivers it. From Marshall McLuhan's *The Medium Is the Message*, with its assertion that television would bind humanity into a global village and end world conflict, to recent statements about the transforming power of the Internet, we have heard that information technology will change not only how we work but who we are. One important point we will make in this book is that the medium is *not* the message, though it may strongly affect the message. The thing delivered is more important than the delivery vehicle. Having a telephone does not guarantee or even encourage brilliant conversations; owning a state-of-the-art CD player is pointless if you use it only to listen to polkas played by a kazoo ensemble. In the early days of television, many commentators said that the new medium would raise the level of cultural and political discourse in the nation, a prediction that clearly did not come true. The corollary for today's managers is that having more information technology will not necessarily improve the state of information.

Knowledge

Most people have an intuitive sense that knowledge is broader, deeper, and richer than data or information. People speak of a "knowledgeable individual," and mean someone with a thorough, informed, and reliable grasp of a subject, someone both educated and intelligent. They are unlikely to talk about a "knowledgeable" or even a "knowledge-full" memo, handbook, or database, even though these might be produced by knowledgeable individuals or groups.

Since epistemologists spend their lives trying to understand what it means to know something, we will not pretend to provide a definitive account ourselves. What we offer is a working definition of knowledge, a pragmatic description that helps us communicate what we mean when we talk about *Knowledge derives from minds at work.* knowledge in organizations. Our definition expresses the characteristics that make knowledge valuable and the characteristics—often the same ones—that make it difficult to manage well:

> Knowledge is a fluid mix of framed experience, values, contextual information, and expert insight that provides a framework for evaluating and incorporating new experiences and information. It originates and is applied in the minds of knowers. In organizations, it often becomes embedded not only in documents or repositories but also in organizational routines, processes, practices, and norms.

What this definition immediately makes clear is that knowledge is not neat or simple. It is a mixture of various elements; it is fluid as well as formally structured; it is intuitive and therefore hard to capture in words or understand completely in logical terms. Knowledge exists within people, part and parcel of human complexity and unpredictability. Although we traditionally think of assets as definable and "concrete," knowledge assets are much harder to pin down. Just as an atomic particle can appear to be either a wave or a particle, depending on how scientists track it, knowledge can be seen as both process and stock.

Knowledge derives from information as information derives from data. If information is to become knowledge, humans must do virtually all the work. This transformation happens through such *C* words as:

- *Comparison:* how does information about this situation compare to other situations we have known?

- *Consequences:* what implications does the information have for decisions and actions?

- *Connections:* how does this bit of knowledge relate to others?

- *Conversation:* what do other people think about this information?

Clearly, these knowledge-creating activities take place within and between humans. While we find data in records or transactions, and information in messages, we obtain knowledge from individuals or groups of knowers, or sometimes in organizational routines. It is delivered through structured media such as books and documents, and person-to-person contacts ranging from conversations to apprenticeships.

Knowledge in Action

One of the reasons that we find knowledge valuable is that it is close—and closer than data or information—to action. Knowledge can and should be evaluated by the decisions or actions to which it leads. Better knowledge can lead, for example, to measurable efficiencies in product development and production. We can use it to make wiser decisions about strategy, competitors, customers, distribution channels, and product and service life cycles. We'll describe the characteristics of knowledge-intensive organizations later in this chapter and throughout the book. Of course, since knowledge and decisions usually reside in people's heads, it can be difficult to trace the path between knowledge and action.

We've observed and analyzed over a hundred attempts to manage knowledge in organizations. To the managers of most of them we've posed the question, "How do you make the distinction between data, information, and knowledge?" Many make no hard distinction in practice, and most of these initiatives involve a mixture of knowledge and information, if not some data as well. Many pointed out that they just tried to add value to what they had—to move it up the scale from data toward knowledge.

Chrysler, for example, stores knowledge for new car development in a series of repositories called "Engineering Books of Knowledge." The goal of these "books," which are actually computer files, is to be an "electronic memory" for the knowledge gained by automobile platform teams. The manager of one such "book" was given a series of crash test results for inclusion in the repository. However, he classified the results as data and encouraged the submitter to add some value. What was the context of the results—why were the crash tests performed? How about comparisons to the results of other models, previous years, and competitors' cars? What consequences did the results suggest for bumper or chassis redesign? It may be difficult to note the exact points at which data becomes information or knowledge, but it's easy to see how to move it up the chain.

Knowledge can also move down the value chain, returning to information and data. The most common reason for what we call "de-knowledging" is too much volume. As one Andersen Consulting knowledge manager told us, "We've got so much knowledge (not to mention a lot of data and information too) in our Knowledge Xchange repository that our consultants can no longer make sense of it. For many of them it has become data." Aeschylus made a similar point clearly twenty-five centuries ago: "Who knows useful things, not many things, is wise."

Because knowledge is such a slippery concept, it's worth reflecting a bit on some of its key components, such as experience, truth, judgment, and rules of thumb.

Experience

Knowledge develops over time, through experience that includes what we absorb from courses, books, and mentors as well as informal learning. Experience refers to what we have done and what has happened to us in the past. "Experience" and "expert" are related words, both derived from a Latin verb meaning "to put to the test." Experts—people with deep knowledge of a subject—have been tested and trained by experience.

One of the prime benefits of experience is that it provides a historical perspective from which to view and understand new situations and events. Knowledge born of experience recognizes familiar patterns and can make connections between what is happening now and what happened then. The application of experience in business may be as simple as an old hand's identifying a downturn in sales as a seasonal phenomenon and therefore no cause for alarm. It may be as complex as a manager's noticing subtle signs of the corporate complacency that led to problems in the past, or a scientist's having a sense of which new avenues of research will likely lead to useful results. These experience-based insights are what firms pay premiums for; they show why experience *counts*.

When firms hire experts, they're buying experience-based insights.

Ground Truth

Experience changes ideas about what *should* happen into knowledge of what *does* happen. Knowledge has "ground truth," to borrow the phrase the U.S. Army's Center for Army Lessons Learned (CALL) uses to describe the rich truths of real situations experienced close up: on the ground, rather than from the heights of theory or generalization.

For obvious reasons, effective knowledge transfer is a critical issue for the army. Knowing what to expect and what to do in military situations can be literally a life-or-death matter. Ground truth means knowing what really works and what doesn't. Experts from CALL take part in real military operations as learning observers and disseminate the knowledge they gather through photos, video tapes, briefings, and simulations. Lessons learned in Somalia and Rwanda in the early '90s, for example, were passed on to the troops involved in the 1994 Haitian mission. The experiences of the first units in Haiti that went from house to house looking for weapons were also videotaped to provide guidance to those who followed.

A key aspect of the army's success at knowledge management was its "After Action Review" (AAR) program. This exercise involves an examination of what was supposed to happen in a mission or action, what actually happened, why there was a difference between the two, and what can be learned from the disparities. Enlisted soldiers and officers meet together in a climate of openness, collaboration, and trust. Results from the AAR are quickly incorporated into army "doctrine," or its formally documented procedures, and training programs. The AAR program was developed not as a knowledge management vehicle but rather as a means to return to values of integrity and accountability. These values had suffered considerably during the Vietnam War, and army leaders adopted the AAR and an orientation to ground truth to restore them—initially in training missions, and later for all types of missions. Over the past few years the army has realized that it had a knowledge and learning tool in the AAR.

Another breakthrough in the army's extensive knowledge experience grew out of the reflections of a senior officer who, late in his career, read Tolstoy's *War and Peace.* He was struck by the difference between Tolstoy's depictions of Napoleonic War battles and the way those battles were taught in classes at military academies. How rich, true, and grounded were Tolstoy's descriptions (he had actually interviewed veterans of those campaigns) compared with the bloodless, rational abstractions taught in the classroom! The gap between ground truth and rational analysis prompted such innovations as CALL.[4]

We could make a similar distinction between how business strategy actually happens and how it is taught in business schools.[5] However, we believe that managers recognize the importance of real-life knowledge or ground truth. This is suggested by some of the language they use. They exchange "war stories" and talk about "life in the trenches." In other words, they share the detail and meaning of real experiences because they understand that knowledge of the everyday, complex, often messy reality of work is generally more valuable than theories about it.

Complexity

The importance of experience and ground truth in knowledge is one indication of knowledge's ability to deal with complexity. Knowledge is not a rigid structure that excludes what doesn't fit; it can deal with complexity in a complex way. This is one essential source of its value. Although it is tempting to look for simple answers to complex problems and deal with uncertainties by pretending they don't exist, knowing more usually leads to better decisions than knowing less, even if the "less" seems clearer and more definite. Certainty and clarity often come at the price of ignoring essential factors. Being both certain and wrong is a common occurrence. In *Sensemaking in Organizations,* Karl Weick observes that "it takes a complex sensing system to register and regulate a complex object,"[6] and elsewhere he remarks:

> The illusions of accuracy can be created if people avoid comparison . . . ,
> but in a dynamic, competitive, changing environment, illusions of accuracy

are short-lived, and they fall apart without warning. Reliance on a single, uncontradicted data source can give people a feeling of omniscience, but because those data are flawed in unrecognized ways, they lead to nonadaptive action.[7]

Knowledge is aware of what it doesn't know. Many wise men and women have pointed out that the more knowledgeable one becomes, the more humble one feels about what one knows. Since what you don't know *can* hurt you, this awareness is extremely important. Recently, a genetic-engineering firm created a new tomato that farmers could pick and ship later than current varieties and that therefore would be more flavorful than the tomatoes available in supermarkets. The firm's scientists had all the expertise needed to develop the new tomato but didn't know enough about farming to know that there were essential things they didn't know. For instance, any farmer with experience growing tomatoes could have told them that any given single variety does not do equally well in all climates. Their new tomato was derived from only one variety. It grew successfully in some areas but not in others, and their scientific triumph was a commercial failure.

Judgment

Unlike data and information, knowledge contains judgment. Not only can it judge new situations and information in light of what is already known, it judges and refines itself in response to new situations and information. Knowledge can be likened to a living system, growing and changing as it interacts with the environment.

Of course, everyone has met "experts" whose knowledge seems to consist of stock responses and who offer the same old answer to any new question: every problem looks like a nail to a person who has only a single conceptual hammer in his toolbox. We would argue that the expertise of these experts ceases to be real knowledge when it refuses to examine itself and evolve. It becomes opinion or dogma instead.

When knowledge stops evolving, it turns into opinion or dogma.

Rules of Thumb and Intuition

Knowledge works through rules of thumb: flexible guides to action that developed through trial and error and over long experience and observation. Rules of thumb (or, in the language of the artificial-intelligence community, heuristics) are shortcuts to solutions to new problems that resemble problems previously solved by experienced workers. Those with knowledge see known patterns in new situations and can respond appropriately. They don't have to build an answer from scratch every time. So knowledge offers speed; it allows its possessors to deal with situations quickly, even some very complex ones that would baffle a novice.

Roger Schank, a computer scientist at Northwestern University, calls these internalized responses "scripts." Like play scripts (or computer program codes), they are efficient guides to complex situations. Scripts are patterns of internalized experience, routes through a maze of alternatives, saving us the trouble of consciously analyzing and choosing at every step along the way. Scripts can be played so quickly that we may not even be aware of them: We arrive at an answer intuitively, without knowing how we got there. That does not mean the steps do not exist—intuition is not mystical. It means we have so thoroughly learned the steps that they happen automatically, without conscious thought, and therefore at great speed. Karl Weick calls intuition "compressed expertise," a phrase that vividly suggests how knowledge works and what it can do.

> *One researcher calls intuition "compressed expertise."*

The skill of an experienced driver provides an example of this kind of intuition. She *knows* how to drive, rapidly accomplishing a series of complex actions without having to think about them, as a beginner would. The veteran driver also develops an intuitive sense of what to expect on the road. Hundreds of hours of driving have led her to "know" that another driver is going to pull out of a side street or change lanes without looking. Experience has made her aware of minute signs that the beginning driver would almost certainly miss and that may be too subtle to verbalize. Like an experienced businessperson, she sizes up a situation quickly without going through a definable process or even being able to explain her "reasoning."

Values and Beliefs

It may seem odd to include values and beliefs in a discussion of knowledge in organizations. Many people assume that organizations are objective and neutral; their purpose is to create a product or provide a service, and that goal may seem unrelated to values. In fact, people's values and beliefs have a powerful impact on organizational knowledge. Organizations are, after all, made up of people whose values and beliefs inescapably influence their thoughts and actions. The organizations themselves have histories, derived from people's actions and words, that also express corporate values and beliefs.

Values and beliefs are integral to knowledge, determining in large part what the knower sees, absorbs, and concludes from his observations. People with different values "see" different things in the same situation and organize their knowledge by their values. Someone who values the bustle of urban life may find energy and variety in a crowded city street. Someone who prefers rural quiet may see only chaos and danger in the same scene. A publishing executive who values risk and change may see a new opportunity in the same on-line technology that a competitor views as a threat to traditionally successful print products.

Nonaka and Takeuchi say that "knowledge, unlike information, is about *beliefs* and *commitment*."[8] The power of knowledge to organize, select, learn, and judge comes from values and beliefs as much as, and probably more than, from information and logic.

Knowledge as a Corporate Asset

People in organizations have always sought, used, and valued knowledge, at least implicitly. Companies hire for experience more often than for intelligence or education because they understand the value of knowledge that has been developed and proven over time. Managers making difficult decisions are much more likely to go to people they respect and avail themselves of their knowledge than they are to look for information in databases. Studies have shown that managers get two-thirds of their information and knowledge from face-to-face meetings or phone conversations. Only one-third comes from documents.[9] Most people in organizations consult a few knowledgeable people when they need expert advice on a particular subject. As we have said, knowledge is what makes organizations go. Knowledge is not new.

Explicitly recognizing knowledge as a corporate asset is new, however, as is understanding the need to manage and invest it with the same care paid to getting value from other, more tangible assets. The need to make the most of organizational knowledge, to get as much value as possible from it, is greater now than in the past.

The Changing Global Economy

Fifty years ago, the United States accounted for about 53 percent of the world GDP. The demand for American goods at home and abroad was so great that almost any product could find a market. Today, the U.S. share of the world GDP is approximately 18 percent. Although the "pie" is much bigger than it was, American companies no longer dominate the world market. There is fierce international competition for every marginal dollar of profit. A rapidly globalizing economy unified by improved communication and transportation gives consumers an unprecedented choice of goods and services and an endless cavalcade of new and better offerings from global companies.

In short, companies can no longer expect that the products and practices that made them successful in the past will keep them viable in the future. Pricing pressures leave no room for inefficient production. The cycle time for developing new products and getting them on the market is becoming more and more compressed. Companies now *require* quality, value, service, innovation, and speed to market for business success, and these factors will be even more critical in the future.

Increasingly, companies will differentiate themselves on the basis of what they know. A relevant variation on Sidney Winter's definition of a business firm as "an organization that knows how to do things" would define a business firm that thrives over the next decade as "an organization that *knows* how to do new things well and quickly."

In their search for new efficiencies, global corporations have outsourced much of the labor of manufacturing to countries where the cost of labor is still relatively low. Clearly, the knowledge-based activities of developing products and processes are becoming the primary internal functions of firms and the ones with the greatest potential for providing competitive advantage.[10]

In a global economy, knowledge may be a company's greatest competitive advantage.

Product and Service Convergence

Increasingly, knowledge and related intangibles not only make businesses go but are part or all of the "products" firms offer. Old distinctions between manufactured objects, services, and ideas are breaking down. Not surprisingly, distinctions between manufacturing and service firms are disappearing too. Alan Webber described the change in a 1993 article:

> Not so long ago, observers predicted with confidence the arrival of a "postindustrial" service economy, where the central role played by manufacturing in the economy would be steadily replaced by new service industries and service jobs. Now we know that the real impact of the information economy is to explode the distinction between manufacturing and services altogether.[11]

Fortune magazine recognized the same trend in 1993, when it replaced its separate Fortune 500 industrial-firm and service-firm issues with a combined issue. The decision to make that change resulted from an internal debate about whether Microsoft was an "industrial" or a "service" firm, and furthermore, whether it mattered. The editors saw that it was no longer meaningful or even possible to decide which firms fit which category.

Software companies sell products that are essentially ideas—intellectual property—embodied in lines of code. We can classify software as a service: a set of functions delivered in digital form. It's no wonder that Microsoft works so diligently to hire smart workers. The software business is a new kind of knowledge-based industry, but even traditional manufacturing firms are increasingly both users and sellers of knowledge. Once-traditional manufacturing firms differentiate themselves from competitors by offering "smart" products ranging from automatic breadmakers to cars that sense driver habits and adjust to them. Xerox calls itself "the document company," not "the copier/printer company." It sells solutions to business problems, not just office machinery. Ford focuses on "quality." IBM markets "industry-solution units." 3M calls itself a knowledge company, and Steelcase, the office equipment firm, has placed full-page ads touting itself as selling "knowledge." These self-definitions are not just market hype but a genuine recognition of the type of value these firms need to offer their customers.

These changes and pressures make knowledge vital to organizations. As James Brian Quinn points out, the intangibles that add value to most products and services are knowledge-based: technical know-how, product design, marketing presentation, understanding the customer, personal creativity, and innovation.[12] The powers of knowledge that we have described—speed, complexity, a sense of history and context, judgment, and flexibility—are precisely those needed in a rapidly changing, increasingly competitive global economy.

A small but telling case in point: The NEC factory in Honjo, Japan, has been replacing assembly-line robots with human workers, because human flexibility and intelligence makes them more efficient at dealing with change. Assembling a new model of mobile phone, humans reached target efficiency after making 8,000 units (compared with the 64,000 units robots needed) and were 45 percent more productive than the machines after both reached peak efficiency. The cost of a model change fell from $9.5 million to between $1 million and $2 million, a significant savings given that NEC is making model changes every six months rather than every two years, as in the past. Tomiaki Mizukami, president of NEC's Saitama plant, says, "Before, we ended up using people as robots. But now we must use their intelligence. Using robots was good, but now we're discovering that using people is actually faster."[13] Even assembly-line work, often considered merely mechanical, benefits from the experience, skill, and adaptability of human expertise.

Similarly, firms that have replaced some accounts-payable personnel with computers are finding that overpayments have increased because automated systems don't catch errors that would be obvious to experienced employees. Although the financial cost of additional overpayments is in many cases more than offset by the savings in salaries and benefits, the errors can cause strained relationships between firms and suppliers. Again, the human dimensions—the knowledge dimensions—of a supposedly mechanical task become apparent when machines try to accomplish them. Richard Loder, president of Loder Drew & Associates, a payables consulting firm, comments, "Payable clerks are blessed with intuition, memory recognition and the ability to make educated guesses. Computers are dumb and dumber in these areas."[14]

Konosuke Matsushita, founder of Matsushita Electric, Ltd., has said, "Business, we know, is now so complex and difficult, the survival of firms so hazardous in an environment increasingly unpredictable, competitive and fraught with danger, that their continued existence depends on the day-to-day mobilization of every ounce of intelligence."[15] Managers around the world have come to realize that they need to understand what they know how to do well and take advantage of that knowledge as effectively as possible.

Sustainable Competitive Advantage

Centuries ago, manufacturers and nations maintained commercial supremacy by keeping material and processes secret. Guilds protected their special knowledge; governments prohibited the export of economically important skills. France, for instance, made exporting lace-making expertise a capital crime: Anyone caught teaching the skill to foreigners could be put to death. Today, real trade secrets are a rarity. There are a few well-known examples (like the formula for Coca-Cola) and a few specialized ones (the Zildjian cymbal company, owned by the same family since its origin in alchemical experiments centuries ago, still guards the formula for the exact composition of the alloy used in its cymbals). For the most part, though, it is virtually impossible to prevent competitors from copying and even improving on new products and production methods fairly quickly in an era characterized by mobility, the free flow of ideas, reverse engineering, and widely available technology.

Alan Webber, the editor of *Fast Company* magazine, has referred to this phenomenon as the "self-canceling technological advantage." "As technology transforms the logic of competition," he explains, "technology disappears as a sustainable source of competitive advantage."[16] Because essentially the same technology is available to everyone, it cannot provide a long-term edge to anyone. A global marketplace for ideas has developed and there are very few concepts and formulae that are not generally available. Competitors can quickly duplicate most products and services. When only Citibank and Chemical had automated teller machines, they briefly had a significant advantage over their competitors, offering a service that customers wanted and they alone could provide. But ATMs soon became available throughout the industry, and what had been a competitive advantage was simply a baseline requirement for consumer-oriented banks. There is no way to make the ATM or any other piece of technology a trade secret for long—even if you build it yourself, as Citibank did.

The advantages of new products and efficiencies are more and more difficult to sustain. VF, the company that sells Lee Jeans and other apparel, has experienced 20 percent annual growth for five years, thanks in part to technical innovations. These include an electronic market response system that informs both the company's shipping and manufacturing departments of every sale made within hours. But Jerry Johnson, VF's chief financial officer, says, "The half-life of innovation is getting shorter and shorter. A couple of years ago we thought we had established a definitive lead in service to our customers. Now it's become the industry standard."[17] Robert Stasey, the director of quality improvement for Analog Devices, another growing company, expresses a similar idea when he says that Analog "is basically a new product engine. Life cycles are short and we want to obsolete our own products before the competition does."[18]

Knowledge, by contrast, can provide a sustainable advantage. Eventually, competitors can almost always match the quality and price of a market leader's current product or service. By the time that happens, though, the knowledge-rich, knowledge-managing company will have moved on to a new level of quality, creativity, or efficiency. The knowledge advantage is sustainable because it generates increasing returns and continuing advantages. Unlike material assets,

> *A knowledge advantage is a sustainable advantage.*

which decrease as they are used, knowledge assets increase with use: Ideas breed new ideas, and shared knowledge stays with the giver while it enriches the receiver. The potential for new ideas arising from the stock of knowledge in any firm is practically limitless—particularly if the people in the firm are given opportunities to think, to learn, and to talk with one another. Paul Romer, who has worked at the leading edge of knowledge economics, argues that only knowledge resources—ideas—have unlimited potential for growth:

> In a world with physical limits, it is discoveries of big ideas (for example, how to make high-temperature superconductors) together with the discovery of millions of little ideas (better ways to sew a shirt), that make persistent economic growth possible. Ideas are the instructions that let us combine limited physical resources in arrangements that are ever more valuable.[19]

And, he goes on to say, the number of potential combinations of the steps that make up processes or the components of a product is virtually inexhaustible.

Corporate Size and Knowledge Management

At a time when firms need to "know what they know" and must use that knowledge effectively, the size and geographic dispersion of many of them make it especially difficult to locate existing knowledge and get it to where it is needed. In a small, localized company a manager probably knows who has experience in a particular aspect of the business and can walk across the hall and talk to him. Our studies have shown that the maximum size of an organization in which people know one another well enough to have a reliable grasp of collective organizational knowledge is two hundred to three hundred people. The stock of knowledge in a global enterprise with scattered offices and plants and a complex mix of products and functions is vast, but that potential boon is part of the problem. How do you find what you need? The mere existence of knowledge somewhere in the organization is of little benefit; it becomes a valuable corporate asset only if it is accessible, and its value increases with the level of accessibility. Managers in large corporations know how common it is to reinvent the wheel, solving the same problems from scratch again and again, duplicating effort because knowledge of already developed solutions has not been shared within the company. This was one of Chrysler's motivations in formulating its "Engineering Books of Knowledge"; the company had forgotten some things it had previously learned about building cars. If there is no system in place to locate the most appropriate knowledge resources, employees make do with what is most easily available. That knowledge may be reasonably good, but in today's competitive environment reasonably good is not good enough. Hence the attempts by many companies, including one described below by the worldwide oil firm BP, to apply technology to the problem of global knowledge transfer.

Computer Networks and Knowledge Exchange

The low cost of computers and networks has created a potential infrastructure for knowledge exchange and opened up important knowledge management opportunities. The computational power of computers has little relevance to knowledge work, but the communication and storage capabilities of networked computers make them knowledge enablers. Through e-mail, groupware, the Internet, and intranets, computers and networks can point to people with knowledge and connect people who need to share knowledge over a distance. Desktop videoconferencing and multimedia computing that transmits sound and video as well as text make it possible to communicate some of the richness and subtlety of one person's knowledge to another.

What we must remember is that this new information technology is only the pipeline and storage system for knowledge exchange. It does not create knowledge and cannot guarantee or even promote knowledge generation or knowledge sharing in a corporate culture that doesn't favor those activities. The proverbial phrase "if we build it, they will come" does not apply to information technology.[20] The availability of Lotus Notes does not change a knowledge-hoarding culture into a knowledge-sharing one, alas.[21] The medium turns out not to be the message and does not even guarantee that there will *be* a message.

A Case in Point: British Petroleum's Virtual Teamwork Program

In 1993, BP Exploration, the division of BP that finds and produces oil and gas, organized its regional operating centers into forty-two separate business assets. BP Managing Director John Browne, who oversaw the transformation of BPX into what he called "a federation of assets," wanted these units to have the freedom to develop processes and solutions appropriate to their particular problems. The best and most adaptable local innovations could be used elsewhere in the larger company. In effect, BPX would be able to draw on the variety and creative power of forty-two moderate-sized companies. This idea of a corporate federation is similar to the "multilocal" structure Nonaka and Takeuchi describe in *The Knowledge-Creating Company* as part of Matsushita's corporate aim of becoming a "possibility-searching company." They remark on "the importance of transcending the dichotomy between localization and globalization," an apt description of Browne's aim.[22] Fully aware that the competitiveness of the global marketplace had made efficiency and innovation necessary for continuing success, he wanted BP to combine the agility of a small company with the resources of a large one. Browne understood that even giants will need to be light on their feet in the 1990s and beyond.

Planning

The communication capabilities BPX needed to realize the idea of a federation—and to create the possibility of "local" connections over distance—were provided by recent developments in cheap computing and related technologies. As the result of a discussion of these technologies at an upper-management technology meeting late in 1994, BPX launched an eighteen-month pilot project called the Virtual Teamwork Program. Its purpose was to develop effective ways for members of teams to collaborate across different locations.

Although BPX managers did not explicitly label it a knowledge management project, from the beginning the aims and operating principles of the program reflected an understanding of the importance of knowledge and the need to develop appropriate ways to share it. The primary aim of the initiative was to let knowledgeable people talk to each other, not to try to capture or tabulate their expertise. The Virtual Teamwork Program's goal was to build a network of people, not a storehouse of data, information, or knowledge. The hardware and software chosen for the Virtual Teamwork stations included desktop videoconferencing equipment, multimedia e-mail, application sharing, shared chalkboards, a document scanner, tools to record videoclips, groupware, and a Web browser. The emphasis was on richness of communication, on duplicating as much as possible the nuances, variety, and human dimension of face-to-face contact. The project team understood that the value of individual expertise resides largely in just those subtleties and intuitions, which words alone cannot convey.

BP's Virtual Teamwork Program stressed richness of communication.

A key early decision, made by John Cross, head of Information Technology (IT), was that an independent group, not the IT function, should undertake the project. He believed that the program would be less likely to fall into familiar IT patterns if a group drawn from different parts of the company ran it. Also, the intentional absence of IT control would make clear that the project was about communication, business change, and corporate behavior, not technology for its own sake. The idea of technology as a tool, not an end in itself, was reinforced by the "coaching" program developed by the Change Management Team, a subgroup of the Virtual Teamwork Program Team. This program showed participants how to use the technology *and* helped them understand how it could further their work. Project leaders referred to "coaching" rather than "training" to emphasize that the process would be a personal interaction: a "coach" working with "players," not a trainer presenting information to passive recipients. The coaches and team members communicated with each other using the VT stations, an ongoing real-life demonstration of the system's value as a tool for collaborative work and knowledge exchange. Discussions between the Change Management Team and what eventually became known as the Knowledge Management Team kept the focus on the broad goal (also suggested by the coaching metaphor) of encouraging project team members to discover untapped potential in themselves and the system. The emphasis was on person-to-person contact and human needs, not on system requirements or an electronic knowledge repository. Only 20 percent of the coaches' time was designated for training in how to use the system. The rest was devoted to helping team members link their business objectives to the capabilities of the system, and challenging them to consider the new ways of working that the VT equipment made possible. Coaching meant not only "how to" but "what" and "why." The core team spent approximately half of the pilot's budget on coaching.

Results

The success of virtual teamworking in four of the five groups that took part in the pilot was demonstrated by volume of use, participant enthusiasm, and measurable savings in time and money. Tellingly, the single failure occurred in the Petrotechnical group, whose members were mainly interested in exchanging data, not knowledge; the VT clients' potential for delivering richly varied communication did not particularly interest them. In addition, that was the one group that, for budgetary reasons, did not have the benefit of coaching.

When equipment failure brought operations to a halt on a North Sea mobile drilling ship one day in 1995, the ship's drilling engineers hauled the faulty hardware in front of a tiny video camera connected to one of British Petroleum's Virtual Teamwork stations. Using a satellite link, they dialed up the Aberdeen office of a drilling equipment expert who examined the malfunctioning part visually while talking to the shipboard engineers. He quickly diagnosed the problem and guided them through the necessary repairs. In the past a shutdown of this kind would have necessitated flying an expert out by helicopter or sending the ship (leased at a cost of $150,000 a day) back to port and out of commission for several days. This shutdown lasted only a few hours.

This episode illustrates how virtual teamworking technology can get knowledge where it is needed. Technology brought the expert and the situation that required his expertise together. The VT clients allowed him to see the problem while talking to people who were actually on the scene. His virtual presence gave the shipboard engineers the benefit of his skill and experience, enabling them to understand and solve the problem quickly. In this type of situation, the person-to-person connection is a much more expedient way of transferring knowledge than trying to extract it from the expert and distributing it in a form that those already at the site would then have to interpret. However, it is not more efficient for a recurring problem, so BP is also developing a repository of solutions to frequently encountered problems.

Another case in which virtual teamworking proved its effectiveness was the Andrew Project, a joint endeavor by BP, Brown and Root (a design and engineering firm based in Houston with an office in Wimbledon), and Trafalgar House (a construction company based in Scotland) to build a new oil platform in the North Sea. Andrew team members took advantage of the application-sharing feature of the VT clients to write joint memos in just ten or fifteen minutes. These previously involved hours or days of sending drafts back and forth by mail. Virtual meetings and VT work sharing led to quantifiable benefits on the Andrew Project, including significant reductions in travel costs and expenses associated with bringing vendors on site. There were also measurable productivity improvements related to more efficient information searches and issue resolution, and reductions in duplication and wasted travel time. Virtual teamworking contributed significantly to the project's meeting its target date, to lower offshore costs, and to a much lower total cost of bringing forward first oil, a key milestone in the development of a new field. The technology did not eliminate the need for personal meetings, which BP employees still required to establish mutual trust and understanding and to hash out important issues that involved large numbers of team members. Once they had met in person, though, participants found that videoconferencing maintained a sense of trust and direct personal contact that phone calls, e-mail, or memos could not match. One indication of the difference was that participants honored commitments made electronically "face-to-face" using the VT stations much more consistently than commitments made by phone or mail.

BP managers tend to downplay the importance of incremental efficiency gains. They are more interested in the changes in how work is done and the explosions of creativity that they believe virtual teamworking can help spark. VT station users have also begun communicating across projects. Members of the Andrew Project in Aberdeen, for instance, are connecting with members of the offshore Miller Team to apply their experience on the mature Miller oil field in the North Sea to the emerging Andrew field. This type of collaboration inspired the core team's imaginary headline "Scottish oil discovered in Alaska!" to suggest the potential of virtual teamworking to nullify distance and create a team out of widely scattered individuals.

BP has also instituted what it calls Virtual Teamwork Business Networking Centers, which are used once a week for virtual coffee breaks. Up to twenty people at eight separate locations have joined in video conversations with no set agenda. Like co-workers around the water cooler or Japanese R&D people in the "talk rooms" provided by their companies, they discuss current work and describe problems they've been struggling with or ideas they've come across. Their hope—and British Petroleum's—is that the conversations will pay off in serendipitous ways. Two participants might discover a surprising, useful connection between their projects, or a suggestion from an unexpected source might help solve a difficult problem. The conversations may simply give participants a better sense of what's happening elsewhere in the company, but that too is beneficial. Openness to the unexpected was one of the operating principles of the project, since the creative innovations BP is looking for are by definition unforeseen.

At the end of the pilot program, BP executives approved plans to expand by a significant number of new units in 1996. Initiatives are under way to apply VT technology and knowledge principles to better understanding the joint ventures and drilling firm's skills in processes. In particular, the VT technology will now support BP's entire senior management team. Project staff expect that the technology and coaching will lead to a more collaborative culture of executive decision making across the organization. In recognition of the fact that the VT project is about sharing knowledge, the Knowledge Management and Change Management teams have been combined into a single group called Knowledge and Teamworking Services. The core team hopes to provide virtual teamworking equipment to a high proportion of BP's professional staff by the end of 1997—the critical mass needed to transform the far-flung company into a close-knit federation of business units and workers. Their goal and Browne's is to create a collaborative learning organization with the agility and creativity to thrive in the new century. They view shared knowledge as a key factor in innovation and productivity.

Lessons Learned

British Petroleum's experience with its Virtual Teamworking project illustrates some of the characteristics of knowledge and the principles and benefits of knowledge management that we have described in this chapter. It also points to topics and concepts that we will tackle systematically later in this book. By way of summary and preview, here are the important features of the program and the principles they reflect.

BP's Virtual Teamwork Program	Knowledge Management Principles
• Members of knowledge communities were identified, then linked by technology.	• Knowledge originates and resides in people's minds.
• Relationships were built through actual and virtual face-to-face meetings.	• Knowledge sharing requires trust.
• Technology was used for communication and collaboration; training emphasized goals, not hardware and software.	• Technology enables new knowledge behaviors.
• Training and upper-management support emphasized the importance of new behaviors.	• Knowledge sharing must be encouraged and rewarded.
• Upper management initiated the project and authorized funds and the core team.	• Management support and resources are essential.
• Five test groups allowed for variety and clear, limited goals.	• Knowledge initiatives should begin with a pilot program.
• Savings and productivity increases were quantified; expanding VT use and participant enthusiasm were qualitative measures.	• Quantitative and qualitative measurements are needed to evaluate the initiative.
• In addition to having specific goals, the project left room for the unexpected.	• Knowledge is creative and should be encouraged to develop in unexpected ways.

Grace is given of God,
  but knowledge is bought
  in the market.
  —Arthur Hugh Clough

2

The Promise and Challenge of Knowledge Markets

R A P I D L Y or slowly, usefully or unproductively, knowledge moves through organizations. It is exchanged, bought, bartered, found, generated, and applied to work. In contrast to individual knowledge, organizational knowledge is highly dynamic: it is moved by a variety of forces. If we want knowledge to move and be utilized more effectively, we need to better understand the forces that drive it.

We believe market forces power its movement, working similarly to markets for more tangible goods. There is a genuine market for knowledge in organizations.[1] Like markets for goods and services, the knowledge market has buyers and sellers who negotiate to reach a mutually satisfactory price for the goods exchanged. It has brokers who bring buyers and sellers together and even entrepreneurs who use their market knowledge to create internal power bases. Knowledge market transactions occur because all of the participants in them believe that they will benefit from them in some particular way. In economists' jargon, they expect the transactions to provide "utility."

People search for knowledge because they expect it to help them succeed in their work. Knowledge is the most sought-after remedy to uncertainty. We all try to reach knowledgeable people when we see the need to deliver a solution to a problem. When we supply knowledge, we expect to benefit too. Within organizations cash is usually not involved in these transactions, but that should not disguise the fact that a market price system exists and payment is made or assumed. The knowledge market, like any other, is a system in which participants exchange a scarce unit for present or future value.

25

Understanding that there are knowledge markets and that they operate similarly to other markets is essential to managing knowledge successfully in organizations. Many knowledge initiatives have been based on the utopian assumption that knowledge moves without friction or motivating force, that people will share knowledge with no concern for what they may gain or lose by doing so. Companies install e-mail or collaborative software and expect knowledge to flow freely through the electronic pipeline. When it doesn't happen, they are more likely to blame the software or inadequate training than to face a fact of life: people rarely give away valuable possessions (including knowledge) without expecting something in return. This may be especially true in our current business climate. Even if only partially mindful of doing so, people make choices about how to spend their limited time and energy and base those choices on perceived self-interest. We don't expect a car salesman to sell us a car at cost, sacrificing his commission simply because we want to pay less. Nor does the salesman expect us to hand him money and walk out of the showroom without a vehicle. No one believes that such one-sided transactions happen in the marketplace or in most of life—even social transactions are generally based on some sort of exchange, as many sociological studies in exchange theory have shown. Just because the object of exchange is intangible does not mean that the market forces are less strong. Knowledge initiatives that ignore the dynamics of markets (and, of course, human nature) are doomed to fail.

Don't expect software to solve your knowledge problem.

We will describe these markets for knowledge in organizations and develop a preliminary taxonomy of that market. We believe the only way to have a market that works well is, first of all, to recognize that market forces exist; second, to try to understand how it functions; and third, to make it more efficient. By talking about knowledge market inefficiencies—and diseconomies—we can get at some of the problems that inhibit knowledge exchange and the transformation of corporate knowledge into value, and can sketch the outlines of a more efficient market.

The first step in any knowledge initiative is recognizing that there are markets for knowledge.

The Political Economy of Knowledge Markets

There really are no such things as "pure" markets—markets that can be understood solely in economic terms. As analysts from John Stuart Mill to Karl Marx to Thorstein Veblen to James March have argued, every market system is embedded in and affected by social and political realities. The value of anything exchanged depends strongly on the context of the transaction. Someone who pays $20,000 for a wristwatch no more accurate than a $20 Timex is obviously not buying a mechanism for telling time. The value of the $20,000 watch is mainly social; it buys the owner status in a society that looks up to or envies people who can afford to purchase and display such items.

Sociologist Harrison White has said that sociology, economics, and political science are the three lenses needed to see organizations fully; no one discipline can capture their whole meaning.[2] We strongly agree that social, economic, and political realities must be taken fully into account to understand markets for knowledge. If the political reality of an organization is such that calculating and secretive hoarders of knowledge thrive, then potential knowledge buyers will have no currency valuable enough to tempt them to share their expertise. Knowledge exchange will be minimal. If it is considered a sign of weakness or incompetence within the culture of an organization to admit to a problem you can't solve on your own, then the social cost of "buying" knowledge will be too high. Once again, the knowledge market won't operate well. At Mobil Oil, where disapproval of "bragging" is embedded in the culture, the efficiency of the knowledge market was reduced because knowledge owners are reluctant to "advertise" their knowledge and were distrusted by their colleagues if they did. Similarly, a Hewlett-Packard vice-president who transferred from the United States to Australia found it difficult to encourage people to advertise their individual expertise in a democratic culture of "mateship" that discourages calling attention to individual performance. While these cultural norms can have positive impacts too, they inhibit internal knowledge markets.

We will look first at the players in the knowledge market: the buyers, sellers, and brokers who take part in knowledge transactions and drive knowledge markets. An individual can perform all three roles in a single day and sometimes plays more than one role simultaneously. It is quite common, for instance, to be a knowledge buyer, seller, and broker during the same conversation. To ensure clarity in the following discussion, we will look at the roles separately.

Buyers

Knowledge buyers or seekers are usually people trying to resolve an issue whose complexity and uncertainty precludes an easy answer. Clearly, asking for the GNP of France or a list of the twenty largest U.S. banks is not a knowledge search; it is a request for data. Knowledge seekers are looking for insights, judgments, and understanding. They want answers to questions such as "What is this particular client like?" or "How did we manage to win that sale?" that require complex answers—answers imbued with all the emotional subtexts so important to our sensemaking. They seek knowledge because it has distinct value to them. It will help them make a sale or accomplish a task more efficiently; it will improve their judgments and skills and help them make better decisions. In short, it will make them more successful at their work.[3]

This task of searching for knowledge accounts for a fairly substantial part of what many managers and executives do. A recent informal study done at Hughes Aerospace by Arian Ward estimated that between 15 and 20 percent of managerial time is spent specifically in knowledge search and responding to requests for knowledge.

Sellers

Knowledge sellers are people in an organization with an internal market reputation for having substantial knowledge about a process or subject. They may sell their knowledge by the piece or, more likely, in a "bundle," in exchange for a salary. Although virtually everyone is a knowledge buyer at one time or another, not everyone is necessarily a seller. Some people are skilled but unable to articulate their tacit knowledge. Others have knowledge that is too specialized, personal, or limited to be of much value on the knowledge market.

Some potential knowledge sellers keep themselves out of the market because they believe they benefit more from hoarding their knowledge than they would from sharing it. In many organizations, of course, this is a rational belief. If knowledge is power, then the owners of knowledge have power that may dissipate if other people come to know what they know. This is a reality of knowledge politics that managers need to deal with in designing knowledge initiatives. One of the challenges of knowledge management is to ensure that knowledge sharing is rewarded more than knowledge hoarding.[4]

Brokers

Knowledge brokers (also known as "gatekeepers" and "boundary spanners") make connections between buyers and sellers: those who need knowledge and those who have it.[5] According to a study we developed for a client, about 10 percent of managers across industries are boundary spanners and therefore potential knowledge brokers. They enjoy exploring their organizations, finding out what people do and who knows what. They like to understand the big picture, which puts them in a position to know where to go for knowledge, especially if it falls outside their official area of responsibility.

Librarians frequently act as covert knowledge brokers, suited by temperament and their role as information guides to the task of making people-to-people as well as people-to-text connections. For instance, when someone in a high-tech firm asks the corporate librarian to do research on the next generation of reduced instruction set chips, the librarian is likely to say, "Did you know that John Smith has been asking about the same subject? You might want to talk to him." Because corporate libraries often serve the whole organization, *Corporate librarians can be indispensable knowledge brokers.* librarians are among the few employees who have contact with people from many departments. In the course of their work, they come to understand a great deal about the various knowledge needs and resources of the company. Traditionally, librarians value customer service and have highly developed techniques for finding out what they don't already know. All of these factors make them natural knowledge brokers. One of us had a consulting experience that vividly illustrates the contribution of corporate librarians in this area.

About eight years ago, NYNEX decided to develop benchmarks for all major technical and managerial functions and asked for help in identifying which library activities should be compared to those in other firms. The director of the corporate resource center developed a list of the most valuable services the library provided. Between us, we had twenty-five years of experience in library and information science, so we should have been able to figure out what libraries do. We came up with eight activities and sent the list to a diverse group of NYNEX library users, asking if these were truly the most valued library activities. To our astonishment, we had omitted the single most valuable function: knowledge brokering. We had left it out because it was informal and undocumented, but it was the service that people cared about most. Librarians were key players in creating efficient knowledge markets, in helping buyers and sellers find each other.

Firms often do not realize the importance of librarians' roles as knowledge workers and managers, and their status and compensation seldom reflect their real value to a firm. In fact, knowledge brokers of all kinds are frequently underrated, though they play an essential role in the knowledge market. Because of their broad, boundary-spanning interests, rational-minded analysts may view them as unfocused or undisciplined, or even "nosy" or "gossipy."[6] Making knowledge connections mainly by talking to people, they are sometimes criticized for spending their time "chatting" rather than doing "real work." Since they are facilitators of other people's success, their contribution may not be visible to managers who think in terms of traditional productivity. The merits of their activities are never measured or captured by human resource systems based on how many people they direct. It is much harder to measure the profit they help generate than the cost to the company of their salaries and benefits. One of the first things firms do when they cut costs (and one of the last things they should do!) is close the corporate library.[7] They see it as pure expense—the cost of staff, space, books, periodicals, and on-line subscriptions. They have no familiar ways to quantify the benefits of the library as an information source and knowledge marketplace. Even though they "know" value exists there, their inability to express it in traditional accounting or financial terms makes them behave as if it didn't.

Some informal knowledge brokers are really knowledge entrepreneurs. They intentionally set out to become experts on who has knowledge and how to exploit it. They then "sell" this expertise, not for money but in exchange for future favors and repute. In effect, they develop an internal knowledge business.

The Price System

All markets have a price system so that value exchanges can be efficiently rendered and recorded. What is the price system of the knowledge market? What sort of currency do participants exchange? What are the necessary market conditions?

When firms buy knowledge from outside their organizations, they frequently (though not invariably) pay with cash. A lawyer, an investment banker, or a consultant can make several thousand dollars per day because the client company perceives that his or her special knowledge is worth that much. Within organizations, the medium of exchange is seldom money, but there are agreed-upon currencies (or "entities," in the language of exchange theory) that drive the knowledge market. As we have said, sellers as well as buyers exchange knowledge because they believe they gain from the transaction. Look at this example, a common experience for knowledge sellers.

> It's six o'clock on a mid-winter evening and snowing again. If I leave my office now, I can be home by seven. That's when my family expects me. I'm looking forward to a quiet evening at home: a nice hot dinner, maybe a fire in the fireplace. As I'm putting my coat on, the phone rings. It's a consultant from another area of the company—not someone I know well; I met him once or twice at meetings. He apologizes for calling at the last minute and says he's just been told he has to fly out to see a major company client in the morning. He knows I've worked with this client in the past. Would I tell him about them? Who are the best people to talk to? What is the company culture like? What do they value? What are they looking for from us?
>
> My caller wants knowledge, not data or even information, so I can't answer him in just a few sentences or merely direct him to an on-line repository. While these gestures might help him, they wouldn't be sufficient. It will take me at least half an hour to give him a useful response. If I choose to stay in my office and talk to him (delaying my return home and possibly ruining a pleasant evening), what do I get in return? How does the silent auctioneer in my head weigh considerable inconvenience against possible help to a fellow consultant? What sort of payment could I receive for sharing my knowledge that would make it worthwhile for me to extend my long day and disrupt my personal life?

This scenario raises the question of what kinds of payment exist in the knowledge market. We have come to the conclusion that there are at least three factors at work. In order of significance from greatest to least, they are reciprocity, repute, and altruism. We will discuss each of these factors briefly, then consider the vital importance of trust, without which no knowledge market can operate effectively.

Reciprocity

A knowledge seller will spend the time and effort needed to share knowledge effectively if he expects the buyers to be willing sellers when *he* is in the market for their knowledge. This is what Tom Wolfe calls "the favor bank" in *Bonfire of the Vanities*. I may choose to miss my dinner and help my fellow consultant if I believe that the caller has knowledge that *I* may need to elicit in the future. If the caller knows nothing that could possibly be of use to me in the future, I may claim that I have no knowledge to offer and decide to go home instead.

Time, energy, and knowledge are finite. They are very scarce resources in most people's workdays. In general, we won't spend scarce resources unless the expenditure brings a meaningful return. As nice a person as I may be—as much as I might like to help a colleague who has a problem—I don't have the time or strength to respond to every knowledge request that comes my way. The choices I make will usually depend on my perceived self-interest.

Reciprocity may be achieved less directly than by getting knowledge back from others as payment for providing it to them. In firms structured as partnerships, knowledge sharing that improves profitability will return a benefit to the sharer, now and in the future. Individuals who have significant stock options in a firm are in a similar position. Whether or not a knowledge seller expects to be paid with equally valuable knowledge from the buyer, he may believe that his being known for sharing knowledge readily will make others in the company more willing to share with him. That is a rational assumption, since his reputation as a seller of valuable knowledge will make others confident of *his* willingness to reciprocate when he is the buyer and they have knowledge to sell: His knowledge credit is good. I may stand in my office with my coat on and talk to my colleague to enhance my own reputation as a knowledge seller. Perhaps that will make it more likely that people throughout the company will respond in kind when I need their knowledge. So reciprocity and repute are related.

Repute

A knowledge seller usually wants others to know him as a knowledgeable person with valuable expertise that he is willing to share with others in the company. Repute may seem intangible, but it can produce tangible results. As we have suggested, having a reputation for knowledge sharing makes achieving reciprocity more likely: being known as a knowledge seller makes one a more effective knowledge buyer. Having a reputation as a valuable knowledge source can also lead to the tangible benefits of job security, promotion, and all the rewards and trappings of a company guru. Although a seller does not receive cash directly, he may receive a higher salary or bonus from sharing knowledge with others. In many consulting firms, consultants' bonuses are tied to demonstrated knowledge generation and transfer. In any organization, however, the value of repute in the knowledge market will depend on the political and social structures of the organization. Knowledge sharing has no fixed or universal market value but has, rather, a range of measures from penalties (for "wasting time" talking to people instead of "working") to significant advancement based mainly on knowledge contributions.

In businesses such as consulting, investment banking, and entertainment, success hinges on repute. In most businesses today, the importance of repute is increasing as the old social contract between firm and worker based on length of service and loyalty erodes. As the promise of continued employment in exchange for long, loyal service fades, workers at all levels feel considerable pressure to heighten their individual repute for their demonstrated knowledge, skills, and competencies.

In our winter evening case, the hope of enhancing our reputations may lead us to stay late at the office and answer our colleague's questions. If this consultant tells others how helpful and knowledgeable Prusak or Davenport is, especially via the firm's informal networks, that may enhance our reputations. (It may also lead to further requests for knowledge sharing, one of the potential drawbacks of being a successful seller.) If our company formally tracks and rewards knowledge sharing, the likelihood of our cooperation leading to some future tangible benefit will increase.

Altruism

It is possible, of course, that a knowledge sharer may be a nice guy who wants to help whether or not he gets anything beyond a "thank you" in return. Or he may be so passionate about his knowledge that he is happy to share it whenever he gets a chance. Such people do exist. Many knowledge sharers are motivated in part by a love of their subject and to some degree by altruism, whether "for the good of the firm" or based on a natural impulse to help others. We all know individuals who simply like helping.

Mentoring is a form of knowledge transfer based in part on altruism. Erik Erikson, among others, has pointed out that people go through a "generative stage" (usually in later middle age) when it becomes important to them to pass on what they have learned to others. Firms cannot create this impulse, but they can encourage or discourage it. Formally recognizing mentoring relationships, giving managers time to pass on their knowledge, and understanding that experienced employees *have* valuable knowledge are ways to foster mentoring. Many firms ignore the contribution that older workers can make to their younger colleagues because they have no way of evaluating or efficiently capturing exactly what it is that the older worker *knows*.

We've mentioned an interesting exception at Chrysler Corporation, where knowledge managers understand that master mechanics and engineers have a stock of productive knowledge that is essential to the firm's viability. The "Engineering Books of Knowledge" they developed serve as a kind of formalized mentoring tool. Contributing to the books is based, at least in part, on altruism. Chrysler is encouraging the formation of the trust and relationships that lead to altruism by creating "tech clubs" for engineers with similar backgrounds and orientations.

Knowledge altruism is real and can be encouraged. It flourishes in organizations that hire nice people and treat them nicely. We constrain it, though, by increasing demands on the time and energy of employees and by cultural factors. C.B. MacPherson argues that our national culture is one of "possessive individualism." It clearly doesn't make sense to depend entirely on goodwill to cultivate something as important as knowledge sharing.

Trust

Trust can trump the other factors that positively affect the efficiency of knowledge markets. Without trust, knowledge initiatives will fail, regardless of how thoroughly they are supported by technology and rhetoric and even if the survival of the organization depends on effective knowledge transfer.[8] For the knowledge market to operate in an organization, trust must be established in the following three ways:

1. *Trust must be visible.* The members of the organization must see people get credit for knowledge sharing. They must directly experience reciprocity. There must be direct evidence of trust; a declara-

tion of the importance of trust in the corporate mission statement is not sufficient.

2. *Trust must be ubiquitous.* If part of the internal knowledge market is untrustworthy, the market becomes asymmetric and less efficient.

3. *Trustworthiness must start at the top.* Trust tends to flow downward through organizations. Upper management's example can often define the norms and values of the firm. If top managers are trustworthy, trust will seep through and come to characterize the whole firm. If they cynically exploit others' knowledge for personal gain, distrust will propagate throughout the company. Their values become known to the firm through signals, signs, and symbols.

Personal contact and trust are intimately related. The U.S. Army recognizes what it calls "face time" as an essential element in building trust within groups and measures it as one of the determinants of successful treatment. In addition to being a necessary condition for knowledge exchange, trust can be a product of it as well. British Petroleum's Virtual Teamworking project succeeded because of the atmosphere of mutual trust established by management, the VT project team, and the participants. Face-to-face meetings among participants established rapport. The frequent videoconferences during which participants exchanged knowledge raised the level of trust and led to measurable improvements in honoring commitments to meet the delivery dates of promised work.

Trust is an essential condition of a functioning knowledge market, as it is of any market that does not depend on binding and enforceable contracts. Of course, even transactions bound by written contracts entail some degree of trust. But the knowledge market—with no written contracts and no court of appeals—is very much based *A firm's knowledge market must be founded on mutual trust.* on credit, not cash. The word "credit" means "to believe" or "to trust," and mutual trust is at the heart of knowledge exchange. When we sell knowledge within an organization, our receiving adequate payment now or in the future depends on the trustworthiness of the buyer and of management. In most cases, we will gain repute for a knowledge transaction only if the buyer gives us credit for it. If he pretends the knowledge was his all along, we gain nothing. If someone claims our research results as his own, we are no more likely to make further knowledge available to him than we are to offer our house to someone who stole our car. A buyer who fails to give credit and recognize his debt to us is also unlikely to reciprocate when we need knowledge. Similarly, management that pays lip service to the value it attaches to knowledge sharing but rewards employees who hoard knowledge will not create the level of trust needed to make the knowledge market effective.

The role of trust in knowledge transactions helps explain why knowledge initiatives based solely on the belief that infrastructure creates communication seldom deliver the expected benefits. The impersonality of groupware allows anyone to post information and invites anonymous access to that information. However, it does not create the same confidence in the quality of knowledge that personal acquaintance and reputation can inspire. The promise of reciprocity in such a system is also weak. The buyer who downloads an item from a server does not feel the same obligation to the provider that he would if he got the same material through a phone call or meeting. This is why the most successful groupware systems are moderated to assure that posted material is accurate and timely. Some even have mechanisms for metering the use of posted items and crediting the suppliers.

Knowledge Market Signals

By "market signals" we mean information that indicates both where knowledge actually resides in the organization and how to gain access to it. Accessibility is another way of looking at cost, since it is a measure of the time and effort that buyers must expend to get knowledge and the kind of return the seller expects. There are formal and informal signals in knowledge markets. The informal ones are generally more accurate guides to where knowledge can be "bought," but they often require personal interaction.

Position and Education

Title or position is the most common formal signal indicating who has or should have valuable knowledge. If we need to learn about a particular research project, it makes sense to go to the project manager; if we need to know what is happening in marketing, why not ask the director of the marketing department? This commonsense approach can work, but not consistently. In fact, the organizational chart is generally not an effective guide to company knowledge. The project director may be unwilling to share his knowledge, or he may have had no direct involvement with the aspects of the project we need to understand. It may be that the marketing director once knew a lot about marketing but now knows mainly about the politics of running a marketing department. Clearly, advancement within a firm is not based solely on knowledge— even tacit or social knowledge—but influenced by other key variables such as drive, ambition, energy, intuition, judgment, ego (or lack thereof), and luck. The expert who knows exactly what we need to learn and would be willing to tell us may be sitting in one of the cubicles we pass on the way to the director's office. The trick is to know which one.

Similarly, education is a formal market signal that may or may not be helpful. If Lorraine has a Ph.D. in a subject we need to find out about, it is logical to go to her: she is a subject-matter expert and has the credentials to prove it. ("Credentials," like "credit," comes from a root meaning "to believe.") She may have just the knowledge we want, but it is possible that Lorraine hasn't learned anything new since she defended her thesis a couple of decades ago. Or her knowledge may be too academic to apply usefully to a practical situation. Or again, she may not be willing to tell us what she knows.

Informal Networks

Probably the best knowledge market signals—though they are still imperfect—flow through the informal networks of practice that develop in organizations. Within these webs, people ask each other who knows what—who has previously provided knowledge that turned out to be reliable and useful. If the person you ask where to go for specific knowledge doesn't know an appropriate seller, she probably knows someone else who does know. Much of the work that goes on in firms gets done because people continually ask one another, through informal networks, who knows how to do things. The informal networks of buyers, brokers, and sellers move knowledge through the organization. Knowledge markets cluster around formal and informal networks, so providing information about these networks is a good way to make knowledge visible.

Informal networks have the benefits and drawbacks of their informality. Because they function through personal contact and word of mouth, they engender the trust that is an essential engine of successful knowledge exchange. A recommendation that comes from someone we know and respect within the firm is more likely to lead us to a trustworthy seller with appropriate knowledge than would a cold call based on the organizational chart or corporate phone directory. Such informal networks are also dynamic. Because they consist of people more or less continually in communication with one another, they tend to update themselves as conditions change. People share information about who has left the company or moved to new projects, who has recently become surprisingly useful sources of knowledge, and who has become unexpectedly reticent.

If this sounds a lot like gossip, it is. Most corporate gossip is a form of knowledge transfer about internal processes. As the eminent organizational expert James March has noted, gossip in the workplace—often considered wasted time—is the way the company's knowledge network updates itself. More formal systems, such as printed or electronic repositories of employee skills and interests, begin to get stale as soon as they are established. They also generally lack the interactivity that makes informal networks work.

What sounds like workplace gossip is often a knowledge network updating itself.

The main disadvantage of these networks is that, by being informal and undocumented, they are not readily available to all who need them. Their viability depends on chance conversations and local connections that sometimes work well but other times do not happen at all. Imagine that information about new cars or restaurants came only through similar informal networks and there were no advertisements, articles, or reviews. We would have to rely entirely on advice from acquaintances. The informal network may help us avoid some bad decisions but it would not give us the full spectrum of choices in our area. To get even a reasonably wide range of recommendations, we would have to spend a good deal of time following the branches of personal, undocumented connections. Such searching can be slow, and the results often unreliable.

Communities of Practice

Sometimes co-workers who have complementary knowledge will form a group. Often called "communities of practice," these self-organized groups are generally initiated by employees who communicate with one another because they share common work practices, interests, or aims.[9] If their communications prove useful over time, they may formalize the arrangement, giving themselves a group name and establishing a regular system of interchange. For example, a number of BP scientists and engineers with a shared interest in water produced as a by-product of drilling formed themselves into a group that eventually communicated through e-mail, newsletters, and occasional meetings. The Produced-Water Group later became one of the Virtual Teamwork pilot groups and used VT videoconferencing technology to enrich the closeness of their interaction. Similarly, the people involved in Citibank's commercial lending activities in the Southeast Asian region organized themselves into a group so they could pool expertise and solve problems together. Academics with common interests have been forming such groups for years—often with the help of the Internet.

Managers should regard communities of practice as company assets and look for ways to preserve them. Too literal an application of reengineering principles, with their emphasis on efficiency, has weakened some of these informal knowledge networks and groups. Some companies have driven out the "slack" necessary for such groups to function well. A reengineered organization is likely to have eliminated the jobs of some of the knowledge brokers whose role is not recognized as essential to the firm's work, though they hold the knowledge networks together. By focusing on measurable "work" and underestimating the value of talk, reengineering can discourage the conversations and self-forming groups in which so much of the firm's knowledge work is done.

Managers shouldn't underestimate the value of talk.

Knowledge Market Inefficiencies

In efficient markets, buyers and sellers find each other and exchange their goods readily. A clear pricing system enables them to agree on the value of the goods being sold with the least possible friction. They have identical or similar ideas of the value of the currency used to buy the goods. In practice, efficient markets generate the most good at the least cost. Markets for knowledge, however, are notably inefficient in most organizations. The right seller is often hard to locate, and can be hard to reach even if we know her location. It is also difficult if not impossible to judge the quality of knowledge before we "purchase" it. Both the knowledge value and likelihood of eventual payment are uncertain.

To get a feel for the inefficiencies of the knowledge market, compare it to the market for new cars. In the car market, we can easily get information about the sellers and products. The Yellow Pages list all car dealers. Newspapers regularly print information about what cars are available, where to buy them, and what they cost. *Consumer Reports* and a host of other publications provide detailed independent evaluations of cars and reveal dealer costs. In many cases, a buyer will have a choice of vendors for the same product. The shopper has opportunities to examine and test cars before buying one. A written contract defines what is being bought and how much we must pay for it. Warranties and laws protect the buyer if the product is defective. Sellers have legal recourse if the buyer fails to pay.

Knowledge markets are obviously much murkier. The value of the knowledge is rarely as tangible or explicit as the value of a car. There are no *Consumer Reports* articles on knowledge sellers and brokers. As our discussion of the price system makes clear, payment is much less certain and less tangible than in the new car market. Information about where knowledge resides in the organization is highly imperfect. Much of the current interest in knowledge management derives from the fact that organizations lack good information about where their knowledge is and therefore have difficulty getting it and making use of it.

Three Key Factors

Our studies show that three factors in particular often cause knowledge markets to operate inefficiently in organizations: the incompleteness of information about the knowledge market; the asymmetry of knowledge; and the localness of knowledge.

Incompleteness of Information. Remember that much of the interest in knowledge management arises when firms realize they do not know where to find their own existing knowledge. The lack of maps and "Yellow Pages" (both of which we will consider later) to guide a knowledge buyer to a seller is a fundamental problem. The absence of explicit information about the pricing structure is also a source of inefficiency, with knowledge transactions inhibited by uncertainty about what the likely return on shared knowledge will be.

Asymmetry of Knowledge. There often is abundant knowledge on a subject in one department of an organization and a shortage somewhere else. Marketing may have extensive knowledge about a particular set of customers that Sales needs but lacks. Strategic knowledge that resides at the top may not be available to the middle managers who need to implement it. A certain amount of asymmetry must exist in any market. As we have said, markets cannot exist without scarcity. But strong asymmetry prevents knowledge from getting where it is needed. Buyers and sellers won't meet. There are always knowledge feasts and famines in organizations. As is true of other kinds of famines, the problem usually has more to do with information patterns, purchasing power, and distribution systems than with an absolute scarcity.

Localness of Knowledge. People usually get knowledge from their organizational neighbors. The knowledge market depends on trust, and individuals generally trust the people they know. Face-to-face meetings are often the best way to get knowledge; and as we have said, reliable information about more distant knowledge sources is usually not available. Also, mechanisms for getting access to distant knowledge tend to be weak or nonexistent. People will buy whatever knowledge the person in the next office may have rather than deal with the effort and uncertainty of trying to discover who in the company may know more. Simon and March use the term "satisficing" to describe the human tendency to settle for the knowledge or information that is "good enough" for their purposes. Knowledge initiatives will run into problems if they are based on the assumption that individuals will go to considerable lengths to get the best possible knowledge, since this is rarely borne out in practice.[10] High search cost for optimal knowledge is probably the biggest constraint to a completely efficient knowledge market within a firm, especially in large organizations. Localness adds to market inefficiency because it causes people to make do with less than optimal knowledge while a much better "product" goes unsold and unused. The distance between buyer and seller prevents a transaction from taking place.

A Case in Point: Javelin Development Corporation

Javelin Development Corporation, a real but disguised engineering and construction company, developed a plan to make knowledge available across projects in hopes of reducing construction time and costs. The idea was to apply existing design solutions to new situations. The centerpiece of the initiative was an on-line knowledge "warehouse" that engineers could draw from as they developed their designs. A year after implementation began, less than 5 percent of the planned features were in place and support for the initiative seemed to be fading.

We can analyze these disappointing results in terms of knowledge market inefficiencies. Chief among them was the lack of a clear price paid to individuals who shared their knowledge. Having been through a period of layoffs and fearing that more were coming, employees saw their unique knowledge as a source of job security and felt that sharing it would weaken their position. Like many engineering cultures, Javelin's also valued the creation of new knowledge over the re-use of existing designs. Although management supported knowledge sharing in a general way, its actions did not communicate assurance that sharing knowledge was genuinely important and would be rewarded. For instance, employees were expected to learn on their own time, not during office hours, a company norm that implied that acquiring knowledge wasn't "real work." The knowledge initiative had verbal support, but managers did not back it up with a sufficient investment of money and personnel. Some designated knowledge facilitators spent only 10 percent of their time on the project. No one created a mechanism for evaluating knowledge sharing in performance evaluations. As a result of all these signals, trust in the genuineness of corporate commitment to knowledge exchange remained low.

In addition, Javelin's knowledge warehouse was a bust as a marketplace. Potential sellers felt they gained little from adding to the stock of on-line knowledge. Potential buyers did not like the organization of the warehouse content. Project designers had favored a rather loosely structured organization so that knowledge would not be forced into old categories. But the engineers who were the intended users of the system favored a hierarchical system that would make it easy for them to find just the information they needed to solve a specific problem.

With uncertainty and skepticism about the value of offering or acquiring knowledge, lukewarm management support, and a marketplace poorly matched to the habits of potential buyers, the knowledge market at Javelin could not function efficiently. The company's serious localness problem was perhaps best exemplified by the experience of a very senior executive who had recently joined the firm. In his previous position at another organization, he had been the primary champion for a very successful knowledge management initiative, yet the organizers of Javelin's knowledge project knew nothing of his interest and expertise. Overall, the company has not yet begun to see the benefits it hoped to get from its knowledge project.

Knowledge Market Pathologies

Some knowledge markets have deep flaws that we call knowledge market pathologies: distortions that drastically inhibit the flow of knowledge. The pathologies described below overlap to some extent, but the distinctions suggested by the analogies to external markets may help identify and explain serious knowledge market problems in organizations.

Monopolies

If only one person or group holds knowledge that others need, a knowledge monopoly exists. The effect is similar to that of monopolies in the market for goods and services: the knowledge will come at a high price because there is no competition to moderate it. Everyone who has worked in an organization knows individuals who have exclusive control of key corporate knowledge and use that fact to establish a position of power. Such a person may "rent" his expertise to accomplish a task or solve a problem rather than sell his knowledge—even at a high price—since his monopoly will cease to exist once his knowledge is genuinely shared. (In this regard, a knowledge monopoly is different from a monopoly on goods or services.) The drawbacks for the organization are obvious. Important knowledge locked in a monopoly will not always be available when and where people need it to benefit the company. It will also not benefit from the interplay of knowledge that can generate new knowledge. According to Nonaka and Takeuchi, one of the conditions that encourages knowledge creation is "redundancy." They describe redundancy as shared information that allows individuals to "invade" one another's boundaries and offer advice and a new perspective.[11] The idea of redundancy, which we will consider in more detail in the next chapter, is clearly the antithesis of monopolistic thinking.

Artificial Scarcity

A knowledge monopoly is one form of artificial scarcity. In general, a corporate culture in which knowledge hoarding is the norm creates scarcity. Knowledge becomes very expensive not because it doesn't exist but because it is hard to get. Departments and groups may lack the knowledge they need to work effectively because the hoarding culture keeps it scarce.

Downsizing can also create knowledge scarcity by eliminating employees whose absence shows them to be owners of essential knowledge. The cost of losing this knowledge is high, leading to failed processes or the expense of luring back the laid-off workers or buying the equivalent of their knowledge from outside sources. In the post–Cold War retrench-ment of the defense industry,

Knowledge often walks out the door during downsizing.

for example, many aerospace companies offered buyout pack-ages as part of their downsiz-ing programs. They saw knowledge walk out the door with employees who took the offer, and had to rehire (often at higher consulting rates) the same people they had encouraged to leave.

To prevent this kind of "brain drain" from jeopardizing the American thermonuclear weapons program, Sandia National Laboratories, in New Mexico, undertook a knowledge preservation program at a time when many of its weapons experts were nearing retirement. It videotaped the experts in wide-ranging conversations about their knowledge, and then created transcripts. Though they hope that the United States will never need the knowledge again, Sandia's managers feel that they could trans-fer it to a new generation of researchers if necessary.

Trade Barriers

A variety of trade barriers hampers organizational markets. The hoarding that characterizes monopolies and artificial scarcity is a barrier erected by the possessiveness of the hoarding individual or department. The not-invented-here mentality that refuses to accept new knowledge is a mirror image of the barrier created by hoarding, a refusal to buy knowl-edge rather than a refusal to sell it. A variation on knowledge hoarding and the not-invented-here barrier is what we might call a class barrier: an unwillingness to give knowledge to or accept it from people in the organization who have relatively low status.

A barrier—even a trade ban—is sometimes established by an execu-tive who has the power to enforce a corporate orthodoxy by banning subjects that threaten it. In the early 1980s, Ken Olsen, the founder of Digital Equipment Corporation, insisted that the word "personal com-puter" and the concepts behind it could not be discussed at Digital. This blanket edict largely closed off the possibility of work in an area that should have been getting attention. Rather than face the challenge of microcomputer open systems, Olsen tried to pretend that it did not exist, and by doing so, damaged his company. Digital employees were power-less to respond to a threat that they could not publicly discuss.

Trade barriers can also arise when companies lack a good knowledge transfer infrastructure or effective market mechanisms. An obvious example is the lack of an effective computer network or communications system. Without the technology needed to codify knowledge and make it widely available, knowledge transactions will be limited and local. The absence of virtual and real places for buyers and sellers to meet is an infrastructure problem, as is the shortage of time for knowledge seeking, knowledge generation, and knowledge exchange. Both downsizing and reengineering, which tend to reduce the time available to look for and share knowledge, are likely to damage the knowledge market infrastructure.

Developing Effective Knowledge Markets

There are a number of ways firms can overcome the inefficiencies and pathologies of their knowledge markets. We will discuss these steps in detail in later chapters, but here are three areas in which initiatives are particularly important.

Using Information Technology Wisely

Technological developments and innovations have the potential to change market dynamics dramatically. In 1400 Western Europe was a commercial backwater compared with the rich, active markets of the Chinese, Islamic, and Indian empires. It was Europe's development of the armed ship that forced open markets for them and shifted the balance of power so that by 1600 market dominance had shifted to the West.[12]

There are many pitfalls and limitations in using information technology for knowledge work—trying to force fluid knowledge into rigid data structures, for example, or focusing too much on the system and not enough on content. But networks and desktop computers, with their ability to connect people and store and retrieve virtually unlimited amounts of content, can dramatically improve knowledge market efficiency. They can provide an infrastructure for moving knowledge and information about knowledge as well as for building virtual knowledge marketplaces.

Some organizations have developed electronic knowledge "Yellow Pages" to provide better information about where knowledge resides in the firm and how to get it. British Petroleum's Virtual Teamworking project is, in effect, an effort to expand the definition of "local" by linking team members electronically. A co-worker you can reach (and talk to and see) by clicking a button on your computer monitor may seem more "local" than someone three floors up in your own building, although he is physically a thousand miles away.

Building Marketplaces

Recognizing knowledge exchange as a market leads to commonsense strategies that can make the market more robust. One step, which we will consider in more detail in our discussion of knowledge transfer in Chapter 5, is to create market*places*—physical and virtual spaces dedicated to knowledge exchange. The rationale is the same as for the sale of goods and services: buying and selling are human activities, and people need a place to meet so they can carry them out. The ancient Greek Agora and Roman Forum were places of assembly for political discussion and decision, sharing the day's news, and buying and selling goods. They are striking archetypes for the public space that's essential for a society (or an organization) to function. Tellingly, NationsBank gave the name "Project Agora" to an internal knowledge project.

Many Japanese firms, including Dai-Ichi Pharmaceuticals, have established "talk rooms" where researchers are expected to have a cup of tea and spend twenty minutes or half an hour discussing one another's work. There is no agenda set for a talk room and no conference table, only an expectation that discussion among colleagues will benefit them and the company. Talk rooms are formalized and sanctioned locations for conversation that, in American companies, occurs more often at the water cooler, coffee machine, or cafeteria.

Several organizations have held knowledge fairs at which knowledge sellers display their expertise and buyers can search for what they need or serendipitously find knowledge that they did not know they needed but can use. Like a trade show or farmers' market, a knowledge fair is a temporary gathering of sellers that attracts potential buyers. One of the authors visited a "Share Fair" devoted to the sharing of "best practices" knowledge, held by Texas Instruments in Dallas. The energy generated by workers and managers intermingling—in many cases, for the first time—was palpable. Perhaps the most frequently heard comment was, "I didn't know we had people doing *that!*"

Corporate universities and live and electronic forums that bring people together to consider subjects of mutual interest are other examples of knowledge marketplaces. Although typically more structured than knowledge fairs, successful forums leave time and space for participants to talk informally. As much or more valuable knowledge exchange is likely to happen in the hallway among participants as in the auditorium during official presentations.

Electronic knowledge markets such as the Internet, intranet discussion groups, and groupware discussion databases have much the same advantages and drawbacks as commercial electronic shopping. The pluses are convenience and choice, with desktop access to a vast variety of material. The downside is variable quality and a lack of personal contact, which tends to reduce trust and commitment. In the electronic home-shopping industry, the result is a lot more browsing than buying. In the electronic knowledge market, it is likely to mean a devaluing of on-line knowledge, which will probably be ignored or treated with suspicion unless it has been evaluated and edited by a respected on-line broker.

Implicit in building a marketplace—even an electronic one—is the need to give members of the organization enough time to shop for knowledge, or to sell it. A Catch-22 of the corporate world is that employees are too busy working to take time to learn things that will help them work more efficiently. Engineers may spend weeks or months solving a problem because they can't find the time

Members of an organization must be given time to shop for knowledge.

to ask if anyone else in the company has dealt with it before. If a company's most influential employees are the very ones who are too busy to attend a knowledge fair or forum, then the knowledge market is not working well.

Creating and Defining Knowledge Market Value

As the Javelin case demonstrates, the absence of reliable information about the apparent value attached to sharing knowledge (or evidence that the value is low) will stifle market activity. The surest way of establishing value is through empirical means; direct evidence of employees being recognized, promoted, and rewarded for sharing knowledge proves that value exists. We have found that firms "get what they pay for" in creating knowledge rewards. Short-term "trinkets," such as frequent-flyer miles or ice cream bars, may motivate a single use of a knowledge management system. One office of a professional-services firm handed out mouse pads to acknowledge use of a knowledge-sharing system—but later realized that the firm's professionals used laptops without mice! To establish a consistent culture of knowledge sharing, you need to use valuable currency: substantial monetary rewards, salary increases, promotions, and so forth.

A firm's investment in knowledge exchange is another kind of empirical signal that it genuinely values knowledge. Putting highly regarded people in knowledge-enabling jobs (rather than making those jobs the part-time responsibility of employees who don't have much else to do), holding well-attended fairs and forums, and giving people time to learn and exchange knowledge are forms of commitment that have much more power than a mission statement. "Put your money where your mouth is" or "walk the talk" is appropriate advice for developing a healthy knowledge market.

A number of consulting companies have made knowledge sharing one of the basic criteria of the performance-evaluation process, which is yet another concrete method of paying a reasonable market price for knowledge. These companies are also practicing good motivational psychology, realizing that recognized and rewarded behaviors will flourish while those that are ignored or penalized will wither.

Knowledge evangelists can also help establish a thriving knowledge market. Enthusiastic, talented managers who are committed to knowledge work and can effectively make the case for it to senior management can have an important impact. When knowledge management is essentially a personal crusade, however, its existence may be precarious, especially at the beginning. If the manager leaves or is assigned to a new, demanding task, the knowledge project may well collapse.

The Peripheral Benefits of Knowledge Markets

The direct benefits of an efficient knowledge market accrue to both the firm as a whole and its employees as individuals. When knowledge flows freely, its potential value becomes actual. Productivity increases and innovations spring from the timely application of existing knowledge and the generation of new ideas in the knowledge marketplace. Knowledge buyers, sellers, and brokers get the knowledge they need to do their work well and get appropriate payment for knowledge they share in the form of recognition and advancement.

A thriving knowledge market also creates benefits that are peripheral to the principal market aim of making knowledge available when and where it is needed. These gains, which we call nonmarket benefits, also contribute to the success of the firm.

Higher Workforce Morale

A healthy knowledge market means that employees see that their expertise is valuable and know that others in the organization will cooperate with them when they need expert assistance. They may be more satisfied with their work and work harder than those frustrated by lack of communication, wasted effort, and uninformed decision making. Employee cynicism ("This company never does anything right"; "They never ask the people who really know"; "The empty suits get the promotions") can have a devastating effect on corporate success.

Greater Corporate Coherence[13]

An active exchange of information and ideas in an atmosphere of openness and trust enables employees at all levels to understand what is happening in the company. James Walsh and Geraldo Ungson, two academics who have researched the idea of "organizational memory," in part define an organization as "a network of . . . shared meanings."[14] A shared awareness of corporate goals and strategies gives individuals cues for directing their own work toward a cooperative goal and makes them feel that their work is meaningful as part of a larger aim. Nonaka and Takeuchi touch on this point when they talk about the importance of making individuals aware of an overall "organizational intention."[15] Kao, Japan's largest household- and chemical-products maker, values corporate coherence so highly that any meeting in the company, including top-management meetings, is open to any employee. Thanks to this policy, every meeting at Kao potentially functions as a productive knowledge marketplace. As Nonaka and Takeuchi remark, "Through this practice, top management can acquire insights from those most familiar with the issues at hand, while employees can gain a better understanding of the general corporate policy."[16]

Richer Knowledge Stock

Knowledge markets are unlike markets for goods in that every sale increases the total stock of knowledge in the organization. The seller both keeps his knowledge and gives it away; more importantly, the transaction itself often generates new knowledge. Newly acquired knowledge interacts with existing knowledge to spark ideas that neither buyer nor seller has had before. One of the major sources of new knowledge (discussed further in our next chapter, on knowledge generation) is *fusion*, bringing together people with different ideas to work on the same problem.

A knowledge transaction, especially a face-to-face exchange, tests the validity of the knowledge that's offered. Buyers seldom receive knowledge passively. They evaluate it and test it in action, since they made the purchase to meet a specific need.

A thriving knowledge market continually tests and refines organizational knowledge.

An active knowledge market thus continually validates and refines organizational knowledge.

Stronger Meritocracy of Ideas

A genuinely open knowledge market will test official beliefs and expose the flaws of the faulty ones before they can do much damage. If Ken Olsen had not been able to dominate the knowledge market at Digital, the company's response to changes in the computer industry probably would have come sooner and been more effective. At Polaroid, Edwin Land's insistence that Polavision (an instant movie film) would be a marquee product inhibited discussion almost to the point of crippling that company. Dr. An Wang's tight control over knowledge about the future direction of the computer industry had a similar effect at Wang Labs.

Knowledge markets tend to break down or circumvent hierarchies, much as the emerging middle classes in Europe began eroding the power of the church and aristocracy in the sixteenth century. They follow networks of knowers, not the architecture of a reporting structure. Usefully knowledgeable people exist at all levels in organizations. The knowledge market has its own shifting hierarchy based on who knows what and how helpful they are. A healthy, undistorted market is a meritocracy of ideas. Talking about Apple Computer during its most creative years, Steve Jobs said, "It doesn't make sense to hire smart people and then tell them what to do; we hired smart people so they could tell us what to do."

Thinking in Market Terms

Even familiar markets for material goods are complex and difficult to analyze and influence. The knowledge market, less tangible and until recently not even viewed in market terms, is no easier to understand.

But applying what we do know about markets to knowledge exchange in organizations helps ground us in the reality of why exchange does and doesn't happen. In giving us a clear framework for understanding knowledge transfer, it gives us the means to improve it. We believe all knowledge management can be fruitfully seen as an effort to increase the efficiency of knowledge markets.

The three chapters that follow—on the generation, codification, and transfer of knowledge—are devoted to the "process" of knowledge management. Any firm that wants to excel at managing knowledge will have to perform these three "subprocesses" well. Although generating, codifying, and using knowledge are rarely analyzed in process terms, the activities that take place under those banners can all be viewed as attempts to make knowledge markets work more efficiently and effectively.

These chapters will also explore some of the constraints firms have to contend with to turn corporate knowledge into corporate value. We will consider the market realities that drive knowledge exchange, how people generate knowledge, the requirements and limits of knowledge codification, and how knowledge is—and is not—transferred and made use of in organizations. We will also look at the relationship between knowledge and technology, specific knowledge roles in organizations, and summarize a variety of knowledge projects.

Bad times have a scientific value.
These are the occasions
a good learner would not miss.
—Ralph Waldo Emerson

3

Knowledge Generation

ALL HEALTHY organizations generate and use knowledge. As organizations interact with their environments, they absorb information, turn it into knowledge, and take action based on it in combination with their experiences, values, and internal rules. They sense and respond. Without knowledge, an organization could not organize itself; it would be unable to maintain itself as a functioning enterprise.

What concerns us in this chapter is the conscious and intentional generation of knowledge—the specific activities and initiatives firms undertake to increase their stock of corporate knowledge. In general, this has been the least systematic of knowledge management activities. Many companies approach knowledge generation as a "black box," essentially just trying to hire smart people and then leaving them alone. One of us (Davenport) studied thirty attempts to improve knowledge work in a process context with two coauthors. We found that most successful initiatives addressed not the process of knowledge generation itself but rather the external circumstances of work, including location and team structure.[1]

Some important literature on this subject has been published in recent years, including Nonaka and Takeuchi's *The Knowledge-Creating Company* and Dorothy Leonard-Barton's *Wellsprings of Knowledge*.[2] Many of their examples involve Japanese firms, which have aggressively pursued knowledge generation as a means of achieving business success. Our discussion is influenced by these sources as well as by our own observation and research with several companies (a few of them Japanese as well).

In this chapter we will consider five modes of knowledge generation: acquisition; dedicated resources; fusion; adaptation; and knowledge networking. In each case, the conventions of language force us to discuss knowledge as a "thing" that can be "managed." We want to emphasize again, however, that knowledge is as much an act or process as an artifact or thing.

Acquisition

When we talk about knowledge generation, we mean the knowledge acquired by an organization as well as that developed within it. Acquired knowledge does not have to be newly created, only new to the organization. British Petroleum gives a "Thief of the Year" award to the person who has "stolen" the best ideas in application development. They recognize that, when it comes to organizational knowledge, originality is less important than usefulness. Texas Instruments has created a "Not Invented Here,

The proverb "Well stolen is half done" is sound reasoning if you're in the knowledge business.

but I Did It Anyway" award for borrowing a practice from either inside or outside the company. The Spanish proverb "Well stolen is half done" sums up this idea succinctly. The knowledge-focused firm needs to have appropriate knowledge available when and where it can be applied, not to generate new ideas for their own sake.

The most direct and often most effective way to acquire knowledge is to buy it—that is, to buy an organization or hire individuals that have it.[3] Of course, not all corporate purchases are knowledge acquisitions. Companies buy other companies for various reasons: to generate additional revenue; to achieve a strategic size or product mix; to get access to new markets; or to gain the skills of a senior management team (this last reason, however, borders on knowledge acquisition). Sometimes knowledge may emerge as a by-product of a purchase made primarily for other reasons. Increasingly, though, firms acquire other companies specifically for their knowledge. They are often willing to pay a premium over the market value of the company purchased because of the value they expect to get from adding that new knowledge to their own knowledge stock. One recent example of this thinking is IBM's 1995 purchase of Lotus. IBM paid $3.5 billion, which was fourteen times Lotus's book valuation of $250 million. Clearly, IBM did not pay that amount of money for the current revenue generated by Notes and other Lotus products or for Lotus's manufacturing and sales capabilities. The $3.25 billion premium IBM paid represents their appraisal of Lotus's unique knowledge of Notes and other collaborative software applications. The minds that invented Notes are more valuable than the software itself; they have the ability to envision the next generation of communications and information-sharing software. They have the skills, experience, and creativity that IBM needs to apply *its* knowledge to the new world of collaborative software. IBM's implied belief is that this capability Lotus has—its knowledge—adds more value than any purely financial reckoning can demonstrate.

AT&T's purchase of NCR is another well-known example of attempted knowledge acquisition. AT&T bought NCR to get into the computer business, but NCR's general-purpose computer business was not in good shape. The factors that made this acquisition unsuccessful are too complex (and some too sketchy) for us to enumerate here, but this failure within a few years of the deal, by no means unusual, suggests how problematical knowledge acquisitions can be. This is particularly true when the objective is to combine one type of knowledge with another—in this instance, NCR's knowledge of computing with AT&T's communications expertise. As we have discussed, a company generates knowledge in the context of its specific culture, and it is thus more resistant to transfer than most other corporate resources.

A company that acquires another firm for its knowledge is buying people (that is, the knowledge that exists in people's heads and within communities of knowers), perhaps some structured knowledge in document or computerized form, and the routines and processes that embody the purchased company's knowledge. Since reliable analytical tools for measuring the value of this knowledge do not yet exist, determining how much that knowledge is worth is speculative and sometimes unnervingly subjective. All that most "due diligence" investigations can do is to try to ensure that key personnel are "locked up" for a few years with employment contracts or payout agreements.

Attempts to devise formal measures to guide knowledge purchases have so far been imperfect and incomplete. When managers assess the level of employee education, for example, they often fail to distinguish between very general capabilities and knowledge that is of genuine value to a firm. They also frequently ignore undocumented and tacit expertise. That knowledge and talent are not synonymous with university degrees is epitomized by the fact that the chairman of Microsoft never graduated from college. These and other efforts to measure the value of knowledge at least reflect an understanding that knowledge is an asset, but they also show how hard it is to quantify. Sid Schoeffler, a pioneer in valuing knowledge and one of the founders of the PIMS method that seeks to measure strategic market success, has estimated that a firm's balance sheet reflects only 20 to 25 percent of its real value. In other words, there are no standard methods for accurately analyzing the largest components of a company's worth. Economic and trade institutions such as FASB, GATT, OECD, EC, and U.S. government agencies are currently attempting to develop metrics based on available financial information as rough proxies for quantifying knowledge.[4] As this research continues and analytic tools improve, markets for company knowledge may become more efficient and the number of acquisitions based on measurable knowledge will surely increase.

Beyond the problems of measuring the value of purchased knowledge, the acquiring firm may find it difficult to determine exactly where the knowledge resides. Many of the people whose knowledge makes an organization work are not often identified or officially responsible for the results that they achieve. Leonard-Barton describes the 1988 purchase of Grimes by EL Products, both manufacturers of electroluminescent lamps. In addition to eliminating a competitor, EL Products expected to benefit from what seemed to be Grimes's greater expertise in producing high-quality lamps efficiently. In other words, ELP was buying Grimes's knowledge. Yet the company failed to

The knowledge you think you're buying may walk out the door.

realize that the critical expertise was the tacit knowledge of line employees, who didn't transfer to the new operation. Naturally, the transferred process did not work successfully because the key knowledge workers were missing.[5] This is a classic problem in the consulting industry, where knowledge and knowledge-based skills are highly visible. Many consulting firms are reluctant to make acquisitions because the "human assets" they buy, having reaped financial rewards, can then walk out the door forever.

A knowledge-rich organization, even a robust one, may prove to be fragile in that much of its knowledge may not survive the upheaval of an acquisition. The organic connection of knowledge to particular people and a particular environment means that a purchaser may end up with only a fraction of the knowledge that existed before the sale. The uncertainty of a corporate takeover and the disruption of internal work processes and networks often lead some talented personnel to explore new options and, sometimes, to leave the company, taking their knowledge with them.

More subtle but no less real losses may result from changes in the work environment. Organizational size, focus, management, and intangibles like trust and atmosphere may change in ways that disrupt the knowledge culture. We said in Chapter 1 that the tendency of knowledge to thrive only in the environment where it develops is one of its advantages. That "stickiness" prevents competitors from easily appropriating knowledge that required a significant investment of time and money to develop. The willingness to acquire a company for its knowledge (and pay a premium to do so) comes from a recognition that it is not possible to pick up another firm's knowledge simply by hiring a few employees or borrowing some ideas. However, even acquisition of the whole company may not buy its knowledge if the acquisition process disrupts the ecology of the knowledge-creating environment.

Finally, the acquiring company may not succeed in integrating new knowledge effectively. Although the purchase is proof of a desire to increase the corporate knowledge stock, there may be cultural and political barriers to accepting and absorbing the acquisition's knowledge fully.[6] Entrenched interests in the purchasing company may resist being told how to do things by new employees, even when the newly acquired procedures are demonstrably superior. This reluctance can be reinforced by a common tendency to view purchaser and acquisition as conqueror and conquered. This attitude contributed to the failures of AT&T's takeover of NCR and IBM's purchase of ROLM.

These potential problems suggest that a knowledge acquisition must be handled with considerable care. Success may depend on extensive efforts to locate and evaluate the knowledge of the acquired company, to protect its knowledge workers and environment during and after the purchase, and to encourage the smooth meshing of existing and newly acquired knowledge.

Rental

In addition to being purchased, outside knowledge can be leased or rented. A common type of leasing is a firm's financial support of university or institutional research in exchange for the right to first commercial use of promising results. Joseph Badaracco, Jr., says that approximately two hundred industry-university consortia were operating under the

1984 National Cooperative Research Act by 1987.[7] These firms in effect outsourced all or part of their research and development. They give up a certain amount of control in exchange for reduced financial and organizational burdens. The drug company Hoeschst, for example, supports research at the Molecular Biological Institute at Massachusetts General Hospital in hopes that it will lead to the development of profitable new drugs. CSIRO, the Australian national R&D consortium, establishes these kinds of relationships between research institutions and industry. R&D efforts are always speculative, and it is not easy to predict when or if research will pay off. However, it should be possible over time and in the aggregate to calculate the value of leased knowledge in terms of the eventual returns that derive from the funded research. The initial decision to support a particular research institution or department is based on the same useful but imperfect measures currently applied to the purchase of a knowledge-rich company: the reputations of the organization and the people in it, their past success, and the opinions of experts on future research potential.[8]

Renting knowledge really means renting a knowledge source. Hiring a consultant for a project is an obvious example. Using reputation as a key measure of value, a company will pay a consultant a fee to share his knowledge with them or apply it to a particular issue. Unlike rentals of equipment or facilities, knowledge rentals are likely to involve some degree of knowledge transfer. Although the knowledge source is temporary, some of the knowledge is likely to stay with the firm. Some clients we have worked with now specify in their consulting con-

If you're renting knowledge, make sure you take steps to retain it too.

tracts that consultants' knowledge be made available to clients in some structured, codifiable format. And consultants are beginning to market their services partly on the basis of transferring knowledge to clients. For example, more than one high-tech consulting firm now offers to provide technical training for the software package SAP if the client employs these firms to implement the package.

Of course, if an expert's knowledge has substantial depth, only a small portion of it is transferable in a short consulting engagement or even in a structured knowledge base. Hiring firms may also have different aims. If a company is renting assistance in solving a particular problem, they are probably more interested in the consultant's recommendations than the knowledge behind them. In other cases, a company may attempt to learn as much as possible from the outside expert. As with so many investments in knowledge generation, intentions are important: a firm needs to know what it wants to have a good chance of getting it. High-level consultants are sometimes surprised at how little clients ask of them in terms of knowledge transfer. Firms that hire them for a day or a week at considerable expense might be expected to squeeze as much knowledge out of them as possible. But they usually do not ask the questions that would help them absorb that expertise in practical ways.

Dedicated Resources

A customary way to generate knowledge in an organization is to establish units or groups specifically for that purpose. Research and development departments are the standard example. Their whole aim is to come up with new knowledge—new ways of doing things. Ernst & Young's Center for Business Innovation is a kind of R&D department. Andersen Consulting has established technology research centers in Silicon Valley and southern France. IBM Consulting has established dedicated competency-development groups in key consulting domains. Motorola, Merck, and McDonald's universities, Xerox PARC, and other corporate research and training facilities are all resources more or less designed to generate knowledge. Some corporate libraries are also variations on R&D departments, expected to provide new knowledge to the organization. This is especially prevalent when the library is tied to a specific knowledge process or function, as is true in many consulting firms.

Since the financial returns on research take time to materialize and may be difficult to measure when they do come, a focus on near-term profits may create pressure to cut costs by cutting R&D. While no part of a business can be funded indefinitely if it generates no measurable value, a narrowly bottom-line view of that return can lead to "savings" that deplete vital knowledge-generating resources.

Because dedicated knowledge resources are by definition somewhat distinct from the everyday work of an organization, transferring knowledge to where it can be used is often complicated. In general, patentable new ideas, which can be made explicit, are easier to transfer than what we might call "internal" knowledge—the more subjective process-type knowledge of how to do things and think about things.

The premise behind separating R&D from other parts of the firm is to give researchers the freedom to explore ideas without the constraints imposed by a preoccupation with profits and deadlines. However, this distance may be difficult to bridge when the time comes to transfer the results of R&D to the wider organization. Knowledge creators and users may not even speak the same language. Probably the most notorious case of a costly transfer gap occurred at Xerox's Palo Alto Research Center in the mid-1970s. The knowledge workers at Xerox PARC invented key elements of the graphical interface computer, including the mouse, graphical icons, and menus. Ironically, the independence that made this breakthrough possible probably contributed to Xerox's inability to understand its importance and potential value. They were not close enough to the research to evaluate the newly created knowledge. Steve Jobs, on the other hand, was prepared for those new ideas by his work at Apple (as well as by culture and temperament) and quickly grasped their significance (although he paid no attention himself to some object technologies under development at Xerox PARC, which he regretted later). A brief tour of Xerox PARC was all he needed to gather the fruits of research funded for years by Xerox. He went back to Apple and built the Macintosh essentially at Xerox's expense.[9] Xerox eventually was able to capitalize on some research at PARC (for example, the development of the large-scale laser printer), but a major commercial opportunity had been lost.

To avoid snafus of this kind, managers must take explicit steps to ensure that knowledge generated by dedicated resources will be made available throughout the company. At Sharp, the results of research by corporate R&D groups are formally transferred to the research laboratories of Sharp's nine business groups and then to business division labs. Corporate-level researchers may move down to the group or divisional level, taking their knowledge with them. These procedures exist for the express purpose of getting the knowledge to where it will be useful. A series of regular high-level meetings focuses on evaluating and integrating new knowledge. Senior management and business group lab managers meet monthly to discuss R&D projects. A regular Laboratory Director's Conference gives lab directors, the director of R&D planning, and the director of the Intellectual Property Office opportunities to plan R&D directions and ways to transfer newly developed knowledge to business groups.[10]

Fusion

Whereas the R&D approach is predicated on reducing the pressure and distractions that can stifle productive research, knowledge generation through fusion purposely introduces complexity and even conflict to create new synergy. It brings together people with different perspectives to work on a problem or project, forcing them to come up with a joint answer.

Borrowing a phrase from Gerald Hirshberg, director of Nissan Design International, Dorothy Leonard-Barton calls this process "creative abrasion" and describes how intentionally combining people with different skills, ideas, and values can generate creative solutions. "Innovation," she says, "occurs at the boundaries between mind-sets, not within the provincial territory of one knowledge and skill base."[11] Nissan Design International believes strongly in the creative potential of fusion. The company makes hiring decisions specifically to promote cognitive diversity within the firm, matching, for instance, an analytical and rational new hire with an intuitive and aesthetically inclined one. Hirshberg talks about this kind of diversity as "a rich and yeasty opportunity for a kind of abrasion that I wanted to turn into light rather than heat."[12]

In *The Knowledge-Creating Company,* Nonaka and Takeuchi say that bringing together people with different knowledge and experience is one of the necessary conditions for knowledge creation. They borrow a term from cybernetics, "requisite variety," to describe both the productive conflict of creative abrasion (what Nonaka and Takeuchi call "creative chaos") and the value of having a larger, more complex pool of ideas to work with. The differences among individuals prevents the group from falling into routine solutions to problems.

Don't be afraid of a little "creative chaos."

Since the group has no familiar solutions in common, individuals must develop new ideas together or combine their old ideas in new ways. One argument in favor of workforce diversity is the prospect of pooling a variety of talents and backgrounds, which increases the chances of a successful outcome. The complexity and diversity of the forces brought to bear on a problem should match (or at least be proportional to) the complexity and diversity of the problem. As we have said, a prime value of knowledge is its ability to handle complex issues efficiently but not reductively.

Nonaka and Takeuchi cite Matsushita's development of the first automatic breadmaking machine as an example of requisite variety and creative chaos in action. Matsushita combined three product divisions with different cultures to develop a successful breadmaking machine, realizing that it needed the variety of knowledge possessed by groups that had previously made rice cookers, toasters and coffeemakers, and food processors. The new product combined the computer-control expertise of the first group, the second's experience with induction heater technology, and the third's knowledge of rotating motors. The creative chaos came from a breakdown of old assumptions and ways of working, an intentional shake-up of the status quo that, as conventionally portrayed, is not innovative. The combined groups (a total of 1,400 employees) initially almost "spoke different languages."[13]

Total chaos is not creative, though. Leonard-Barton argues that innovation occurs "at the boundaries between mind-sets," but the mind-sets must connect for boundaries to exist. Creative abrasion or fusion requires some common ground. Group members must develop enough of a common language to understand one another. There must be some shared knowledge before collaboration can take place. (Nonaka and Takeuchi call this overlapping knowledge "redundancy," and identify it as a necessary condition for knowledge creation.) Matsushita used a three-day retreat for middle managers and a regular newspaper for factory workers to help establish a common language—in effect, a territory that diverse knowledge workers must inhabit to work together. They also articulated an organizational intention—a shared goal or concept to unify the efforts of the diverse members of the group. (In this case it was "easy and rich." The Japanese are comfortable with metaphorical or—to American ears—cryptic phrases that point the group in a common direction but don't inhibit creativity by being too definite.)

Knowledge generation, clearly worthwhile in itself, is not the only valuable outcome of knowledge activities. IDEO, a large and successful product design firm, "routinely innovates" for its clients.[14] The firm is rigorously committed to formalized brainstorming—one- to two-hour meetings of three to ten participants dedicated to generating "an array of possible solutions." The sessions employ specific behavior rules, clear facilitator roles, and various inputs.

The benefits of these sessions often have less to do with the volume and quality of generated ideas than with "spillover" effects, which include supporting organizational memory, providing skill variety, and promulgating an "attitude of wisdom." IDEO defines wisdom as the quality possessed by skilled practitioners who openly acknowledge what they don't know and question the validity of their individual and organizational knowledge. Needless to say, this attitude is extremely rare in most organizations, yet it's an important atmosphere to create for knowledge generation to flourish. If we were to construct a single test for how open to knowledge generation an organization is, we would ask how often its executives question their own knowledge.

Although fusion can lead to powerful results that are unobtainable in other ways, it is not a shortcut to knowledge generation. A significant commitment of time and effort is required to give group members enough shared knowledge and shared language to be able to work together. Careful management is also necessary to make sure that the collaboration of different styles and ideas is positive, not merely confrontational. As Hirshberg says, abrasion should generate "light rather than heat."

Here are five knowledge management principles that can help make fusion work effectively:

1. Foster awareness of the value of the knowledge sought and a willingness to invest in the process of generating it.

2. Identify key knowledge workers who can be effectively brought together in a fusion effort.

3. Emphasize the creative potential inherent in the complexity and diversity of ideas, seeing differences as positive, rather than sources of conflict, and avoiding simple answers to complex questions.

4. Make the need for knowledge generation clear so as to encourage, reward, and direct it toward a common goal.

5. Introduce measures and milestones of success that reflect the true value of knowledge more completely than simple balance-sheet accounting.

Adaptation

In "Microcosmic God," a 1941 science fiction story by Theodore Sturgeon, the main character creates a miniature world of beings who live and evolve extremely rapidly. He forces them to innovate by imposing various environmental threats on them. They react to storms, heat, drought—even a metal plunger moving inexorably down from their "sky"—with a steady stream of inventions and discoveries, from new insulating materials to power sources to super-hard aluminum. The crises in their environment act as catalysts for knowledge generation. "Adapt or die" is their fate, so they adapt and advance.

The story provides a vivid metaphor for the way external (and sometimes internal) changes cause businesses to adapt. New products from competitors, new technologies, and social and economic changes drive knowledge generation because firms that don't change in response to changing conditions will fail. In fact, there is a large and growing body of literature concerning self-organizing and complex adaptive systems and the relevance of these models to organization effectiveness and strategy.[15]

Positive and negative examples abound. We've already mentioned Digital Equipment and Wang Laboratories as once-successful corporate cultures that failed to adapt. Success is often the enemy of innovation; it has been called "the winner's curse."[16] It is difficult to change something that has worked and may still be working. Lulled by past success, companies sometimes fail to see that change is happening or to acknowledge that it can affect them. The appearance of low-cost, high-quality Japanese cars on the U.S. market changed the automotive world, but decades of dominance blinded American automakers to the magnitude of the threat. Similarly, Sears ignored the changes that Wal-Mart was making in the retailing environment until shrinking sales forced them to face reality. Several years ago, one of us (Prusak) was called in by a very successful food products firm to evaluate how it managed its core information (it didn't!) and what improvements could be made. It quickly became apparent that the firm was not really interested in changing its routines since, as one executive said, "We're on a rocket to the moon. Why go off course with changes?" However, rockets may either run out of fuel or be diverted by forces beyond their control.

As one after another of the most successful companies of the '70s and '80s have faced a crisis in the '90s, the business world has become aware that success can lead to an unwillingness to adapt, to recognize challenges and respond to them by generating new knowledge. John F. McDonnell of McDonnell Douglas Corporation (which itself had trouble adapting to change and was recently acquired by Boeing) observes: "While it is difficult to change a company that is struggling, it is next to impossible to change a company that is showing all the outward signs of success. Without the spur of a crisis or a period of great stress, most organizations—like most people—are incapable of changing the habits and attitudes of a lifetime."[17]

Leonard-Barton talks about "core rigidities," which include the tendency of companies and employees to stay on "well-worn and successful paths," and comments: "human minds are the most flexible assets a company has—and the most rigid. People are capable of making astounding leaps in intuition and, at the same time, of tenaciously clinging to the details of petty, unproductive routines."[18]

Striving for continuous innovation, some companies try to instill a sense of crisis before it exists. Like the character in Sturgeon's story, they shake up their organizations, creating obstacles that the firm must overcome by generating new knowledge. Ryuzaburo Kaka, chairman of Canon, has said, "The role of top management is to give employees a sense of crisis as well as a lofty idea."[19] Hewlett-Packard's Lew Platt has stated that creating a sense of artificial crisis is one of his

Instill a sense of crisis before it exists and you might be able to head off a real one.

highest objectives. BP's decision to restructure itself into a large number of fairly autonomous business units was less an adaptation to current problems than an anticipation of future challenges. BP's executives expect new knowledge to keep the company competitive and perhaps to make it the environment-changer to which other firms react.

The various reasons that companies have trouble adapting to changes in their environments all come down to the essential fact that history matters. A firm's ability to do things—even its ability to see and understand things—is developed over time. Its knowledge is a social construct built out of the collective experiences of its workforce, the talents it rewards, and the shared stories of the firm's triumphs and mistakes. The current interest in assessing how the so-called agile company can keep ahead in a volatile competitive environment should not obscure the fact that any company's agility is necessarily limited. Neither firms nor the people in them are chameleons, able to adapt to any change. They can only build on their inherent capabilities. A firm may make significant changes, but it cannot transform itself into a different animal altogether.

The attention managers have devoted in recent years to classifying core competencies reflects firms' efforts to understand the ways they can and cannot change. Core competencies can be broken down into discrete parcels of knowledge explaining precisely how certain things are done. Wal-Mart's widely discussed cross-docking competency, for example, is knowledge of how to orchestrate a complex ballet of people, trucks, and forklifts in a distribution center, and how to build the facilities and information systems infrastructures that allow the activity to take place daily. These knowledge assets *are* the firm. It may be necessary to find ways to apply them to new products and services when external changes make the old ones uncompetitive, but it is not possible to throw them out and start from scratch, any more than an individual can totally remake his personality or a country remake its culture. The firm may learn to do new things, but those skills will be similar to what they have done in the past.[20]

A firm's ability to adapt is based on two principal factors: first, having existing internal resources and capabilities that can be utilized in new ways, and second, being open to change or having a high "absorptive capacity." While a full discussion of these factors is beyond the scope of this book, both of them have specific knowledge management implications. The most important adaptive resources are employees who can acquire new knowledge and skills easily. Since the best predictor of mental nimbleness

Employees who are willing and able to learn new things are vital to an adapting company.

is proven experience in taking on new tasks, firms should seek out employees who have already mastered a variety of roles and skills. After they've been hired, employees should also be encouraged to change jobs often, to build and manage their own skill portfolios, and to take "learning sabbaticals" to master new work-related disciplines.

Employees whose backgrounds suggest an openness to change should therefore be given hiring preferences. But this attribute can be reinforced by exposing workers and managers to a wide variety of knowledge, particularly at times when change is seen as vital. At Monsanto's Agricultural Chemicals Division, for example, chemical researchers were given access to a wide variety of external market information shortly before patents expired on key products. Standard Life, a large U.K. insurer, immersed its senior managers in new sources of competitor knowledge at a time when the country's insurance market was rapidly diversifying. Of course, it's important to start digesting and creating new knowledge before a business crisis occurs; by the time the crisis hits it may be too late to respond.

Networks

Knowledge is also generated by informal, self-organizing networks within organizations that may over time become more formalized.[21]

Communities of knowers, brought together by common interests, usually talk together in person, on the telephone, and via e-mail and groupware to share expertise and solve problems together. When networks of this kind share enough knowledge in common to be able to communicate and collaborate effectively, their ongoing conversation often generates new knowledge within firms. Although it may be difficult to codify, this process can add to the knowledge of the entire company. As we'll describe in Chapter 6, such networks often need help from professional knowledge editors or network facilitators, who can record knowledge that would otherwise remain in the heads of experts. In addition, the early or initial users of the network may play a key role in putting knowledge into practice. New technologies, for instance, are often adopted by lead users and passed along by networks. In that way a particular practice can gradually become part of the active knowledge capital of the firm.[22]

Given that their product is knowledge itself, it is not surprising that many consulting and service firms have organized their previously informal communities of practice into formal networks, with budgets for enabling technologies, knowledge coordinators, librarians, writers, and administrative staff. Some smaller consulting and service firms have chosen not to do this, either from a reluctance to add overhead or a feeling that too much managerial oversight can stifle the spontaneity and passion of informal networks.

In the absence of formal knowledge policies and processes, networks act as critical conduits for much innovative thinking. Consider, for example, a series of events that occurred recently at Hoeschst-Celanese, a large fabric manufacturer in North Carolina. During a lunch with colleagues, a Hoeschst R&D technician who had recently come back from a conference on synthetic fiber manufacturing in Europe mentioned a particular presentation regarding a new material. One of his colleagues passed on some details of the lunchtime discussion to about eighteen global peers via an informal e-mail network. Three weeks later, one of these networked researchers mentioned the e-mail message to a company executive during a plane ride they took together to visit a client. The executive brought the matter up with a team he was on whose mandate was to look at new business opportunities. Soon Hoeschst formed a small executive group to look further into this promising material.

This story undoubtedly resonates with readers familiar with how knowledge "gets around" in organizations. It shows how extensively an informal network can generate knowledge when each participant adds an incremental portion. At the same time, it is obvious how large a role chance played in getting the knowledge where it could be used in this particular instance. How easily the knowledge brought back from the conference might never have reached the group that needed it! In our consulting work, we use this story as a "prompt" to stimulate thinking about what the management of Hoeschst-Celanese should (or should not!) do to make this informal process more effective and efficient in the future.

Common Factors

The common denominator for all these efforts is a need for adequate time and space devoted to knowledge creation or acquisition. In companies committed to dedicated resources, space not only means the laboratories and libraries in which discoveries can be made but also the meeting places where knowledge workers can congregate. In some instances, the shared space may be electronic, but meeting places of some kind must exist. Unfortunately, time, not physical space, is the corporate resource most likely to be begrudged to knowledge activists. It is the scarcest of all resources, the one impossible to replicate and yet most essential to genuine knowledge generation.

A third critical factor is a recognition by managers that knowledge generation is both an important activity for business success and a process that can be nurtured. Knowledge generation is admittedly difficult to measure, and botched interventions can be catastrophic. But since it is axiomatic that a firm's greatest asset is its knowledge, then the firm that fails to generate new knowledge will probably cease to exist.

Only those ideas that are least truly ours
can be adequately expressed
in words.
—Henri Bergson

4

Knowledge Codification and Coordination

T H E A I M of codification is to put organizational knowledge into a form that makes it accessible to those who need it. It literally turns knowledge into a code (though not necessarily a computer code) to make it as organized, explicit, portable, and easy to understand as possible. An analogous example is the legal system, where the laws and decisions that act as precedents are codified in many texts (and now on-line and in CD-ROM-based systems). These references, of course, represent only part of what "the law" is and how it is practiced; they do not encompass the tacit skills of lawyers and judges. However, this codified material embodies and makes accessible a significant portion of articulated legal knowledge.

Codification in organizations similarly converts knowledge into accessible and applicable formats. Knowledge managers and users can categorize knowledge, describe it, map and model it, simulate it, and embed it in rules and recipes. Each of these approaches has its own specific set of values and limitations, and they can be applied singly or in combination. Obviously, new technologies play an important role in knowledge codification and make the prospects for these activities increasingly promising.

The Basic Principles of Knowledge Codification

The primary difficulty encountered in codification work is the question of how to codify knowledge without losing its distinctive properties and turning it into less vibrant information or data. In other words, some structure for knowledge is necessary, but too much kills it. Companies

68

that want to codify knowledge successfully should therefore keep in mind the following four principles:

1. Managers must decide what business goals the codified knowledge will serve (for example, firms whose strategic intent involves getting closer to the customer may choose to codify customer knowledge).

2. Managers must be able to identify knowledge existing in various forms appropriate to reaching those goals.

3. Knowledge managers must evaluate knowledge for usefulness and appropriateness for codification.

4. Codifiers must identify an appropriate medium for codification and distribution.

Codifying all corporate knowledge would be an immense and futile undertaking, similar to and even more difficult than the mostly futile efforts undertaken to deploy enterprise-wide data modeling. As Patricia Seemann, a consultant and former managing director of the Right First Time knowledge project at Hoffmann-LaRoche, says, "Relevance is far more important than completeness." Since the purpose of codification is to put knowledge in usable form, the corporation needs some idea of what uses it has in mind. The definition of usefulness should not be too narrow, however. Honda, for instance, keeps track of "failed" development ideas because it recognizes that they may be successful in the future; ideas that are promising though currently unfeasible need to be recognized and preserved. To be worthwhile, however, a knowledge codification project needs more specific aims than just making knowledge generally available.

At Senco Products, an innovative Cincinnati-based metal fastener manufacturer, there is a corporate initiative to try to diagram the "logic trail" leading to major decisions. The goal is to understand what failures of knowledge or reason occurred when a decision turns out poorly. Of course, firms can only undertake this kind of analysis if they have a high-trust culture, or the politics around it could be devastating!

Finding the sources of the knowledge you want to codify is obviously essential. If you don't know where it is, you can't do anything with it and are unlikely to know *what* it is. Mapping corporate knowledge sources, discussed in detail below, is an important part of the codification process. Once found, someone must evaluate the knowledge to assess its usefulness and importance to the organization, and to determine what kind of knowledge it is. Is it the rich, tacit, intuitive knowledge of a seasoned expert, or is it rules-based, schematic, explicit knowledge (or something in between)? *Whether* you should do anything with the knowledge depends on its importance; *what* you should do to it depends on its type. Careful evaluation—labor-intensive and demanding significant skill and company knowledge—is an expensive but essential requirement for successful codification. The cost of this evaluation is a prime reason for focusing codification efforts on a particular goal or set of goals.

Codifying Different Types of Knowledge

Knowledge in organizations ranges from the complex, accumulated expertise that resides in individuals and is partly or largely inexpressible to much more structured and explicit content. The following chart, adapted from Sidney Winter's work, outlines some appropriate codification strategies for different kinds of knowledge.[1] Along with providing an overview of codification options, it suggests the tension between the benefit of capturing the rich knowledge that has the greatest potential value to an organization and the difficulty of representing that knowledge effectively.

Codification Dimensions of Knowledge

Tacit _____ Articulable

Not teachable _____ Teachable

Not articulated _____ Articulated

Not observable in use _____ Observable in use

Rich _____ Schematic

Complex _____ Simple

Undocumented _____ Documented

Codifying Tacit Knowledge

Tacit, complex knowledge, developed and internalized by the knower over a long period of time, is almost impossible to reproduce in a document or database.[2] Such knowledge incorporates so much accrued and embedded learning that its rules may be impossible to separate from how an individual acts. The distinctive style of a master musician can barely be described in words, much less externalized in a way that would allow someone else to play in an identical way. The knowledge a creative research scientist uses to decide which line of inquiry to follow likewise cannot be turned into a step-by-step list or a report. If it were possible to extract knowledge from the knower in this way, it would radically change our compensation and education policies.

We simply can't represent some knowledge effectively outside the human mind. To dramatize this point, here is a personal story from Larry Prusak's childhood:

> When I was in eighth grade, I was on a baseball team with my classmates. My class only had nine boys, so they had to put me on the team to have enough players. Because of an injury I had suffered at birth, I was by far the worst hitter on the team. I couldn't hit at all (though I *could* run and field). My teammates gave me a hard time, of course: They were fiercely competitive and wanted every edge they could get. When my father saw how unhappy I was about the situation, he bought me a copy of Ted Williams's *The Art of Hitting*. My father didn't know much about baseball but he loved books, so it was the one thing he could think of doing to help me. Ted Williams understood hitting as well as any man alive and he tried to put what he knew into his book. I couldn't hit, but I could read, so I read it twice—practically memorized it. Result: I still couldn't hit much. I made only a very modest improvement, perhaps based on a newfound self-confidence. Of course, I wasn't much of an athlete. But even if I were, I'd say that hitting can't be taught by a book. The skills involved are too complex and subtle, too internal; they just can't be expressed in words that can be put to much use.

In other words, they cannot be *effectively* codified, at least in print; a document cannot capture Ted Williams's knowledge, skill, expertise, understanding, passion, and delight in hitting. As his book's title suggests, hitting is an art, and arts are difficult to boil down into rules and formulations. Even if this kind of knowledge could be successfully codified, the process of getting it on paper would be prohibitively laborious. Trying to get down everything a skilled knowledge worker knows would be similarly arduous and futile. As Michael Polanyi, the philosopher who first articulated the concept of tacit versus explicit knowledge, remarks, to understand tacit experience, try explaining in detail how you swim or ride a bicycle.[3]

This is why the codification process for the richest tacit knowledge in organizations is generally limited to locating someone with the knowledge, pointing the seeker to it, and encouraging them to interact. Arian Ward, a manager at Hughes Space and Communications, created a system to try to address problem solving with tacit knowledge in satellite development—the need, for example, for a last-minute supplier substitution. Not only supplier knowledge is involved here, but also knowledge of how to work the procurement system to make things happen quickly. The system connects people who have problems with those who can solve them. Because certain problems tended to recur, Ward eventually began to structure the patterns of tacit knowledge and capture solutions in a repository. He called the system the "Knowledge Highway." British Petroleum's Virtual Teamwork project is also based on the understanding that providing access to people with tacit knowledge is more efficient than trying to capture and codify that knowledge electronically or on paper. The traditional apprentice system, so successful in transferring skills in the industrial age, attests to these truths.

Mapping and Modeling Knowledge

A knowledge map—whether it is an actual map, a knowledge "Yellow Pages," or a cleverly constructed database—points to knowledge but doesn't contain it. It is a guide, not a repository. Developing a knowledge map involves locating important knowledge in the organization and then publishing some sort of list or picture that shows where to find it. Knowledge maps typically point to people as well as to documents and databases.

The principal purpose and clearest benefit of a knowledge map is to show people in the organization where to go when they need expertise. Rather than making do with accessible but imperfect answers or spending time tracking down better knowledge (essentially building one's own map on the fly), the employee with a good knowledge map has access to knowledge sources that would otherwise be difficult or impossible to find.

A knowledge map can also serve as an inventory. Just as a city map shows both what resources (libraries, hospitals, train stations, schools) are available and how to get to them, a knowledge map is a picture of what exists in the company as well as where it is located. It therefore can be used as a tool to evaluate the corporate knowledge stock, revealing strengths to be exploited and gaps that need to be filled.

As we have already suggested, a firm's organizational chart is a poor substitute for a knowledge map. In some cases, a job title can be a reliable proxy for knowledge (for instance, a regional sales director is

often the best source of knowledge about customers in that region), but generally the organization chart will not tell you where people actually go to find knowledge. For one thing, most organizational charts are hierarchical, describing formal reporting structures with far more detail at the top than the bottom. But key knowledge can and does exist anywhere in the company. Effective knowledge seekers almost
always need to cross departmental boundaries and ignore re-

A good knowledge map goes beyond conventional departmental boundaries.

porting structures to get what they need. This means that knowledge maps may lead to political tensions. Expertise not reflected in people's titles and job descriptions doesn't show up on an organizational chart. Moreover, the chart has nothing to say about accessibility. Key knowledge personnel don't simply have knowledge; they are willing and able to share it.

At least initially, knowledge mapping should focus on a clearly defined need. A health products firm where we consulted, for example, had a strategic focus on health maintenance organizations and other nonhospital care providers, but managers realized that knowledge of these customers was highly diffused and disorganized. Arian Ward, developer of the Hughes Communications Knowledge Highway, talks about starting with areas that "scream to be mapped."[4] The knowledge map developed at Hoffmann-LaRoche was specifically designed to help process new drug applications more efficiently and comply quickly with questions about them.

Assembling the Map

The information needed to create a knowledge map often already exists in organizations, but it's usually in a fragmented and undocumented form. Every employee has a little piece of the map in her head, knowing about her own expertise and where she goes to get certain questions answered. Creating an organizational map is a matter of combining these individual "mini-maps." Organizations that develop knowledge maps often use surveys that ask employees what knowledge they have and where they get the knowledge they need to do their jobs. They analyze and stitch together the responses, assembling a public map out of many private ones.[5]

Mapmakers may also follow a trail of recommendations, taking what sociologists call a "snowball sample." Talking to the knowledge sources suggested by one person, then following up with the people *they* mention and then the people those people suggest can eventually lead to just about whatever information you need, no matter how specialized or distant it is: The widening cascade of referrals leads everywhere. (The title of John Guare's play, *Six Degrees of Separation,* refers to the notion that there are no more than six steps—from all the people I know to all the people they know to all the people those people know, and so forth—separating any one individual from everyone else on earth.)

Here's an example of an effective map of knowledge at work both inside and outside an organization, showing how a trail of associations can lead to the most esoteric information.

A few years ago, one of the senior fact checkers at Time Life's massive and well-established Information Center got a call from a staff writer who said, "I need to know if spiders get car sick." The writer was doing an article for *Time* on Rodeo Drive jewelry stores that were putting tarantulas in the shop windows to discourage smash-and-grab thieves. The tarantulas were dying after a few days on the job, but no one knew why. One theory was that the long truck ride that brought them from Latin America was making them sick. Like all of the 240 full-time researchers at the center, the fact checker had a file of cards listing experts in various fields. There were four specialists on arachnids listed on her knowledge map. (That's what the cards actually were—a map can take many forms.) Two of the scholars were identified as having some expertise in spider illnesses. She called one. Although he didn't have the answer, he gave her the name and number of a colleague who specialized in arachnid disturbances. He was able to provide the information she needed (which was, by the way, that spiders lack inner ears and do not suffer from motion sickness; they were dying because not enough air circulated through the shop windows). The fact checker added the name of the new expert to her card file, expanding and improving her knowledge map. Had he not known the answer to her question, he probably would have been able to suggest a colleague who did. These Time Life researchers continuously pooled their sources (and sources of new sources). The critical mass of knowledge seeking and sharing gave the organization superb access to knowledge.

A Case in Point: Microsoft's Knowledge Map

As we've noted, the knowledge map can refer to documents and structured knowledge, to people, or to both. The most elaborate knowledge maps for people can be quite complex because knowledge structures are complex, knowledge changes over time, subjectivity comes into play, and expertise involves power. One of the best examples of a people-oriented knowledge map can be found at Microsoft, where the information systems group decided to map the knowledge of system developers. A 1995 pilot in an application-development group was successful, and full implementation is proceeding. The project, called Skills Planning "und" Development (or "SPUD"), is focused not just on entry-level knowledge but rather on that needed to stay on the leading edge of the industry.

The project objective is to improve the matching of employees to jobs and work teams. Microsoft also believes that once its IT employees have a better idea of what knowledge is required of them, they will be better consumers of educational offerings within and outside of the company. Eventually the project may be extended throughout Microsoft and into products and services for customers.

There are five major stages to the project:

1. Developing a structure of knowledge competency types and levels.
2. Defining the knowledge required for particular jobs.
3. Rating the performance of individual employees in particular jobs by knowledge competencies.
4. Implementing the knowledge competencies in an on-line system.
5. Linking the knowledge model to training programs.

The SPUD project uses a four-type knowledge structure to evaluate employee competency. Entry-level competencies come under the heading of foundation knowledge. Above the foundation level there are local or unique knowledge competencies—advanced skills that apply to a particular job type. A network analyst, for example, might need a fault diagnosis competency for LANs. The next level of knowledge is global, which applies to all employees within a particular function or organization. Every worker in the controller organization, for example, would be knowledgeable in financial analysis; every IT employee would have expertise in technology architectures. The highest level in the knowledge structure comprises the universal competencies for all employees in the company. Examples include knowledge of the overall business the company is in, the products it sells, and the drivers of the industry.

Within each of the four knowledge competency levels there are two different categories. Explicit knowledge competencies involve expertise in specific tools or methods (for example, Excel or SQL 6.0) and change frequently with the marketplace. Implicit competencies, such as requirements definition, involve more abstract thinking and reasoning skills. All told there are 137 implicit competencies and 200 explicit ones in the Microsoft knowledge structure. Within each type of knowledge competency there are also four defined skill levels: basic, working, leadership, and expert. Each skill level for each knowledge competency is described in several bullet points that make the level clear and measurable.

Each job in Microsoft IT has to be rated by a manager in terms of the forty to sixty knowledge competencies required to perform it. Workers are also evaluated in terms of the knowledge they have exhibited in their current jobs. The initial rating is built in an iterative fashion by the employee and his or her supervisor; eventually the entire work team participates.

Microsoft is using the employee rating process to build an on-line knowledge map that can be accessed company-wide. A manager building a team for a new project can query the on-line system and ask, "Give me the top five candidates who have leadership skill levels on 80 percent of the knowledge competencies for this job and who are based in Redmond [Microsoft's headquarters location in Washington State]." The system runs on an SQL Server and has a Web front end for easy intranet access around the world.

The system's knowledge types and levels are also linked to specific course opportunities inside and outside Microsoft. Ultimately, the Learning and Communications Resources group hopes to be able to recommend not only specific courses but even specific material or segments within a course that would be aimed at the targeted knowledge level.

Microsoft's knowledge map demonstrates that the company's management values knowledge and supports its exchange. Their commitment of time and money is a symbolic action that has value apart from the actual ability of the map itself. The map simultaneously makes knowledge easier to find and promotes the idea that corporate knowledge belongs to the corporation as a whole, not to a particular group or individual. Since the success or

Don't underestimate the symbolic value of a knowledge map to your company's culture.

failure of knowledge work depends so heavily on culture, this benefit of the knowledge map should not be underestimated.

The Technology of Mapping Knowledge

As the Microsoft case suggests, computer technology can help make knowledge maps work. On-line Yellow Pages or an electronic database of knowledge workers can be made accessible to everyone on the corporate network. It will generally allow users to search by topic or key word, making it easy to locate and compare potential knowledge sources. Most important, an electronic map can be revised more frequently than a printed one. Organizations are dynamic; knowledge maps begin to go out of date as soon as they are created. More-or-less continuously edited electronic Yellow Pages will be more useful and credible than an increasingly inaccurate paper document. Computers also have the potential to communicate a better sense of the knowledge owners as people than a print entry. In many companies, knowledge Yellow Pages show an image of the person listed. A few organizations include a brief video clip instead, an even richer personalization. Since successful knowledge transactions depend so heavily on trust and compatibility, personalizing the entries in these ways can make the map more effective.

Lotus Notes and Web browser/intranet systems are common tools for publishing corporate knowledge maps. Hewlett-Packard's research laboratory uses Web technology to make the knowledge of researchers more accessible; the company also has a similar system in place for corporate trainers and educators. McKinsey, Ernst & Young, and IBM Global Services all use Notes for their knowledge maps. British Petroleum, which is creating an electronic Yellow Pages for its virtual teamworking network, has both groupware and Web browsers as part of their suite of communications software.

At a more rudimentary level, general human resources (HR) packages such as PeopleSoft and SAP have limited capabilities to inventory the skills and knowledge of employees and the expertise required for particular positions. Because these broad packages are typically used for payroll as well, companies can link compensation to knowledge. But the knowledge categories are simple and generic, and few companies take advantage of them.

At the next level of functionality in HR systems are resume-oriented packages, which are often interfaced with broader systems like People-Soft. These systems, including Restrac and Resumix, work by scanning in resumes, extracting key concepts from resume text, and comparing them to expertise desired in particular jobs. They can be used for either internal or external job candidates, though most companies are more focused on the external labor market. They can also analyze resumes submitted from the Internet or an intranet.

Resume-oriented systems are primarily geared toward reducing the cost and time of the staffing process, rather than aimed at evaluating the knowledge of employees. The knowledge categories, while better than general HR systems, are still limited and generic. Even in terms of assessing the capabilities of applicants, the concept-analysis and search capabilities of these systems are only a starting point. Some of the systems now allow line managers to search and browse the applicant databases directly, rather than having to go through the HR function.

Some small vendors are attacking the knowledge issue directly, producing systems that are oriented to specific knowledge domains, notably information technology. For example, Success Factor Systems has a software tool that allows firms to specify the success factors ("knowledge, skills, abilities, and behaviors") for the organization, and then to evaluate the match between jobs and applicants. Within the IT function, a program called Skillview allows evaluation of up to three hundred IT-oriented skills by employees, supervisors, peers, or clients. The skills are granular enough so that an employee's skill profile can be used to create an individualized training program.

Despite these useful features, technology alone cannot ensure that the knowledge map will be used effectively in an organization. Here, as elsewhere in knowledge work, the $33\frac{1}{3}$ percent rule applies: If more than a third of the total time and money resources of a project is spent on technology, the project becomes an IT project, not a knowledge project. Clarity of purpose, accuracy, availability, and ease of use are the essentials of a good knowledge map. Although technology can help achieve them, those characteristics are what make the map valuable. In fact, some of the most successful maps are not electronic at all.

At Chemical (now Chase) Bank, a paper phone directory was once produced for the entire IT organization—several thousand people. It categorized employees for the first time by what they actually *did*. Like many directories, it used traditional listing categories of alphabetical last name, geography, and division. The innovation was to list employees by what they did in their jobs (and presumably were knowledgeable about).

For the first time, for example, all the C++ programmers were listed together. The book was a huge success with employees, many of whom noted that they'd never been able to find likeminded and skilled co-workers before it was created.

The Rolodexes once used by Time Life fact checkers were a highly effective low-tech knowledge map. An electronic version of the same information would improve search speed and make updating easier (in fact, Time Life later put the Rolodex system on-line to get those benefits), but clearly the value of the map was the quality and depth of information much more than the bells and whistles of a sophisticated storage and retrieval system.

The Politics of Mapping Knowledge

Most maps have a political dimension. A map is a representation of reality, but if that reality is ambiguous or in dispute, any one map will be seen as favoring one viewpoint over another. The map itself becomes a force in creating the reality it is supposed to describe. The old saying "The map is not the territory" may be literally true, but the map can *influence* the territory, defining as well as describing it.

Organizational knowledge maps are political documents too. Questions about who has the most useful knowledge are open to interpretation (unlike, say, the question of where water fountains are located in an office building). If knowledge is genuinely important to an organization and those who have it are recognized and rewarded, then the knowledge map will be a picture of status and success as well as a knowledge locator. For example, although the fact checkers at Time Life were able to share their knowledge, an effort to document and share sources among editors and writers at one of the company's magazines later failed. Giving away one's proprietary sources of knowledge in that particular setting was viewed as giving away power and influence. In any listing of who knows what, people will also care about whether or not they are on the map and will try to influence the mapmakers to include them. When one high-tech firm we work with tried to create a map depicting the key human and technical knowledge repositories for new product development, the project almost foundered because of the intense maneuvering to be "situated well" on the map. As one of us has noted in a recent article, "If politics plays no part in a knowledge management initiative, it is a safe bet that the organization perceives nothing of value is at issue."[6]

So in one sense political wrangling over a corporate knowledge map is a good sign: It shows that knowledge matters. But it raises issues of how to keep politics from distorting a map that is supposed to reflect knowledge, not power. When he created a directory of employee skills in the late 1980s, Ted Lumley, chief of technical computing at Mobil Exploration and Producing, asked people to rate their own levels of expertise. He found that the "experts were modest about their capabilities, and the neophytes overestimated theirs." How much this had to do with the newer employees honestly not understanding the dimensions of real expertise and how much was political jockeying for status is hard to say, but Lumley felt politics played a significant part. When he developed a new map a few years later, he left out ratings altogether.[7]

> *Political wrangling can be a good sign—it tells you that knowledge matters.*

Modeling Knowledge

Dynamic modeling has a lengthy history and a generally favorable reputation when it is used to help managers understand and improve a specific operation. As operations research, modeling has proven quite useful when rules, entities, and routines are stable, but there is still much to discover about the value of its application to knowledge-centered operations.

One large consumer products firm we have worked with has constructed a dynamic model of how new products are developed in its key units. The model uses various types and forms of knowledge as inputs and executive actions as transforming agents, with new products being the output or outcome. One of the most interesting aspects of this project is the firm's attempt to quantify the value of the key variables as well as the "frictions" that impede knowledge flow and utilization. These frictions can be infrastructure failures, social, political, cognitive, and communication impediments, and failures of managerial "will." While this experiment is still being refined and its overall results are not yet known, the very act of undertaking it has signaled the value of knowledge to those in the firm, and ensuing discussions have helped management focus on the subject. In general, the greatest value of modeling knowledge processes lies not in reaching an exact understanding of knowledge input, output, and flow rates but in identifying the variables in the model that can be affected by management action.

Capturing Tacit Knowledge

As difficult as it is to codify tacit knowledge, its substantial value makes it worth the effort. Mapping who knows what in an organization creates an essential knowledge inventory, but does nothing to guarantee the ongoing availability of knowledge. Having access to knowledge only when its "owner" has time to share it or losing it entirely if she leaves the company are significant problems that threaten the value of the organization's knowledge capital. Firms must therefore have strategies for preventing such losses. A partial answer (which we will discuss in the next chapter) is to try to transfer as much knowledge as possible to someone through mentoring or apprenticeship, so that important tacit knowledge is not wholly concentrated in one person. Multimedia computing and the hypertext capabilities of intranets have created the possibility of effectively capturing at least some meaningful fraction of an expert's knowledge, making the tacit explicit. If Larry Prusak had watched films of Ted Williams hitting or, better yet, had been able to use an interactive multimedia computer program to study Ted's swing visually, he *might* have learned a little more about hitting. Companies are beginning to use these technologies to record the narratives and nuances that carry so much of the real value of knowledge. IBM's approach to retaining important knowledge at its Lotus Development subsidiary includes trying to retain key employees by creating special programs to identify and reward essential knowledge workers.[8]

The Value of Narratives

Human beings learn best from stories. As Karl Weick says, "people think narratively rather than argumentatively or paradigmatically."[9] This precept has always been intuitively clear to anyone who teaches; recent research, most notably by Roger Schank at Northwestern University, has tended to underscore its importance.[10] His work has been supported by recent studies examining the role rhetoric plays in conveying knowledge. Donald (now Deidre) McCloskey has looked at rhetoric in economics; Bob Eccles and Nitin Nohria have examined its role in organizational behavior.[11] Other studies have focused on law, theology, and other areas. In all these fields, research shows that knowledge is communicated most effectively through a convincing narrative that is delivered with formal elegance and passion.

In discussing what is needed for sensemaking (which is essentially what knowledge does), Weick says:

> The answer is . . . something that preserves plausibility and coherence, something that is reasonable and memorable, something that embodies past experience and expectations, something that resonates with other people, something that can be constructed retrospectively but also can be used prospectively, something that captures both feeling and thought, something that allows for embellishment to fit current oddities, something that is fun to construct. In short, what is necessary in sensemaking is a good story.[12]

This description of stories—the way they embody experience and apply it to future expectations, their basis in feeling and thought, their essential humanness—is similar to our description of knowledge and suggests why there is a meaningful link between the two.

A good story is often the best way to convey meaningful knowledge.

We have talked about "war stories" that convey "ground truth" as one of the most effective ways of communicating not just information but knowledge: a rich and complex understanding of an event or situation in a human context.

What does the importance of narrative suggest about knowledge codification? Trying to turn knowledge into a "code" would seem to defeat the purpose of communicating it through resonant storytelling. Once we recognize that narratives are the best way to teach and learn complex "stuff," though, we can often *encode* the stories themselves so as to convey meaning without losing much of its leveragable value. Many firms already do something like this when they send videos to branch offices to be shown over lunch. In the past, they were likely to contain a speech or exhortation by a senior executive. Increasingly, though, firms distribute tapes that tell the story of an important business event, such as how a key sale was made. Knowledge is more likely to be absorbed if it adheres to the listeners' sense of ground truth, is delivered with feeling, and is placed in a context or frame that is at least partly shared by its audience. One well-known securities firm sends out a message every morning on its "hoot and holler" network to all its brokerage agents, giving them what is called "useful information" about a particular sale, an upcoming event, or some valuable piece of customer feedback. These messages almost always take the form of a story. At Verifone (a recently acquired subsidiary of Hewlett-Packard), where workers are widely dispersed around the world, stories of desirable business behavior are circulated electronically under the banner of "Excellence in Action."

We have seen many examples of these sorts of efforts failing because the speaker lacks the insight or imagination to understand where his listeners are coming from, that is, the context in which they interpret his words. In one instance, the CEO of a major midwestern manufacturer spoke to all the firm's U.S. employees over a satellite network to announce a reengineering initiative. Unfortunately, his speech was so heavily laden with business jargon that many factory workers couldn't follow. Even more seriously, he failed completely to address the natural anxieties that the workers associated with reengineering. With all the media attention given to the association of reengineering and downsizing, he should have known that employees would interpret even the most neutral proposals in a negative light. Whatever knowledge he intended to share failed to "take" because he didn't communicate with his employees in terms they could understand.

Embedded Knowledge

Some knowledge that is quite complex and initially tacit can be externalized and embedded in a company's products or services. The knowers use their expertise to develop a process or product that contains at least some of what they know. Any manufacturing process, whether automated or formalized in a set of procedures, is constructed from what was once the knowledge of individuals. In theory, this embedded knowledge is independent of those who developed it and therefore has some organizational stability—an individual expert can disappear without bringing the process to a halt or reducing the company's stock of embedded knowledge. In practice, however, it is difficult to locate the dividing line between knowledge that is fully embedded in a process and the tacit, human knowledge that keeps the process going. As we mentioned in Chapter 3, when EL Products, a manufacturer of electroluminescent lamps, bought Grimes, one of its competitors, ELP managers imagined that Grimes's knowledge of how to make dust-free lamps was embedded in an explicit production process. Only when they tried and failed to make that process work without the help of the Grimes line operators did they understand how much essential expertise still existed only in the heads of skilled employees (or, in this case, ex-employees).[13]

Codifying Knowledge in Systems

An expert system represents an explicit attempt to capture or imitate human knowledge by transferring it to a formalized rules-based system. As we'll describe in greater detail in Chapter 7, the history of artificial intelligence has been characterized by excessive claims from proponents who have underestimated the complexity and contextuality of human thought and overestimated the capabilities of computers.

For example, some years ago a major oil company decided to build an expert system to capture the knowledge of one of their interpreters of aerial photographs, a man reputed to be the best in the world at locating potential drilling sites. Wanting to formalize this valuable knowledge so they would still have it should the employee not be available, the company hired an expert on artificial intelligence to develop the system. He went through a process of watching the photograph analyzer work, asking him questions about how he evaluated and weighed what he saw in the photographs, what clues he looked for, and what principles he applied. The process was lengthy and complex: long sessions spent clarifying the analyst's expertise, followed by writing elaborate computer code to embody that knowledge, followed by further clarification and code writing. Even so, the first prototype was discarded and the project failed. The expertise was too subtle and complex to be written into the computer; the artificial photo analyst could not begin to match the human's knowledge.

However, expert systems and artificially intelligent systems can play a limited role in the codification of knowledge. The more bounded, unambiguous, and rules-based that knowledge is, the more easily it can be embedded in an expert system. Chess-playing computers, like IBM's Deep Blue, can now compete with the best human players because chess, though complex, is a closed system of unchanging and codifiable rules. The size of the board never varies, the rules are unambiguous, the moves of the pieces are clearly defined, and there is absolute agreement about what it means to win or lose. Even with advances in fuzzy logic, computers are not yet well suited to ambiguous and intuitive operations where the rules, if they exist at all, are much harder to define.

Evaluating Explicit Knowledge

Like the tenets of law described early in this chapter, some forms of knowledge are already codified and explicit. Patents are one form of codified knowledge, a representation in text of a process or product developed through the expertise of scientists or inventors. By definition, patented knowledge is knowledge that can be explicitly expressed. The word "patent" means "lying open"—a patent represents knowledge that is protected by being publicly described and connected with an owner. Similarly, reports and other structured documents are examples of knowledge that has already been made explicit.

But the structured, explicit knowledge of patents and reports does not become usable simply by being codified. It needs to be evaluated and made accessible to the people who can do something with it in order to benefit the organization. When Gordon Petrash was appointed Dow Chemical's director of intellectual asset management, he understood that many of the company's 29,000 patents represented intellectual capital that was largely dormant and even hidden because Dow had "forgotten" what they contained. The knowledge codified in them was not being utilized. The first project taken on by Petrash and his group was to evaluate patents to determine which could be used, which might be sold, and which should be abandoned (keeping unused patents in effect is an expensive proposition). The process of weeding out patents with little or no value saved $1 million in fees in the first eighteen months and created the potential to develop valuable new products. Furthermore, making Dow business units and potential business partners aware of the untapped value in other patents offered substantially higher potential returns. As Petrash's initiative makes clear, evaluating codified knowledge and then making it available is an integral part of the entire codification process.[14]

A Case in Point: Monsanto's Knowledge Management Architecture

Monsanto's Knowledge Management Architecture project is an ambitious effort to codify corporate knowledge. Its aim is to allow the company's 30,000 employees to share knowledge and information and, by making global knowledge locally available, to combine the knowledge benefits of a large company (quantity and diversity of knowledge) with the benefits of a small one (accessibility to knowledge). Several features of Monsanto's approach illustrate important codification issues.

In their evaluation of existing knowledge and information, the company makes a distinction between quantitative, structured content and qualitative, relatively unstructured content. The Knowledge Management Architecture provides different tools for capturing, representing, and retrieving the two kinds of material. Structural content is housed in a relational database with desktop access provided by appropriate query software. Unstructured content is represented in Web pages and Lotus Notes. This flexible approach means that relatively amorphous, "soft" knowledge is not destroyed by being forced into a rigid structure. The structured material that does fit comfortably into the database can be retrieved more easily and systematically than if it were stored in a more loosely organized form.

The Knowledge Management Architecture includes what Monsanto calls an Enterprise Reference Data System, which provides global definitions for key terms such as "customer," "product," and "material." Without a common understanding of these terms, the company could not organize intellectual material into a single system. It might seem that such words are too basic to need defining.

Harmonize organizational knowledge, but don't homogenize it.

In fact, multiple and sometimes contradictory meanings for fundamental terms exist in many organizations and create barriers to consolidating information and knowledge.[15] Common definitions are not only required to make a system like the Knowledge Management Architecture work; they are the necessary common ground of communication across a company. Knowledgeable people cannot share expertise efficiently if they mean different things when they use familiar, essential terms. Common ground and orderliness are purchased at a cost; idiosyncratic local definitions may express local truths that get lost when a global standard is adopted. In any codification process, there is an inherent tension between local and global needs, between the value of the particularity of knowledge and the value of making it comprehensible to a variety of people. Only the most essential shared terms should be standardized— and even those are not yet completely standardized at Monsanto. What is called for is just enough uniformity to make the system work. The goal is to harmonize organizational knowledge, not to homogenize it.

Monsanto also recognizes the importance of evaluating and interpreting its knowledge capital. An unedited repository of intellectual material is of little value to an organization. Users need to be guided to important material and given a context in which to understand it. At Monsanto, analysts who had previously been gatekeepers of financial information provide analyses of the content of the company's financial data warehouse, adding their knowledge to what had been relatively undifferentiated data and information. Other employees have the responsibility of evaluating the unstructured intranet and Lotus Notes content, analyzing its relevance to different business units and putting their analyses online as guidelines for users.

The Continuing Codification Challenge

Codifying knowledge is an essential step in leveraging its value in the organization. Codification gives permanence to knowledge that may otherwise exist only inside an individual's mind. It represents or embeds knowledge in forms that can be shared, stored, combined, and manipulated in a variety of ways. The challenge is to codify knowledge and still leave its distinctive attributes intact, putting in place codification structures that can change as rapidly and flexibly as the knowledge itself. As we have discussed, stories and rhetorical strategies provide the richest and most flexible approach to this task. Developing technologies will extend the range of possible applications, but for the foreseeable future codification will continue to be more art than science, the domain of minds rather than machines. As Lofti Zadeh, an early AI pioneer and developer of fuzzy-logic concepts, recently stated, "No computer can summarize what you tell it." That task, vital to knowledge codification, is still a human one.[16]

A man has no ears
for that to which experience
has given him no access.
—Friedrich Nietzsche

5

Knowledge Transfer

H O W   C A N an organization transfer knowledge effectively? The short answer, and the best one, is: hire smart people and let them talk to one another. Unfortunately, the second part of this advice is the more difficult to put into practice. Organizations often hire bright people and then isolate them or burden them with tasks that leave no time for conversation and little time for thought. While we'll consider various knowledge transfer issues and strategies in this chapter, many of them come down to finding effective ways to let people talk and listen to one another.

Knowledge *is* transferred in organizations whether or not we manage the process at all. When an employee asks a colleague in the next cubicle how to put together a budget request, he's requesting a transfer of knowledge. When a sales rep new to a territory asks the retiring rep about the needs of a particular customer, they're exchanging knowledge. When one engineer asks another in an office down the hall if he has ever dealt with a particular problem, the second engineer, if willing and able, will transfer his knowledge.

These everyday knowledge transfers are part of organizational life. They are, however, local and fragmentary. We discuss a business problem with someone down the hall because she is conveniently close and we feel comfortable with her—not necessarily because she is the best person to consult on the subject. Although we make a judgment about who in our immediate area is most likely to be able to help us, we rarely try to find the person in the company who has the deepest knowledge of the subject. We hope to get good enough information from someone nearby. This is yet another example of the implications of bounded rationality— the very human limits on how much information people can absorb and how much effort they will expend to get it. The larger and more complex the firm is, the less likely it is we will find the best expertise in the next office or anywhere at our location. Greater size may increase the chances that the knowledge we need exists somewhere in the company, but it decreases the likelihood that we will know how and where to find it. In a competitive environment, "good enough" is often, in fact, *not* good enough. A company that fails to keep track of components needed in a manufacturing process probably will not thrive. The same is true of companies that don't keep track of their knowledge components—even more so, because knowledge assets are difficult to buy in a market. Knowledge abounds in our organizations, but its existence does not guarantee its use.

Strategies for Knowledge Transfer

Spontaneous, unstructured knowledge transfer is vital to a firm's success. Although the term "knowledge management" implies formalized transfer, one of its essential elements is developing specific strategies to encourage such spontaneous exchanges. This is particularly necessary for organizations whose primary role is to create knowledge. Perhaps we can find the most useful lessons about knowledge transfer from research facilities in Austin, Texas, where two high-tech consortia, Microelectronics and Computer Corporation (MCC) and Sematech, have struggled with the transfer of technologies, ideas, and research results to the companies that funded their research into computer and semiconductor technologies, respectively. According to a thorough account by David V. Gibson and Everett M. Rogers of the two organizations, Sematech has been the more successful at technology or knowledge transfer.[1] As one MCC researcher commented:

> There are lots of known techniques for knowledge transfer—volumes have been written. At MCC we have used liaisons, assignees, workshops, training, technical reports, third-party licenses, production and support of products (as opposed to prototypes), and many other techniques. Again, on the basis of the result we may assess the approach reflected by these techniques as having failed.[2]

The primary reason for Sematech's success has been the organizational and human resource structures devoted to technology transfer. More specifically, the organization pays great attention to the role of "assignees" from sponsoring firms who come to Sematech to participate in research and then take ideas back with them. Indeed, when a technology transfer manager was asked to describe how Sematech transferred knowledge, she commented: "We have documents, document databases, an intranet Web, groupware, you name it. But the assignees and the face-to-face meetings we have are by far the most important channels for transferring knowledge to the member firms."[3]

Tacit and ambiguous knowledge is especially hard to transfer from the resource that creates it to other parts of the organization. Perhaps the most reliable way to put this knowledge into circulation is to emulate Sematech and transfer people in and out of the dedicated resource. Have them spend a year or two absorbing and helping to generate new knowledge, which they then can carry to new assignments. In Japan, for example, it is common to rotate engineering executives into manufacturing and vice-versa so that the managers have an understanding of the entire process of new product development and production.

Water Coolers and Talk Rooms

Conversations at the water cooler or in the company cafeteria are often occasions for knowledge transfer. Influenced by outdated theories of the nature of work, management sometimes assumes that water cooler socializing is wasting time. Although some of the talk will be about sports and the weather, most water cooler conversation focuses on work: people ask each other about current projects; they bounce ideas off one another; they get advice on how to solve problems. Their conversations *are* work. In his article "What's So New About the New Economy?" Alan Webber says, "In the new economy, conversations are the most important form of work. Conversations are the way knowledge workers discover what they know, share it with their colleagues, and in the process create new knowledge for the organization."[4]

When IBM needed to reinvent itself in response to the fact that companies were reducing their reliance on mainframe computers, then-chairman John Akers circulated a memo telling employees to stay away from the water coolers and get back to work. He thought they were avoiding work when in fact they were often trying to find ways out of the company's difficulties. When a business is struggling, people naturally gather to talk through problems and share

In a knowledge-driven economy, talk is real work.

ideas about how to solve them. Those conversations are more likely to generate creative solutions than keeping employees at their desks plugging away at their individual tasks. Akers's memo reflected a traditional management attitude—"Stop talking and get to work!" On the contrary, as Webber says, "Start talking and get to work!" is better advice in an economy driven by knowledge.

Transferring knowledge through personal conversations is being threatened not only by industrial-age managers but also by the move to "virtual offices." Many firms are adopting work arrangements in which workers—particularly those in such customer-oriented functions as sales and service—are encouraged to work at home or at a customer site. While these arrangements offer benefits such as greater employee flexibility and more time with customers, it also lowers the frequency of informal knowledge transfer. Firms that initiate virtual office programs should at least encourage workers to be in the office on the same days, identify ways to make up for lost interaction, and educate workers on effective knowledge transfer through computers and telephones. IBM, for example, has taken some steps to restore knowledge transfers that have been lost or reduced in the transition to virtual offices. The company's managers worried, for example, that virtual field employees who have contact with customers would be less likely to pass on customer comments to researchers, product developers, and marketers. Therefore, each of these functional areas started programs in which previously office-bound workers were expected to spend time directly with customers. In effect, field sales and service personnel are no longer expected to be information intermediaries.

Water cooler knowledge exchanges are also hit-or-miss in terms of dealing with a particular business problem or making a key decision. When faced with a need for specific knowledge at a critical point in a project, it would not be a sensible strategy to stand by the water cooler in hopes of picking up exactly what you're looking for from whoever happens to be thirsty. Similarly, if you've learned something important about a customer, competitor, or supplier, you shouldn't count on unstructured casual conversations to spread the word. But these unstructured transfers of knowledge do have the corresponding advantage of opening the door to serendipity. They are opportunities for spontaneous meetings of the mind that have the potential to generate new ideas or solve old problems in unexpected ways.[5]

Many Japanese firms have set up "talk rooms" to encourage this kind of unpredictable creative blending and exchange. As we mentioned earlier, at Dai-Ichi Pharmaceuticals there are rooms with green tea and attractive lighting that researchers are expected to visit for twenty minutes or so as a normal part of their workday. No meetings are held in the talk rooms; there are no organized discussions. The expectation is that the researchers will chat about their current work with whomever they find and that these more or less random conversations will create value for the firm. It is a kind of Brownian motion theory of knowledge exchange, its very randomness encouraging the discovery of new ideas that a more specifically directed discussion would miss.

In addition, Japanese managers spend many after-work hours together. Group dinners and visits to nightclubs are part of Japan's corporate culture. They function as an important knowledge-sharing mechanism, as well as mechanisms for establishing trust and (with inebriation as an excuse) opportunities for criticism. Japanese businesses do not commonly use e-mail; managers and workers prefer face-to-face meetings. When one of us (Davenport) made a trip to Japan to discuss knowledge management, he suggested to a small group of managers that they could go home earlier if they exchanged ideas electronically. They laughed and said that neither they nor their wives necessarily wanted earlier homecomings!

Davenport also observed the development of a Lotus Notes–based knowledge repository at a very large Japanese financial services firm. At that time the Notes implementation team saw many cultural barriers to effective information and knowledge sharing at the company. "We don't have an output culture," said one team member. "Our know-how is hidden in people. If knowledge is in my brain it will be difficult to get it out. The motivation to share is very difficult." Another team member noted that information is less valuable if widely shared. "Much of our information is secret," he noted. A third team member commented that, "When we share information it is after work over drinks and dinner. We would like for Notes to take over some of those functions, since we are a global company and everyone cannot meet face to face. But it will be difficult."

The lesson here is that knowledge transfer methods should suit the organizational (and national) culture. It is not possible and in many ways would not be desirable to impose the Japanese model on American companies. The attempt described above to impose an American knowledge transfer approach in Japan may also fail. We should recognize the value of both face-to-face and electronic contacts and provide opportunities for both. Above all, we need to broaden our definition of "productivity" to include what may be very productive casual conversations, periods of reflection, and learning.

When you need to transfer knowledge, the method must always suit the culture.

Informal knowledge transfer is endangered by a particularly American sense of what is and isn't "real" work. An employee who dutifully reads and answers e-mail messages and responds promptly with e-mail and memos of his own is supposedly hard at work, regardless of the value of what is being exchanged. On the other hand, an employee who reads a book at his desk—arguably an effective approach to knowledge acquisition—is looked at with suspicion. Doesn't he have work to do? Shouldn't he save his reading to do on his own time? The suspicion exists even if the book may enhance the employee's knowledge in a way that proves beneficial to the organization. If it is unusual to find an employee who enhances his knowledge by reading at work, it is almost unheard of for a co-worker to have the leisure to ask what the book is about and enter into a conversation about it. A company that claims to value knowledge but discourages reading and talking on company time sends mixed messages. The more convincing message is that knowledge is not much valued after all. Managers need to recognize that the availability of "slack" time for learning and thinking may be one of the best metrics of a firm's knowledge orientation.

Knowledge Fairs and Open Forums

There are other ways that organizations can encourage serendipitous knowledge sharing across the lines of departments or business units. They are basically the strategies we outlined in our discussion of knowledge marketplaces: creating locations and occasions for workers to interact informally. Corporate picnics provide opportunities for exchange between employees who never get to talk to one another in the course of their daily work. A knowledge fair is a more orchestrated forum for encouraging the exchange of knowledge but one that still allows for spontaneity. It brings people together without preconceptions about who should talk to whom.

Ernst & Young, a large accountant and consulting firm, held a knowledge fair in Cleveland at which close to thirty separate consulting and research units set up booths to display information and discuss their work. Participants were free to wander around and pick up whatever struck them as useful. The hope, borne out by surveys after the event, was that participants would make new connections and discover new synergies given the opportunity to mingle freely.

CSIRO, a large Australian contract R&D organization, recently held its first knowledge fair near Melbourne, bringing together scientists from across the country who communicated electronically but had never actually met one another in person. One of the authors attended the fair and felt a palpable sense of excitement in the air as these researchers finally had a chance to meet. Although many had had extensive e-mail exchanges, they all said (in one form or another), "I've wanted to chat with that fellow for ages. I can't wait to talk with him."

These knowledge fairs worked in part because they were relatively unstructured. They gave people opportunities to wander and mingle at will as well as ample time to talk. They did not impose a progression; they let visitors create their own itineraries and in effect their own markets. Contrast this approach to that of a large high-tech firm, when it brought together more than three hundred senior managers for a three-day conference intended as a forum for knowledge exchange. Unlike the E&Y and CSIRO knowledge fairs, the conference was organized down to the minute, with a full schedule of speakers, workshops, and events—three long, structured days. There was no time set aside for people to talk about what they were hearing or about their work. Some managers who knew one another from phone conversations but had never met had no chance to interact at the conference. At most they could exchange a word or two as they hurried along to the next activity. Although the event cost a fortune—much more than a knowledge fair—participant surveys rated it a failure. The lesson to be learned is not that fairs are good and conferences are bad, but that in any gathering there needs to be room for choice and time for conversation. Conversation should never be seen as an extra, a spare time activity. A conference that tries to stuff people with knowledge is operating on a false assumption of how knowledge works.

We strongly advocate knowledge transfer through face-to-face meetings and through narratives in addition to more structured forms. The signals that convince people they can communicate effectively are best given in person. But, as we have said, giving people who work at the same location opportunities to talk to one another does not by itself solve the problem of transferring knowledge, especially in large organizations. Conversations must be encouraged to flourish, but they won't ensure that an innovation developed at an oil rig in Texas will be adopted at one in Alaska. They won't keep business units that are half a world apart from duplicating problem-solving efforts, because they provide no good mechanisms for efficiently disseminating knowledge. So we also need to consider more formal and intentional ways of sharing knowledge within organizations.

What Kinds of Knowledge?

As we have made clear throughout our discussion and especially in our chapter on codification, the relative difficulty of capturing and transferring knowledge depends on the kind of knowledge involved. Knowledge that is more or less explicit can be embedded in procedures or represented in documents and databases and transferred with reasonable accuracy. Tacit knowledge transfer generally requires extensive personal contact. The "transfer relationship" may be a partnership, mentoring, or an apprenticeship, but some kind of working relationship is usually essential. Such relationships are likely to involve transferring various kinds of knowledge, from explicit to tacit. Not all of the learning communicated will be complex and intuitive, but it is the tacit knowledge that we cannot readily transfer in any other way.

We described a failed attempt to capture an aerial photo analyst's skill in an expert system in the last chapter. This example illustrates how hard it is to replicate tacit knowledge through a set of rules, even the complex rules of a sophisticated computer program. However, although the system failed to "learn" how to read aerial photographs, the computer scientist who was brought in to develop the system did acquire those skills. The long process of trying to extract and understand the expert's knowledge served as an apprenticeship. Having extensive conversations, looking at photographs together, asking questions, and seeking clarifications taught the consultant a new skill. When the project ended, the expert system was useless, but the system designer was said to be the second best analyzer of aerial photographs in the world!

Companies committed to transferring tacit knowledge often set up formal mentoring programs and make passing on knowledge to young employees an explicit part of the job descriptions of skilled senior staff.

Japanese steel firms, for instance, encourage and expect "older-younger" bonding between employees, with the more experienced senior person passing along his knowledge of the job to the next generation.[6] The consulting firm Booz, Allen & Hamilton redesigned its consultant appraisal process to incorporate knowledge transfer through mentoring. Every consultant is responsible for facilitating the learning and development of a colleague one level below her in seniority.[7]

The infrastructure of tacit knowledge transfer can also include (but should not be limited to) electronic technology. Raychem, a California electronics and telecommunications manufacturer, has set up an Internal Information Interview Network, a database that lists employees who are willing to meet with colleagues and share information.[8] This network is a specialized kind of knowledge map. Knowledge maps are clearly part of the knowledge transfer infrastructure. The BP Virtual Teamwork videoconferencing system is essentially a tacit knowledge pipeline, a mechanism for linking the people with knowledge to the people who need it. Another use of technology to transfer tacit knowledge can be seen in the efforts of several organizations to record the stories and experience of its senior practitioners on video or CD-ROM before they leave the company.

As a general rule, though, the more rich and tacit knowledge is, the more technology should be used to enable people to share that knowledge directly. It's not a good idea to try to contain or represent the knowledge itself using technology. (Explicit knowledge can be more successfully stored in some sort of technological repository, such as Lotus Notes or some more highly structured database.) Extensive knowledge transfer could not happen in large global companies without the tools provided by information technology, but the values, norms, and behaviors that make up a company's culture are the principal determinants of how successfully important knowledge is transferred.

The Culture of Knowledge Transfer

There are many cultural factors that inhibit knowledge transfer. We call the inhibitors "frictions" because they slow or prevent transfer and are likely to erode some of the knowledge as it tries to move through the organization. The following are the most common frictions and ways of overcoming them.

Friction	Possible Solutions
• Lack of trust	• Build relationships and trust through face-to-face meetings
• Different cultures, vocabularies, frames of reference	• Create common ground through education, discussion, publications, teaming, job rotation
• Lack of time and meeting places; narrow idea of productive work	• Establish times and places for knowledge transfers: fairs, talk rooms, conference reports
• Status and rewards go to knowledge owners	• Evaluate performance and provide incentives based on sharing
• Lack of absorptive capacity in recipients	• Educate employees for flexibility; provide time for learning; hire for openness to ideas
• Belief that knowledge is prerogative of particular groups, not-invented-here syndrome	• Encourage nonhierarchical approach to knowledge; quality of ideas more important than status of source
• Intolerance for mistakes or need for help	• Accept and reward creative errors and collaboration; no loss of status from not knowing everything

Trust and Common Ground

In 1990 and 1991, surgical teams at five northern New England medical centers took part in a study of skill sharing. Their goal was to discover whether a skill-sharing process that included observation of one another's work could improve the rate of success for the coronary-artery bypass surgery in which they all specialized. The project began by providing each of the twenty-three surgeons involved with information about his or her success rates compared with others in the medical center and with statistics for the entire region. It included training in continuous improvement techniques and site visits during which visiting professionals observed their counterparts in action.

After these activities had taken place, the hospitals collectively showed a 24 percent reduction in the mortality rate of the surgery—seventy-four fewer deaths per year than predicted. Four of the five medical centers—all but the one that had the lowest mortality rate before the study—showed substantial reductions. In addition, participants attributed the adoption of more than a dozen enhancements in patient evaluation, staff organization, and surgical technique to their site visit experiences.[9]

Some of the details of this successful transfer initiative illuminate issues relevant to other transfer projects. Giving surgeons information about the better success rates of some of their colleagues created a motivation to learn. As David Kanouse and Itzhak Jacoby point out in their study of information transfer in the medical profession, physicians are motivated to change habitual behavior only when they believe that their patients are not experiencing satisfactory outcomes.[10] Why change what works as well as or better than anything else? Professionals in any business ask the same question; we must answer it with a convincing demonstration that a new idea or technique is superior.

A major factor in the success of any knowledge transfer project is the common language of the participants. Sharing almost identical training and experience, working in precisely the same specialized area, the surgeons and other professionals in the heart-surgery study could readily understand one another's words and actions. Research shows time and again that a shared language is essential to productive knowledge transfer. Without it, individuals will neither understand nor trust one another. Brought together, they will clash or simply not connect.

People can't share knowledge if they don't speak a common language.

Nonaka and Takeuchi's emphasis on "redundancy" or overlapping areas of expertise and Thomas Allen's discussion of "cultural mismatch" as a barrier to technology transfer both recognize the importance of common ground. Effective knowledge transfer is far easier when participants speak the same or similar languages (by language we mean not just English or Spanish but also "mechanical engineer" or "field sales") or, as Allen says, when there are gatekeepers or boundary spanners to translate between cultures and value systems.[11] BP, for example, employs consultants to translate observations made by "roughnecks" on North Sea oil rigs into language and concepts that executives in London can better understand.

Sometimes knowledge transfer can work only if the various parties are brought together physically. This was the experience of a large contracting firm that was a key contractor in the Boston Harbor tunnel project. They had overseen a similar project in New Zealand—a tunnel linking two islands that had some of the same characteristics as the Boston project. The tunnelers in New Zealand developed innovative improvements on a particular drilling process that some executives wanted the Boston workers to emulate. They tried to transfer that knowledge in various ways, sending memos and descriptions, creating diagrams and manuals, even hiring consultants to give talks to the Boston crews. The firm strenuously resisted bringing the groups together for two reasons. The expense was one factor, but an even more powerful influence was an entrenched engineering culture that made them believe firmly that some sort of technological mediation *must* be the right way to transfer knowledge. Eventually, though, they had to fly tunnelers from Wellington to Boston and let the two groups of workers spend time together because nothing else worked. Over rounds of Foster's lager, the New Zealand group discussed and demonstrated their innovations with the Boston workers, and were thus able to transfer their knowledge "in bulk." Over time, the Bostonians came to internalize these innovations, and employed them on the tunnel.

This story shows how difficult it can be to make tacit knowledge explicit and transfer it quickly and easily. The particular skills involved in this process did not lend themselves to codified documentation; that form of communication simply could not work. The fact that the knowledge involved may have been too subtle and complex to express in words is only one of the reasons for the failure. The instinctive resistance to change and the need for trust are at least as important. As hands-on people, the Boston tunnelers may not have invested the printed word with enough authority to let it change ingrained behaviors. Like many of us, they may have felt that seeing is believing: only an actual demonstration of the new technique and its advantages was likely to convince them. Why should a few sheets of paper that come from the other side of the world persuade them there's a better way to do what they've been doing for years? Like most of us, they need to size up the people providing the new knowledge before they will accept it. Are they "regular guys"? Are they good workers? Are they genuinely skillful? Are they trustworthy?

People who share the same work culture can communicate better and transfer knowledge more effectively than people who don't. The New Zealanders and the Boston workers could get along together because they had common interests and experiences. They could communicate in the same way military people from around the globe can, often more easily than they can talk to their neighbors. The closer people are to the culture of the knowledge being transferred, the easier it is to share and exchange.

The cases of the surgeons and the tunnelers show how important it is to have a common work language and to communicate in person. Physical proximity helps participants to share that language and to establish a foundation of mutual respect. The U.S. Army, whose CALL system we mentioned earlier, actually budgets "face time" into a knowledge team's plans. They find this direct contact essential to building rapport and to eliminating what they recognize as one of the basic frictions that prevent effective knowledge transfer—the absence of trust.

In some cases, there's no substitute for direct contact.

The Status of the Knower

People judge the information and knowledge they get in significant measure on the basis of who gives it to them. Organizations that ignore this fact are likely to be disappointed by the results of knowledge transfer projects. It is common, for instance, for organizations to send junior engineers to a conference because the company can spare them. Their work isn't considered as important as that of senior staff, who can't take time off from essential projects. The younger engineers often come back from the conference and say, "We learned these things. We think the company can benefit if we change our process in these ways." But few listen to them, whether they're right or wrong. The knowledge they bring back will be rejected for the same reason they were chosen to go to the conference: they are not perceived as esteemed employees. A similar problem bedeviled MCC, the computer research consortium in Austin. Companies sent relatively poor workers as "assignees" because they were expendable. Not only did they not contribute as effectively as star researchers to the research itself but they were also less effective as transfer agents.

The CEO of a large pharmaceuticals firm where one of us was consulting several years ago needed information on market conditions in Malaysia. He asked for reports from the corporate librarian, a marketing director, and a senior vice-president in charge of strategic planning. The librarian's information was by far the best. It was a carefully organized report using recent data from the World Bank and other key sources. The senior VP threw together a couple of articles from weekly business magazines. But the CEO thought that the senior VP's information was the most valuable and gave the librarian's report the lowest rating. The status of the provider (and probably his personal regard for his strategic planner) biased his judgment. When the same material was shown to other managers in the company without any indication of the source, they all judged the librarian's report superior to the others.

The CEO's response was a case of judging by reputation, which is not always a bad thing. We all do it. Reputation is a proxy for value that we use to evaluate the flood of information coming at us. We don't have time to look carefully at everything, so we select what we think will be worthwhile based on the reputation of the sender. We say, "I know Susan is smart, and she's provided useful material in the past, so I'll pay attention to what came from her." But sometimes we can be wrong, especially if we base our decision more on status than past performance.

Transfer = Transmission + Absorption (and Use)

Knowledge transfer involves two actions: transmission (sending or presenting knowledge to a potential recipient) and absorption by that person or group. If knowledge is not absorbed, it has not been transferred. Merely making knowledge available is not transfer. Access is necessary but by no means sufficient to ensure that knowledge will be used. The goal of knowledge transfer is to improve an organization's ability to do things, and therefore increase its value. Even transmission and absorption together have no useful value if

Knowledge that isn't absorbed hasn't really been transferred.

the new knowledge does not lead to some change in behavior, or the development of some new idea that leads to new behavior. It is fairly common for someone to understand and absorb new knowledge but not put it to use for a variety of reasons. Not respecting or trusting the source of the knowledge is an important one. Pride, stubbornness, lack of time, lack of opportunity, a fear of taking risks (in a company that punishes mistakes) are others. Our self-esteem is based on what we know and how we've done things in the past. If someone comes in and says, "My way of doing this is better than what you've been doing for the past five years," we are likely to resist. As Kanouse and Jacoby point out, "There are good reasons to believe that behavior change is a much rarer event than acquisition of knowledge." In *Wellsprings of Knowledge*, Dorothy Leonard-Barton talks about "signature skills," which she defines as the abilities by which a person identifies himself or herself professionally. People's egos are bound up in these skills; their sense of competence and well-being at work depends on using them. They will resist any innovation that may require them to abandon their signature skills in favor of new ones. Resistance to change is powerful, even in the face of indisputable objective evidence that a particular change makes sense. We are hardly wholly rational creatures. Most people in the United States have all the information they need about the dangers of too much fat in their diets. At the same time, Americans are more overweight than ever and sales of fatty junk food are growing. Knowing is not the same as doing.

Velocity and Viscosity

All the factors we've discussed affect the success and efficiency of knowledge transfer in organizations. They will influence the "velocity" of transfer, that is, the speed with which knowledge moves through an organization. How quickly and widely is it disseminated? How quickly do the people who need the knowledge become aware of it and get access to it? Computers and networks, of course, excel at enhancing the velocity of knowledge.

"Viscosity" refers to the richness (or thickness) of the knowledge transferred. How much of what we try to communicate is actually absorbed and used? To what extent does the original knowledge get pared down? Does what was absorbed bear little resemblance to what we tried to transmit and retain little of its original value? Viscosity is influenced by a number of factors, especially the method of transfer. Knowledge transferred by means of a long apprenticeship or mentoring relationship is likely to have a high viscosity: the receiver will gain a tremendous amount of detailed and subtle knowledge over time. Knowledge retrieved from an on-line database or acquired by reading an article will be much thinner.

Obviously, both velocity and viscosity are important concerns for knowledge managers in determining how efficiently a firm uses its knowledge capital. How quickly does it place knowledge where it can generate value and how much of the knowledge assets are actually getting where they need to go? Because genuine learning is such a deeply human endeavor, and because not only absorbing but *accepting* new knowledge involves so many personal and psychological factors, velocity and viscosity are often at odds. What enhances velocity may thin the viscosity. Most knowledge transfer efforts strike a compromise between these two factors.

Mobil Oil provides a useful example. Mobil's engineers developed some sophisticated ways of determining how much steam is required to drill under various conditions. They applied these techniques at their oil fields in Liberal, Kansas, and found that they could dramatically reduce the amount of steam they generated themselves and bought from outside sources. Because they now knew precisely how much they needed, the potential savings were significant, and the financial implications of making this knowledge operational at other Mobil oil fields were immense. So they embedded the techniques in an intricate and intelligent system—focusing on enhancing the knowledge's velocity— and sent a memo to other Mobil drilling operations detailing the new calculations and describing the benefits. They assumed that other sites would quickly adopt an innovation whose value was indisputable. Yet nothing happened. Nothing changed. The effective viscosity level for the new process was zero.

After some investigation, Ted Lumley, an information manager at Mobil, decided that the transmission medium was wrong: a memo was not an effective vehicle to transfer the knowledge. The requisite information could be presented in the memo, but a piece of paper did not have the power to convince experienced people that they should change what they had been doing for years. Like the surgeons who would not alter their tried-and-true methods just because they read about new ones, the Mobil engineers were unlikely to absorb and use new techniques described in a memo. The authors and some colleagues were asked to help them devise a better way. We developed a case study about the breakthrough and even made videos of the people who had designed the new process. We recommended days of debate and intensive discussion so the new techniques could be internalized and socialized, thereby making it possible to present a more convincing case in favor of the change and give people an opportunity to weigh its benefits and make it "their own."

After six months, the adoption rate was 30 percent. Remember, this was a process whose financial benefits were clear and immediate. Probably the rate will climb to 50 percent; it may or may not eventually approach 100 percent. Does this mean that the knowledge transfer process was a failure or poorly handled? We think not. The adoption and application of new knowledge can be a slow and arduous process, and the success rate will be profoundly influenced by the culture of the firm. That is a fact of organizational life. Part of Mobil's corporate culture—a distrust of "bragging"—may have militated against a full expression of the value of the new technique and against receptivity to this success story. But resistance to abandoning procedures that have been successful for years is a universal phenomenon, not one limited to Mobil.

Simply improving a process won't be enough to win over everyone.

A mechanistic model of human behavior would predict high velocity—the rapid acceptance of an innovation that is demonstrably superior to the old way of doing things. "A works better than B, so stop doing B and do A instead" seems to be unassailable logic. But neither organizations nor people are strictly logical. They are much more often "intentionally rational." That is, they do what is rational for themselves based on their own agendas and goals, irrational as these might seem to outside observers. To many people, hang gliding is irrational because of the risks involved; to those who feel that excitement and risk make life worthwhile, it makes perfect sense. Similarly, a manager who chooses to ignore a clear improvement in a process he manages is not simply irrational. His resistance may be based on a reasonable desire to continue to believe that his way is best. He might recall other innovations that didn't pan out, or reflexively opt for the comfort of doing things the old way over the challenge of learning a new one.

A Case in Point: 3M

3M has a justifiable reputation for encouraging new ideas and turning those ideas into products and profits. The company sells over 60,000 different products, with 30 percent of its revenues coming from products less than four years old. Last year 3M produced over 400 new products. The goal of CEO Livio DeSimone is to have 10 percent of the company's revenues generated by products less than a year old by 1997.

Developing innovations on such a scale would almost certainly be impossible without effective knowledge transfer, since new ideas are so often sparked by access to existing ones. Knowledge transfer is even more essential to getting from idea to product. This process requires the cooperation and abilities of numbers of people who are "on the same page" to collaboratively solve the complex problems inherent in creating a new product. With its impressive success in innovation, 3M provides a striking example of a culture that encourages and enables knowledge transfer.

Deeply ingrained beliefs and values at 3M have encouraged knowledge transfer and led to significant investment in the machinery of transfer. Delegating responsibility, tolerating creative mistakes, and respecting individual talents at all levels of the firm have been part of the company's culture almost from the beginning. Researchers at all levels are expected to spend 15 percent of their work time on personal research interests. All are eligible to apply for grants to support their research and encouraged to involve other employees in their projects. One of the most famous results of this openness and encouragement was the invention of Scotch tape by Dick Drew. He was a sandpaper salesman who, in most companies, would have been told that product development was not his job.

Regular meetings and fairs give 3M's researchers time and space to meet and exchange knowledge. A technical council composed of leaders of major 3M laboratories meets once a month to share ideas. The group also holds a three-day retreat once a year. A technical forum of scientists and technologists sponsors an annual three-day knowledge fair and has more frequent meetings for members with common interests. In addition, an on-line database of technology expertise is available throughout the company. 3M has fostered the belief that technical knowledge belongs to the company, not to the individual or group who developed it. Making knowledge widely available and giving researchers time to absorb it and "play around" with it has led to some notable new products. Art Fry's invention of Post-It Notes was instigated in part by a memo from another 3M scientist inviting others in the company to take a look at his newly developed bonding material. It is hard to imagine a clearer example of innovation spurred by effective knowledge transfer within a company. Although information technology plays an important role at 3M and may have been tangentially involved in distributing the memo, the knowledge transfer that resulted in this profitable invention was not caused by technology but by a culture of sharing.[12]

In this chapter we have attempted to discuss knowledge transfer in a broader context than typically encountered. Too often, knowledge transfer has been confined to such concepts as improved access, electronic communication, document repositories, and so forth. We believe it is time for firms to shift their attention to the more human aspects—from access to attention, from velocity to viscosity, from documents to discussions. Obviously, firms need to exploit both the hard and the soft aspects of knowledge transfer, but in the Western business culture there are usually too few advocates of the soft stuff.

Firms need to shift their attention from documents to discussions.

With this chapter we complete our analysis of the process of knowledge—its generation, codification, and transfer. We will now focus on some enablers of knowledge management, including knowledge management roles and information technologies.

We can be knowledgeable
with other men's knowledge,
but we cannot be wise
with other men's wisdom.
—Michel de Montaigne

6

Knowledge Roles and Skills

I F   K N O W L E D G E   management is to thrive, organizations must create a set of roles and skills to do the work of capturing, distributing, and using knowledge. There are many strategic and tactical tasks to perform, and it is unrealistic to assume that a company can simply throw knowledge management activities on top of its existing positions. As we have been emphasizing, humans add the value that turns data and information into knowledge. Employees in dedicated roles with specific responsibilities must therefore perform some aspects of this process. In this chapter we describe some of those roles and the types of skills they require.

On the other hand, knowledge management will also not succeed in an organization if it is solely the responsibility of a small—or even a large—staff group. Ultimately, managers and workers who do other things for a living (designing and engineering, manufacturing, selling and providing service to customers) have to do the bulk of the day-to-day activities of knowledge management. As we will discuss, the most successful organizations are those in which knowledge management is part of everyone's job. Of course, it will usually take the efforts of some full-time knowledge staffers to make knowledge management a pervasive phenomenon.

In this chapter we will begin by addressing the most important knowledge roles—those performed by personnel working throughout the firm. Our goal is to help organizations encourage every employee to become a manager of knowledge. We will then describe front-line knowledge tasks and knowledge project management roles. The chapter concludes with a detailed discussion of the senior-most knowledge role, the "Chief Knowledge Officer," or CKO.

107

Knowledge-Oriented Personnel

While specialists are clearly critical to the success of knowledge management, even more important are the activities and attitudes of those who are paid to do something other than manage knowledge. Planning managers, business analysts, design and manufacturing engineers, marketing professionals, and even secretaries and clerks are the most important managers of knowledge. They all need to create, share, search out, and use knowledge in their daily routines. In this sense, knowledge management must be part of everyone's job.

Managing knowledge should be everybody's business.

Despite the corporate mantra that employee knowledge is a valuable resource, most firms do not make concerted efforts to cultivate the knowledge-oriented activities of their personnel. We will briefly discuss two notable exceptions: one in a knowledge-intensive business, the other in an industry not often viewed in that light.

McKinsey and Company is perhaps the most knowledge-oriented firm in a knowledge-oriented industry. The consulting firm has several roles with the job of managing knowledge, either creating it or storing and distributing it. But there have been some difficulties in conceptualizing and implementing these roles, at least partially because at McKinsey knowledge is everyone's job—or at least almost everyone's. The firm's managing director even calls knowledge "the lifeblood of McKinsey."[1] Consultants are expected to contribute to the firm's knowledge capital and to use it in client work. Line consultants write books and articles as frequently, if not more so, as specialists in industries or functions. Research and practice development projects are typically staffed by regular consultants, who thereafter go back to client service. McKinsey is a model of the organization in which every practitioner is a reflective one.

This isn't to say that the knowledge environment is perfect at McKinsey—at least it wasn't several years ago when one of us (Davenport) worked there. No one expected much of secretaries or administrators, for example, with regard to creating, distributing, or using knowledge. And Tom Peters, a former McKinsey consultant, has pointed out that while the firm's consultants are excellent at learning from one another, they are "average or weak" at learning from outsiders.[2] In our view, this dynamic is partly intrinsic to client work and partly due to an implicit attitude at McKinsey, that its people are the smartest around.

If there's a single factor that is most critical to McKinsey's success in knowledge management, we believe it's at the front end—the kind of people the firm hires from the beginning. Interviews and screening processes are designed to identify bright, intellectually curious, knowledge-seeking individuals. McKinsey's staff consultants are thus fully capable of being knowledge creators, sharers, and users. Ironically, their knowledge orientations make it more difficult for knowledge specialists—experts in a particular business function or industry—to do their work; many consultants feel self-sufficient and not needful of experts. The firm has wrestled with the role of knowledge specialists for years.

The McKinsey case is an impressive example of how knowledge roles work in a knowledge-driven industry. Even more impressive, however, is the example of Chaparral Steel, which Harvard researcher Dorothy Leonard-Barton has described in some detail.[3] The company is a successful mini-mill steel manufacturer, hardly a business where you would expect to find knowledge given much prominence. But at Chaparral, every worker is considered a knowledge worker. Line steelworkers visit customers to better understand their requirements, attend industry seminars, and perform production experiments. Ideas come from everybody in the organization. A visitor to Chaparral once noticed that the security guard was reading a textbook about steelmaking. There is no division of knowledge labor designating some people as thinkers and relegating others to doers.

For this free flow of knowledge to prevail, the organizational culture must be extraordinary. At Chaparral, the organizational structure is remarkably flat, both officially and symbolically. The company has a unique apprenticeship program for all production workers that includes both classroom and on-the-job training. Risk taking is encouraged. Employees are selected for their ability and their attitudes about learning. There are no time clocks, and there is a generous profit-sharing system. These cultural and organizational approaches clearly encourage Chaparral's workers to gain and share knowledge.

Knowledge Management Workers

The first dedicated knowledge roles we'll describe in this chapter involve the day-to-day work of knowledge management. Certain of these functions are strictly technical: writing HTML and Perl scripts for Web sites, structuring and restructuring knowledge bases, and installing and maintaining such knowledge-oriented software packages as Lotus Notes. But pure technology is not enough. Even technologists should have a strong focus on how to make knowledge content appealing and how to persuade those who have knowledge to put it into a rich knowledge base.

The most intriguing new knowledge jobs, however, are knowledge integrators, librarians, synthesizers, reporters, and editors. Let's be honest: few organizations have many workers who are skilled at framing and structuring their own knowledge; even fewer of them have time to sit down and input it into a system. An engineering team may have designed a great new product, but nobody on the team has the time, inclination, or skill to describe what happened in a project and put it into a repository. Thus, organizations need people who will extract knowledge from those who have it, put it in structured form, and maintain or refine it over time. Universities don't really teach these skills, but the closest approximation is found in journalism and library-science curricula. Perhaps some schools will begin educational programs specifically oriented to knowledge management. For now we'll have to view knowledge management education as a by-product of other objectives.

Knowledge management jobs are proliferating rapidly. Andersen Consulting has over two hundred of them; Ernst & Young, McKinsey, and IBM Consulting are probably close to that. Coca-Cola has identified forty; Hewlett-Packard probably has twenty or thirty. One of the challenges of this emerging field is for these knowledge workers to identify one another and begin to develop an occupational community. A greater sense of professional affiliation would be especially valuable given the varying levels of the worker roles. Andersen, for example, has "knowledge integrators," who are sufficiently expert in a particular domain to determine what knowledge is most valuable and synthesize it. The firm also has "knowledge administrators," whose work focuses on capturing, storing, and maintaining the knowledge that others produce.

Good knowledge workers at any level should have a combination of "hard" skills (structured knowledge, technical abilities, and professional experience) with "softer" traits (a

Ideally, knowledge workers possess both technical know-how and intuitive skills.

sure sense of the cultural, political, and personal aspects of knowledge). Well-roundedness isn't necessary for everyone, but it is particularly important for those who work closely with knowledge users. At a minimum, knowledge management teams should combine these orientations, and each member must respect all required skill sets.

Some firms draw knowledge management workers from the ranks of line employees. At Ernst & Young, for example, the employees who compile and maintain knowledge repositories in particular industry or practice areas are consultants who worked in those areas. They cycle in and out of knowledge management roles, remaining in them for one or two years. This arrangement ensures that knowledge management workers are conversant with the domain, even if they lack "professional" knowledge structuring and writing skills.

Organizations are also redesignating existing groups of workers—often librarians—as knowledge managers. Ernst & Young's "Center for Business Knowledge" was previously a library for its consulting practice, though new functions were added with the conversion to the new title. At Owens-Corning, the corporate library became the "Knowledge Resource Center." But the name was not all that was changed. The former librarians got themselves out of the routine of "fetching" information that users knew existed but couldn't find, and encouraged users to fetch their own through database searches or outsourced library-type transactions. They focused on creating navigational tools—knowledge maps, as we called them in Chapter 4—to acquaint their customers with available knowledge resources, and on advising them on how best to use internal and external knowledge resources.[4] If librarians are to thrive in the new world of knowledge management, they will have to change their objectives, activities, and cultural predispositions.[5]

One alternative to knowledge reporters, editors, and librarians is the group that became known as "knowledge engineers" in the heyday of expert systems. Surely some of them would be candidates for knowledge management positions, but many with such jobs tend to be insulated, more concerned about writing well-structured computer code than capturing and leveraging knowledge. Even the term sounds a bit arrogant.

Finally, participants in an on-line discussion group excoriated one of us (Davenport) for not including "technical communicators" as potential managers of knowledge. Some members of this group, who are also known as technical writers, said that they were currently working on knowledge management projects. On reflection, there is actually considerable logic behind the idea that technical writers would be able to understand certain forms of knowledge—particularly technical knowledge—and contribute to an electronic repository. There are undoubtedly other groups in organizations with useful knowledge management skills as well.

Managers of Knowledge Projects

The middle level of the formal knowledge management infrastructure is occupied by the manager of the knowledge project. As we argue in Chapter 8, much of the real work of knowledge management takes place in the context of specific projects to manage specific forms of knowledge, or to improve particular activities related to knowledge. As with any other type of change project, knowledge management initiatives need managers. Knowledge initiative managers should have facility in project management, change management, and technology management. Good candidates may have led successful research, reengineering, or behavior-changing IT projects in the past. Ideally, a knowledge project manager should come from a background that emphasizes the creation, distribution, or use of knowledge.

The manager of a knowledge project performs such typical project management functions as:

- Developing project objectives
- Assembling and managing teams
- Determining and managing customer expectations
- Monitoring project budgets and schedules
- Identifying and resolving project problems

But managing knowledge projects isn't just about project management. The role demands an unusual mix of technological, psychological, and business skills. Managers of such projects should be equally comfortable with Web-accessed databases and with self-managing teams, with knowledge structures and compensation structures. Whatever the types of knowledge workers involved in a particular initiative, the knowledge project manager should speak their languages and understand their value systems.

Depending on the specific type of knowledge management project, the project manager may have to perform other kinds of activities. If the project is a repository, for example, the manager will have to deal with such issues as determining the technology for storing the knowledge, persuading employees to contribute to the repository, and creating a structure for holding the knowledge. If the project involves knowledge transfer, the project manager will have to identify, develop, and monitor both human and automatic channels for knowledge sharing. Knowledge asset management approaches may involve such activities as calculating knowledge valuations, negotiating with internal and external holders of desired intellectual capital, and managing a knowledge asset portfolio. Projects involving infrastructure development typically encompass financial analysis, work with external vendors of technologies and services, and development of human resources management approaches.

The knowledge project manager needs to be on top of both the hard and soft aspects of knowledge management. He or she must be willing and able to discuss the finer points of organizational learning, while at the same time ensuring that knowledge-oriented systems go forward. Of course, the project manager must also complete knowledge-oriented project activities on time and under budget. We've seen too many knowledge project managers who were very good at talking about the subject but didn't walk it very well.

We'll mention one more attribute of the knowledge project manager that you probably haven't considered. Managers who work with knowledge need a certain humility. One knowledge project manager at Hewlett-Packard went even further, arguing for "egolessness." He explained that knowledge is a sensitive subject. If you're the manager of a particular knowledge domain, it's easy to come to believe that you are the primary source and arbiter of knowledge for the organization. It's even easier thereafter for lesser mortals to resent you and withhold their knowledge or their attention from you.

A little humility goes a long way when you're managing a knowledge project.

At Hoffmann-LaRoche, the large pharmaceuticals company, a knowledge project manager confirmed this problem in speaking of a knowledge manager colleague. He represented "the dark side of knowledge management," believing that he knew more about new drug development (the subject of the firm's knowledge repository) than anyone in the firm or perhaps the world. Since there is apparently much deep knowledge about specific aspects of drug development, but very little understanding of the entire process—even in drug companies—he may even have been correct in this belief. His colleagues and customers within the organization, however, bridled at his intellectual arrogance. While the project was successful overall, his domineering personality made the objectives more difficult to accomplish.

The Chief Knowledge Officer

Many firms in the United States, and a few in Europe, have now appointed chief knowledge officers (CKOs) to lead the knowledge management charge. Others have created "chief learning officers," a related role that involves both the management of knowledge and the facilitation of organizational learning. Both of these positions are senior management roles on the level of chief information officers, heads of the human resources organization, and other functional and business unit leaders. Other related positions include director of intellectual capital (a position at Skandia, the Swedish insurance company), director of knowledge transfer (Buckman Laboratories), and global director of intellectual asset/intellectual capital management (Dow Chemical).

The role of a chief knowledge officer is complex and multifaceted. Many firms, of course, don't yet have anything like a CKO. Even if yours doesn't, if you're serious about managing knowledge, someone has to undertake the executive-level tasks. If your firm is considering the creation of such a job, or if you are angling to become a CKO yourself, you must recognize that some will consider the role a passing fad. To make the job real, its specific tasks and responsibilities must be carefully enumerated. The list below of CKO "musts" will provide a good start for a company attempting to shape the role.

The chief knowledge officer in an organization must:

- Advocate or "evangelize" for knowledge and learning from it. Particularly given the important role for knowledge in the strategies and processes of many firms today, long-term changes are necessary in organizational cultures and individual behaviors relative to knowledge. These changes will require sustained and powerful advocacy.

- Design, implement, and oversee a firm's knowledge infrastructure, including its libraries, knowledge bases, human and computer knowledge networks, research centers, and knowledge-oriented organizational structure.

- Manage relationships with external providers of information and knowledge (for example, academic partners or database companies), and negotiate contracts with them. This is already a major expense item for many companies, and efficient and effective management of it is important.

- Provide critical input to the process of knowledge creation and use around the firm (for example, new product development, market research, and business strategy development), and facilitate efforts to improve such processes if necessary.

- Design and implement a firm's knowledge codification approaches, as described in Chapter 3. Such approaches specify key categories of information or knowledge that the organization would address, and entail mapping both the current knowledge inventory and future knowledge models.

- Measure and manage the value of knowledge, either by conventional financial analysis or by "anecdote management." If the organization has no sense of the value of knowledge and its management, the function won't last long.

- Manage the organization's professional knowledge managers, giving them a sense of community, establishing professional standards, and managing their careers. These workers may be "matrixed" between the CKO and managers of the domains where the company focuses knowledge management efforts (for example, a particular market, product set, or type of customer).

- Lead the development of knowledge strategy, focusing the firm's resources on the type of knowledge it needs to manage most, and the knowledge processes with the largest gaps between need and current capability.

Of all of these CKO responsibilities, three are particularly critical: building a knowledge culture, creating a knowledge management infrastructure, and making it all pay off economically. The cultural factors usually entail long-term change, and probably will hinge on the types of people a company hires and the reasons they come to work there in the first place. In the short term, however, a firm can begin to foster a knowledge culture in part through such means as education, incentive programs, and management example.

Setting up a knowledge management infrastructure involves more than making a decision between Lotus Notes and a Web-based intranet system. As we will discuss in Chapter 7, there is a substantial technology component to knowledge management; the task involves workstations, networks, databases, search engines, and even word processing and desktop-publishing tools. But the human resources issues—setting up structures for the development and maintenance of knowledge bases in different functions and departments—are more difficult to create and manage. These include human networks, some of the roles and responsibilities described in this chapter, and even relationships across firms. Only a few organizations have built a fully capable infrastructure. For example, John Peetz, CKO at Ernst & Young, has set up a substantial organizational infrastructure for knowledge management. There are "knowledge councils" at the firm's international level, its national level, and its business unit (audit, tax, consulting) level. Within the consulting organization, which began managing knowledge first, there are "knowledge networks" for each key practice area. It takes substantial time and effort to create and maintain such an infrastructure, but it's necessary if knowledge management is to become institutionalized.

And no knowledge management undertaking will come to much unless there is a close tie to dollars, yen, and marks. The CKO has to determine how better management of knowledge will help the firm make or save money, and must be able to document that connection. Gordon Petrash at Dow Chemical saved his firm more than $4 million through better management of patents alone. At Buckman Laboratories, there are no overall figures for increased revenues available, but "anecdote management" is a key focus. The firm has plenty of examples of how sharing and using knowledge led to big sales that wouldn't have happened otherwise.

Anecdote management can be the best way for a chief knowledge officer to justify knowledge work.

Figures and stories are the ultimate weapons when budget renewal time arrives. Perhaps the best example of measuring the economic value of knowledge is at Skandia. Leif Edvinsson, the firm's director of intellectual capital, has led a comprehensive effort to measure the firm's intellectual capital, and has published several annual reports on the firm's progress in accumulating such capital.

As in any new position in organizations, the personal characteristics of a CKO are critical. As we see it, some of the following attributes would be desirable for a CKO (in addition to the general attributes and skills of a senior executive). If you're thinking you'd like to be a CKO, you can test your own background against these criteria:

- Deep experience in some aspect of knowledge management, including its creation, dissemination, or application.

- Familiarity with knowledge-oriented organizations and technologies (libraries, groupware, and so forth).

- Display of a high level of "knowledgeability" directly related to one's professional stature.

- Comfort (and ideally personal experience) with the primary operational processes of the business.

As this list suggests, CKO positions require a blend of technical, human, and financial skills. Although it is necessary to have some experience with efforts to use technology for knowledge capture and distribution, a good CKO combines an orientation to technology-based, explicit knowledge with a feel for the cultural and behavioral factors that impede or enable knowledge. Faith in the virtues of knowledge is an important characteristic, but it must be combined with a hard-nosed business sense. Executive recruiters and our personal experience tell us that it's difficult to find this combination of hard and soft attributes in one person.

The structure and reporting relationships of the CKO role and its associated organization are also important—not only for day-to-day execution but also for symbolic value. Our research shows that there are generally three options for the location of the CKO role in a firm's organization chart. It can be a senior stand-alone role, or it can be combined with either the human resources (HR) or information systems (IS) functions.

We'll describe later a few firms that have combined knowledge management and HR or IS organizations with some measure of success. Both of these existing functions, however, have many responsibilities that do not involve knowledge in any substantial way. Combining knowledge management with them is bound to dilute the importance of knowledge and send a signal that it is less important than these more traditional roles.

A stand-alone role is therefore the most desirable situation. As described above, the CKO job is an important and complex one, and clearly substantial enough to stand on its own. Furthermore, the establishment of a new role and infrastructure sends an important signal to the organization. To embed it within another function makes it seem less important, and easier to ignore. Naturally, an independent CKO will still have to maintain a close liaison with a firm's information technology and human resources management executives. The stand-alone knowledge organizations we have seen thus far generally report to the president or CEO of a company, though there are also examples of CKO-like roles that report through the senior R&D or technology officer.

A related but confusing issue that bears on the reporting relationships of the senior knowledge executive is establishing parameters for knowledge management, organizational learning, and intellectual capital. While the three provinces are obviously related, the senior roles built around each tend to involve different responsibilities and incumbents with different backgrounds. We believe that firms should integrate these roles, but only a few have done so.

If a company calls the position "chief knowledge officer," chances are good that a primary focus of the role involves capturing and leveraging structured knowledge, with information technology as a key enabler. Managers with these roles often come from technology-oriented backgrounds, though they also typically have experience in cultural and organizational change. For example, Nick Rudd voluntarily surrendered his role as chief information officer at Young & Rubicam, the big advertising agency, for a new CKO role at Wunderman Cato Johnson, one of the Y&R business units. Rudd had been yearning to move in a more knowledge-oriented direction for several years, but he felt that he could have much more direct impact at the business unit level, and this business unit was much more interested in managing knowledge than any other. While he had been a technology manager for more than twenty years, he has a strong predisposition to issues of learning and change as well. Similarly, Mark Demerest, Sequent Computer's CKO, was formerly a manager in the company's technology architecture group, and worked both internally and with customers on architectural planning.

By contrast, if the senior role is designated "chief learning officer" (CLO), you can bet that the key focus of the job has more to do with training and education than with capturing and leveraging structured knowledge. It's also likely to involve the human resources function more than the information systems group. Most of these executives have responsibility for executive development at a minimum, and sometimes all employee training. CLOs tend to come from human resources or organizational development backgrounds. General Electric's CLO, Steve

Kerr, formerly a professor of organizational behavior, presides over GE's education center in Crotonville, New York. Monsanto's first CLO was previously head of human resources. Both managers have some interest in managing explicit knowledge, but their primary focus is executive and employee development.

Positions having "intellectual capital" or "assets" in the title tend to be in the middle, with a strong focus on converting knowledge into revenues and profits. The two most prominent holders of such positions are Leif Edvinsson at Skandia and Gordon Petrash at Dow Chemical. Edvinsson, as described above, concentrates on measuring the value of Skandia's intellectual capital and communicating the value to the investment community. Petrash, whose title is Global Director of Intellectual Asset/Intellectual Capital Management, has a strong R&D background, and emphasizes management of Dow's intellectual property, including patents and licenses.

One of the more balanced approaches to the senior knowledge role can be seen at Coca-Cola. Judith Rosenblum became Coke's first CLO in 1995, and was previously vice-chair for "learning, education, and human resources" at Coopers & Lybrand. Her job at Coke, however, goes well beyond the usual training and HR bureaucracy. It includes organizational learning, knowledge management, and establishing solid links between knowledge and learning and shareholder value. Managers who report to Rosenblum have responsibility for each domain, and her job is to integrate them. Like John Peetz at Ernst & Young, Rosenblum has placed a strong emphasis on building an organizational infrastructure for knowledge and learning, training a large contingent of fast-track managers to lead knowledge efforts all around the firm.

CKO roles are particularly appropriate in firms where knowledge is a critical business resource. Professional service firms have this characteristic, and many of them—including Ernst & Young; IBM Consulting; Coopers & Lybrand; Booz, Allen & Hamilton; and EDS—have established CKO roles. Young & Rubicam and its subsidiaries, one of which created a CKO role, are also businesses that sell advertising and marketing knowledge. Each of these organizations has realized that their clients are seeking not only the services of individual professionals but the aggregated knowledge of their worldwide staffs.

At Ernst & Young, for example, in addition to presiding over the organizational infrastructure described above, the CKO works with technologists to develop a knowledge-oriented infrastructure. It's also his job to translate the strategic directions of the firm's audit, tax, and consulting business units into specific knowledge requirements and desirable knowledge behaviors. In fact, several of the firm's different national practices, including Canada, the United Kingdom, and continental Europe, have each named their own CKOs, and they coordinate their activities through an international knowledge committee.

CKOs are also appropriate in businesses where knowledge is embedded in the products sold, or critical to the services offered to customers. This is a likely situation, for example, in the computer industry. Sequent Computer created its CKO role when managers realized that knowledge management (in the form of an on-line repository called the Corporate Electronic Library) was critical to sales of its high-end servers and to the professional services business it had recently started.

CKOs have also popped up in industries that one wouldn't initially associate with knowledge, such as insurance. Skandia in Sweden and Lincoln National Life in the United States have created CKO-like positions, as have a couple of Canadian insurance companies. But the insurance business actually contains several important knowledge domains, including underwriting knowledge, actuarial knowledge, and investment knowledge. Insurance companies were among the most active developers of computer-based expert systems in the 1980s. Several insurance CEOs have even proclaimed to us that they are really in the knowledge business, not the insurance business—though in our opinion they have yet to explain the implications of these statements.

Still, creating a CKO role is not for every firm. Even in companies where knowledge management is quite popular, there may be circumstances that dictate against establishing a CKO position. The organization may have such a decentralized organizational structure that a central knowledge role would be inappropriate. At Hewlett-Packard, for example, despite the fact that more than a score of knowledge management initiatives are underway throughout various parts of the firm, HP managers doubt that a formal CKO job will ever grace the corporate organization chart. The firm consists of a set of decentralized, autonomous business units, and for a central CKO to try to influence divisional knowledge plans and policies would be wholly inconsistent with the "HP Way."

Another reason firms may decide against establishing a CKO is that all important CKO functions are already being performed by other managers. At Andersen Consulting, there are already more than two hundred knowledge managers working at various industry or competence groups around the firm, but the company has no plans for a CKO. The functions of a CKO are currently divided among several different roles, and like many partnerships, Andersen has an antipathy toward senior "overhead" roles. Most of the necessary knowledge leadership tasks are clearly well covered, however, since Andersen's "Knowledge Xchange" repository is one of the most ambitious and successful knowledge efforts in business today. It has over 40,000 users, thousands of knowledge bases, and many examples of successful application in Andersen's client work.

When there are obstacles to creating a CKO position per se, it may be helpful to combine it with other roles. Several chief information officers, for example, including those at Hewlett-Packard and General Motors, have taken on knowledge management as a component of their overall responsibilities. At Buckman Laboratories, the existing director of information systems became the director of knowledge transfer, but still maintained the oversight of the chemical company's information systems. At Lincoln National, when a CIO left the company, a new "chief information and knowledge officer" took his place. Since there are still substantial responsibilities involved in building and maintaining an organization's IT infrastructure, it will be easier to focus on knowledge if some of the IT activities are shifted to other departments or outsourced. At General Motors, knowledge management started out under the head of IT, but moved into a more marketing-oriented group when a new CIO came on board.

In decentralized organizations, it makes sense to assign CKO functions to a number of different managers.

Most CKOs feel that they can accomplish little by themselves; they manage others who do the tactical work of knowledge management. In at least one case, however, the CKO stands alone, or rather relies on managers and employees who are not knowledge professionals. Nick Rudd, the CKO at the Wunderman Cato Johnson division of Young & Rubicam, intentionally avoided building a staff because he feels the work of managing knowledge is the responsibility of all knowledge workers. He attempts to persuade the direct-marketing firm's managers to start their own projects and to use their own people to carry them out. Wunderman only recently created Rudd's role, and it is probably too early to assess the results.

We have explored four levels of knowledge management roles: line workers who must also manage knowledge within their own jobs; knowledge management workers; knowledge project managers; and the senior knowledge executive. This is a good snapshot of the organizational structure for knowledge in leading corporations. While some firms will have different structures, someone must perform these roles and activities if the company is truly committed to managing knowledge.

But remember that knowledge management is still an emerging field that is being explored primarily at companies where business and organizational environments are changing rapidly. Therefore, any company embarking upon knowledge management should be prepared to adjust its structure and roles frequently. As one researcher put it with regard to organizational structures in fast-changing Silicon Valley firms:

> The pivotal importance of informal networks in high-technology companies is due to the fact that the productivity of knowledge-based entities depends on employees' capabilities, commitments, motivations, and relationships. They cannot be programmed around pre-determined roles and positions in a machine-like hierarchy. Moreover, continuous change typically renders institutionalized roles and positions somewhat obsolete.[6]

If there is one overriding principle to keep in mind regarding knowledge management roles and responsibilities, it is that they should be real jobs requiring dedicated resources. One of the reasons knowledge hasn't been well managed in the past is that no one was clearly responsible for it. In today's harried business environment, few employees will be able to mix corporate knowledge management responsibilities with their existing jobs. They will be lucky enough if they have time to manage their own knowledge and share it with others.

The real danger is not that computers
    will begin to think like men,
        but that men
    will begin to think like computers.
        —Sydney J. Harris

7

Technologies for Knowledge Management

A S W E ' V E asserted throughout this book, knowledge management is
much more than technology, but "techknowledgy" is clearly a part of
knowledge management. Indeed, the availability of certain new technologies such as Lotus Notes and the World Wide Web has been instru-
mental in catalyzing the knowledge management movement. Since
knowledge and the value of harnessing it have always been with us, it
must be the availability of these new technologies that has stoked the
knowledge fire.

A Case in Point: Hewlett-Packard

At Hewlett-Packard, for example, knowledge technologies are bursting
out all over. The firm's information systems managers began to notice
around 1995 that the real growth in applications had less to do with
data than with technologies for managing knowledge, expertise, and
documents containing them. When they convened a workshop to discuss knowledge management applications, they were surprised to hear
about more than twenty. Since most of these applications involved
Web-based intranets or Lotus Nets, HP's IT managers established a
general policy that Notes should be used for discussion-oriented applications, and the Web for publishing purposes. Of course, the actual ways
in which these tools were employed were more complex than these
guidelines.

Today Hewlett-Packard is a showcase of Web-based knowledge management. The company's Electronic Sales Partner (ESP) system contains

123

hundreds of thousands of documents that help HP's computer systems sales force in the sales process. White papers, sales presentations, technical specifications, and pointers to external materials are all available worldwide through an intranet Web. Anyone within HP can submit a document for possible inclusion on ESP; a small group of reviewers determines whether the submitted documents are unique and appropriate for the system. Eventually the selected documents are classified automatically based on metaknowledge—classifications of the type and format of knowledge—furnished by the submitting employee. The system also includes a search engine, a function for browsing documents by category, tools for assessing accesses by HP employees, and archiving capabilities for documents that have not been recently accessed. Based on the numbers of submissions and accesses, as well as anecdotal information about the use of ESP in successful sales efforts, the system appears to be a great success. Calling it the "most successful implementation of software I have seen in twenty years," the manager of the sales support area reports "phenomenal feedback from both submitters [of information] and users." The only difficulty cited by HP involves navigating among the vast number of documents—a problem that will probably get worse before it improves.

HP has another Web-based system, called "Connex," in its R&D laboratories to identify experts. Connex allows an HP employee to search for an HP Labs expert who, for example, has a Ph.D. in electrical engineering, knows ISDN well, and lives in Germany. The company has mastered the technical side of this locator service, but is still wrestling with the issue of how to motivate scientists to include their biographies, and with the controversial connotations of the term "expert." The same system has also been used to identify experts within the training and education community.

Hewlett-Packard uses Notes for both internal and external knowledge applications; a "Trainers' Trading Post" application allows trainers and educators throughout HP to exchange experiences with educational programs and offerings. Externally, a Notes-based application called "HP Network News" allows resellers of HP computer systems to get product and service knowledge without having to make a phone call.

While Notes and the Web are the most visible knowledge tools at HP, there are many underlying infrastructural elements that support knowledge management as well. One reason the firm's various knowledge repositories are so useful is that HP has a common set of tools for word processing, presentations, and spreadsheets. Any document produced within the company therefore can be read and modified by other users. Many of the knowledge applications also incorporate such infrastructural tools as database management systems, document search engines, and HP's worldwide communications network. HP's technology managers are now exploring a new tool called GrapeVINE that allows targeted distribution of knowledge based on content categories that are specified by knowledge users.

The concept of knowledge management, then, would be much less powerful at HP and at many other firms without these knowledge-oriented technologies. Technology's most valuable role in knowledge management is extending the reach and enhancing the speed of knowledge transfer. Information technology enables the knowledge of an individual or group to be extracted and structured, and then used by other members of the organization or its trading partners worldwide. Technology also helps in the codification of knowledge and occasionally even in its generation.

However, knowledge management technology is a broad concept, encompassing much more than Notes and the Web. Firms can apply a wide variety of technologies to the objectives of managing knowledge, some of which have been available for many years. In this chapter we will review these technologies, discuss their application to knowledge management problems, and describe how to combine them with more human-oriented knowledge management approaches to create a dynamic knowledge environment.

Expert Systems and Artificial Intelligence

While knowledge management is a relatively recent field of study, attempts to use technology to capture and manipulate knowledge have been underway for decades. Going under the name of "artificial intelligence," these efforts have typically concentrated on managing narrow domains of knowledge such as configurations of computers or the diagnosis of a particular type of disease. We will review these technologies, which include expert systems, case-based reasoning, and neural networks, only briefly here, since there is an extensive body of literature on the subject.[1] We will mainly look at what has happened with these technologies in business environments, as well as comment on some newer technologies such as Notes and the Web that have become popular for managing business-oriented knowledge.

Like many technology fields, the area of knowledge technology has suffered from overly high expectations and excessive levels of hype, particularly with regard to expert systems. It is fair to say that the vaunted potential of expert systems has never been realized. Here is a typical pronouncement, written a little more than a decade ago:

> It is early yet to estimate the magnitude of the contribution expert systems will make to the extension of human capability and to our effectiveness as managers, and it would be more than a little reckless to rank it now along with steam power and electricity. But the contribution will be in that class and will be indeed profound.[2]

Other authors speculated that expert systems would "change the way businesses operate by altering the way people think about solving problems"; "help America solve its productivity problems"; and "help businesses reorganize themselves into more efficient and effective organizations." With such systems, "managers will be able to monitor more activities and personnel while simultaneously increasing the quality and quantity of decisions"; "training will also be revolutionized"; and "in short, the whole business environment should become much more rational."[3]

The wildest exaggerations came from adherents who envisioned machinery replacing human brainpower. Here, for example, is MIT professor Marvin Minsky's 1970 prediction:

> In from three to eight years, we will have a machine with the general intelligence of an average human being. I mean a machine that will be able to read Shakespeare, grease a car, play office politics, tell a joke, have a fight. At that point, the machine will begin to educate itself with fantastic speed. In a few months, it will be at genius level, and a few months after that, its power will be incalculable.[4]

As we know, neither expert systems nor any other branch of artificial intelligence has lived up to this prediction. Even the prospect of a computer greasing cars is nowhere in sight. Indeed, the limited success of artificial intelligence systems has fostered a greater appreciation for just

The shortcomings of artificial intelligence should heighten our appreciation for human brainpower.

how rich and complex human knowledge is. Take the case of McDonnell

Douglas (now a part of Boeing), which developed an expert system to scan aircraft approaching the runway and determine if they were positioned properly for landing. The company knew that experienced ground crews could tell at a glance if a pilot needed to adjust pitch (raising or lowering the nose), bank, alignment, or speed. After watching thousands of landings, these personnel had internalized a lot of information and knew intuitively what a good landing looked like. But they were not in a position to communicate corrections to the pilots. Moreover, McDonnell Douglas wanted a system that would work in low visibility. So the company decided to build an expert system that captured this human knowledge. They interviewed and tested the ground crews to learn as much as possible about what they saw during that brief over-the-shoulder observation. Then they incorporated that material into a system that eventually proved to be 80 to 85 percent as accurate as the two-second human glance, a level of success that justified the effort, according to McDonnell Douglas. Nevertheless, the fact that it took two years and considerable expense to capture even a relatively small, straightforward amount of human expertise shows how difficult it is to embed tacit knowledge in such a system.

A different branch of artificial intelligence attempts to combine the power of narrative with the codification of knowledge on computers. Called "case-based reasoning" or CBR, the technology involves extraction of knowledge from a series of narratives, or cases, about the problem domain. CBR technology has been commercially successful in resolving customer service problems: over five hundred firms use CBR for this purpose. Unlike expert systems, which require that rules are well structured with no overlaps, case structures can reflect the fluid thinking that goes on in our minds. According to one expert on the technology:

> Case-based reasoning is both a cognitively plausible model of reasoning and a method for building intelligent systems. It is grounded in commonsense premises and observations of human cognition and has applicability to a variety of reasoning tasks, providing for each a means of attaining increased efficiency and better performance.[5]

Whether case-based reasoning can take on other types of knowledge with commercial success, however, remains to be seen. Companies have applied CBR to such tasks as planning, scheduling, design, legal reasoning, story understanding, and robot navigation, but the technology has not achieved broad business application in any of these areas. We describe CBR's considerable successes in the customer service domain, where rapid access to knowledge is at a premium, later in the chapter.

The reality of expert systems and artificial intelligence in business has been much less spectacular than originally anticipated, though certainly not without value. While organizations have implemented technical systems in narrow knowledge domains, humans have not been supplanted as knowledge providers. The field of "knowledge engineering" thrives in a few areas, but has never taken off in a general sense. Therefore, we believe that the foreseeable future will bring evolutionary, not revolutionary, improvements in technology, and a continued heavy role for people as more than passive users of knowledge technologies.

Case-based reasoning programs have been shown to bring about marked improvements in customer service.

Implementing Knowledge Technologies

The concept of knowledge management technologies is not only broad but also a bit slippery to define. Some infrastructure technologies that we don't ordinarily think of in this category can be useful in facilitating knowledge management. Take videoconferencing, for example, or even the telephone. Both of these technologies don't capture or distribute structured knowledge, but they are quite effective at enabling people to transfer tacit knowledge.

The BP Exploration "Virtual Teamwork" project discussed in Chapter 1 involved nothing other than providing a desktop videoconferencing infrastructure to help people exchange knowledge across vast distances. BP experts in Italy and Alaska, for example, fixed a problem with a drill rig compressor in Latin America in a videoconference. Instead of the days it would have taken for the experts to fly in and solve the problem—days when oil wasn't coming out of the ground—the defect was corrected in hours.

We all use telephones for knowledge transfer. And any manager will quickly realize that knowledge workers are unlikely to make effective use of knowledge repositories if they do not have personal computers on their own desktops. Because tools like PCs, videoconferencing, and telephones are well understood, we won't focus any further in this chapter on infrastructural technologies that make knowledge transfer possible. But if you're a manager with the objective of facilitating knowledge, don't overlook them.

Our focus here, however, is on the technologies that capture, store, and distribute structured knowledge for use by people. The goal of these technologies is to take knowledge that exists in human heads and paper documents, and make it widely available throughout an organization. We will also focus on the human dimension of knowledge technologies—how they are used by people in organizations, and what difference they make to organizational processes, structures, and cultures.

Since it is the value added by people—context, experience, and interpretation—that transforms data and information into knowledge, it is the ability to capture and manage those human additions that make information technologies particularly suited to dealing with knowledge. While technologies designed for managing data are structured, typically numerically oriented, and address large volumes of observations, knowledge technologies deal most frequently with text rather than numbers, and text in relatively unstructured forms, such as clauses, sentences, paragraphs, and even stories. Volume may be the friend of data management, but it is the enemy of knowledge management—simply because humans have to sift through the volume to find the desired knowledge. Vast amounts of computerized processing may take place on data without substantial human intervention. Knowledge technologies, however, are more likely to be employed in an interactive and iterative manner by their users. Therefore, the roles of people in knowledge technologies are integral to their success.

The different roles of people is also a key factor in distinguishing the various types of knowledge technologies. Some technologies involve participation by broad groups in the use of knowledge; others involve only a few individuals. An even more critical differentiating factor is the level of knowledge required to successfully use a particular technology. Some knowledge tools effectively require that the user be something of an expert on the topic; others assume that the user is a more passive participant in the knowledge process. This dimension is used to structure much of the discussion below of individual knowledge management tools (see diagram). The other key dimension is the time required to find a knowledge management solution in a particular business application of a tool. Some knowledge-work environments allow time for search, synthesis, and reflection; others, such as those in-

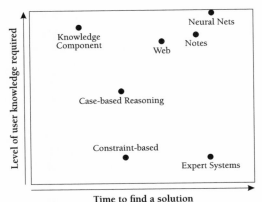

Key Dimensions of Knowledge Management Tools

volving customer inquiries, require real-time or near real-time performance.

Broad Knowledge Repositories

One of the best-known approaches to using technology in knowledge management is the repository of structured, explicit knowledge—usually in document form. Such repositories have been present for decades in the form of computerized databases of published materials, for example, Lexis/Nexis and Dialog. A few companies have used external on-line services to store internal knowledge repositories. Buckman Laboratories, for example, employed a "private" branch of the CompuServe service as its repository for documents and discussion on customer, product, and competitor knowledge. The firm has recently shifted to an intranet, but for four years it employed CompuServe quite successfully, and was able to focus on content issues rather than technology problems.

The best example of a broad knowledge repository is the Internet. As a source of outside knowledge, the Internet can overcome some of the disadvantages of the localness and asymmetry of knowledge, since a subject search will return results from the whole system. Localness is not an issue because it does not matter to the user where material resides. The hypertext that has made the World Wide Web such a success allows related content to be linked regardless of its physical location.

Although these systems partly solve the problem of locating knowledge, they often compound the problem of judging the knowledge that is being provided. As anyone who has carried out an Internet search knows, the overwhelming majority of "hits" supplied by search engines are irrelevant or worthless. A tremendous amount of time can be wasted sorting through trash to find a few treasures. The level of trust in the Internet knowledge market is thus justifiably low. You might recall the former diplomat who brandished a "secret" report that the U.S. military had shot down TWA Flight 800—not realizing that the report had originated on the Internet, where numerous conspiracy theorists ply their trade.

Future technical innovations, such as increased speed and more sophisticated search engines, will probably make the Internet a better knowledge source. But the emergence of human Internet brokers or librarians with reputations for finding quality material would enhance the value of the Internet as a knowledge tool more significantly than purely technical improvements. One information entrepreneur is currently attempting to develop such a network of librarians.

In the past, repositories were largely external to any particular organization; they were used to obtain competitive intelligence, market knowledge, or external technical, legal, or commercial knowledge. Now, however, many firms are creating repositories of internally sourced structured knowledge. They are creating repositories of internal product knowledge, marketing knowledge, customer knowledge, or other types.

Lotus Notes and Intranet-based Webs are the two leading toolsets for managing knowledge repositories today. Although the functionality of these two tools is merging, there are still differences between them. In early 1997, Notes excels at database management, discussion-group creation and management, and replication of databases for remote disconnected use in the field. The Web is ideal for publishing information across multiple types of computer platforms, for multimedia databases, and for displaying knowledge that is linked to other knowledge through hypertext links. In the fairly near future these capabilities will be available on both technologies.

At present, Notes is a more comprehensive out-of-the-box solution that includes many of the capabilities (replication, security, application-development tools) that organizations will eventually have to purchase in using Webs. However, the growth in Web capabilities is much faster, since thousands of companies rather than one are working on them. If you're starting a knowledge management project today involving publishing, discussion, and search, we'd recommend using the Web because of its maturation trajectory and because it's a lot simpler for users to understand. If you've been doing this type of knowledge management for a while, you've probably been doing it in Notes, and we see no reason to switch now. It particularly excels at the "lessons learned" form of knowledge management involving discussion. The Lotus "Domino" Web server allows knowledge to be created in Notes and then distributed over the Web.

Professional services and consulting firms were some of the earliest adopters of Notes for the purpose of knowledge management, and it is safe to say that they have advanced the frontiers of the tool. Firms such as Ernst & Young, Andersen Consulting, Price Waterhouse, and Coopers & Lybrand all have very large repositories of knowledge from serving clients, several of which exceed a thousand different databases. Notes is particularly appealing in professional services because work in that industry often involves travel to the client site, and the replication feature in Notes allows a remote employee to quickly download all new items added to databases of interest and then to peruse them off-line. Firms outside of the professional services industry have also adopted Notes for knowledge applications. Chrysler, for example, has used it to create an "Engineering Book of Knowledge," a set of lessons learned in the design and engineering process about particular car components.

Since it is relatively easy to develop Notes applications, many of them are developed by individual users and can overlap in functionality and content. Most of these firms' "knowledge architectures" in Notes are a bit haphazard; finding the knowledge one wants from so many different places to look is very challenging, even with the "Yellow Pages" or "card catalogue" applications that most of these firms have devised. Andersen Consulting, for example, has developed at least three levels of navigation tools for its enormous "Knowledge Xchange" system, but users still find it difficult to negotiate among the more than twenty-five hundred Notes databases in the repository. Firms will increasingly have to use rigorous management approaches to deal with Notes databases and content in the future, including criteria for application development, naming conventions for data or knowledge bases and the content within them, and the creation of reusable knowledge management templates and objects. This level of structure may seem a bit Procrustean, but it is necessary if the large-volume repository is the mechanism of choice.

Notes-based knowledge management implementations are often accompanied by other tools, particularly where the management of external knowledge is concerned. Two such tools are Hoover, from Sandpoint Systems (a unit of Dun & Bradstreet) and GrapeVINE, from Grapevine Technologies. Hoover searches through selected external databases, "sucking up" knowledge that has been identified as relevant (based on user-specified keywords) to a particular user or group within a company. Hoover's customer does not have to specify or know the sources from which the knowledge is drawn. Notes is typically employed to distribute the found knowledge to the user's desktop. Monsanto, for example, uses Hoover and Notes to distribute external market knowledge to the desks of scientists developing new chemicals and genetic advances. The goal of the initiative is to ensure that scientists develop new products that are not only technically successful but also consistent with the needs of customers and distinct from competitor offerings. Automated search programs similar to Hoover are offered by Individual Inc. (NewsPage), OneSource Information Services (Company Watch), and Bolt Beranek & Newman (Personal Internet Newspaper).

GrapeVINE, a program used for knowledge management at such firms as HP, Andersen Consulting, and Ford, is a somewhat more structured technology for bringing external knowledge into an organization. It can also be combined with Notes for purposes of distribution and alignment with other knowledge management applications. GrapeVINE, like Hoover, searches through external databases. It does its searching, however, not on the basis of simple keywords but rather on a "knowledge chart"—a hierarchical map of an organization's knowledge terms and relationships. The chart is not easy to construct and maintain, but it can allow a more strategic perspective on what knowledge really matters to the organization. GrapeVINE also allows designated knowledge editors to comment on and prioritize—in other words, add value to—external data that GrapeVINE has brought in and "escalate" the importance of an item to ensure it reaches the PCs of the employees and managers who need it. If an organization is willing to make the commitment to the organizational and technical infrastructure demanded by Grape-VINE, it can be a very useful vehicle for managing external knowledge.

Repositories based on the World Wide Web are rapidly picking up steam. The Web is a very intuitive technology, and deals easily with audio, graphic, and video representations of knowledge. Knowledge in a particular domain is often related to other knowledge, and the hypertext structure of the Web makes it very easy to move from one piece of knowledge to another. Most Web-based repositories are smaller and easier to negotiate than those built in Notes. Intranet Webs are therefore the easiest way to get into knowledge management.

However, if you plan to use Web technology for knowledge management (particularly the search-and-retrieval of structured, document-based knowledge), don't think that a Web browser and server software is all that you need. A complex suite of tools is normally necessary to capture the information, store it, and allow broad access. The usual requirements include Hypertext Markup Language (HTML) publishing tools for producing Web documents, a relational database system for storing them, text search-and-retrieval engines, and some approach to managing the "metaknowledge" that describes and facilitates access to the knowledge you've got on hand—plus, of course, your preferred Web browser and server. If this seems rather overwhelming, there are some organizations that sell a bundled Web-based knowledge management capability, for example, Sequent Computer's "Knowledge Depot" products and services.

Sequent used all these tools internally to develop its Sequent Corporate Electronic Library (SCEL), a Web-based repository of information and knowledge. Development of the system began in 1994, making it one of the oldest Web-based repositories. Initially the SCEL was developed to support the sales force; Sequent's vice president of corporate architecture, Dave Rodgers, argued that the system would allow sales representatives to become productive more quickly at a time when the firm had substantial turnover in field sales. Over time, however, the SCEL has become a "one-stop shop" for information and knowledge of all kinds—from the Corporate Mission Statement to lunch menus at its corporate headquarters in Portland, Oregon. While we see the virtues of having one place to go for all computer-based knowledge, the idea of putting highly prosaic content into a knowledge repository does not appeal to us. We're afraid that, as with network television, bad content will drive out good.

Another requirement for search-and-retrieval knowledge management is the development of an on-line thesaurus. Knowledge is unwieldy to structure, and you will find that searchers will be looking for knowledge using terms that you can't always antici-

A good thesaurus is essential to most on-line knowledge repositories.

pate. The idea behind a thesaurus is to connect the terms by which you've structured the knowledge with the terms employed by the searcher. This isn't that tough technically if you've bought a search engine. It is more difficult to compile a set of meaningful terms by which your knowledge repository can be searched.

The underlying technique for both Web and Notes-based knowledge repositories is text search-and-retrieval. While this technology has been around for decades, it has both strengths and shortcomings for knowledge management. On the positive side, the knowledge itself typically has plenty of meaningful context that was created by the original author of the article, legal brief, or biography. However, the knowledge in textual databases is indexed on the basis of keywords and their proximity in the text. These are relatively shallow aspects of the knowledge, and it can be difficult to extract knowledge in search queries on this basis. And if the information about a problem is not already in text form, putting it in that form requires significant time and human labor.

Notes and the Web can be used for other knowledge management applications as well. One popular application, for example, is the expert locator, which allows users to search through a set of biographies for an expert on a particular knowledge domain. This is still a form of repository, but the objective is to locate people rather than documents. Intranet-based Webs combined with database-management software are the most popular technology for this type of application. The data on the expert may include educational background, jobs held within and outside the company, current projects or responsibilities, and particular skills, including languages spoken or computer proficiency. Most importantly, the expert locator should include a keyword-based guide to the domains of expertise in the company. If someone seeks an expert on the topic of "database marketing," for example, it should be easy to connect with experts having that expertise by searching on that keyword.

The technology associated with expert locators is relatively straightforward. In addition to a Web browser and server software, the application will typically require some system of database management and a search engine. As with repositories, the search engine should work with a thesaurus, since the terminology in which expertise is sought may not always match the terms the expert uses to classify that expertise. "Database marketing" searches, for example, should also turn up experts in "interactive marketing," "response management," and "fulfillment."

Companies do, however, often encounter nontechnological difficulties in building expert locator systems. The systems require a considerable time commitment on the part of the expert (or of some intermediary) to enter and update biographies into the database. Motivating experts to perform such tasks may be difficult. As we made clear in our discussion of mapping knowledge, the very idea of designating some employees as "experts" may also be fraught with political peril.

We mentioned Hewlett-Packard's expert locator system at the beginning of the chapter. Another firm that has constructed this type of system is Teltech, where it is at the core of the firm's business. Teltech's system deals with a network of external experts. The company first used conventional textual database systems, and now employs Web technology, to allow both Teltech analysts and clients to search for experts in a wide range of technical domains. The company's thesaurus of technical terminology is critical to the ability of users to match their need for expertise with available experts. Teltech creates the on-line biographies from paper documents, and also has a consulting service to create a locator system for clients.

However, the knowledge management activities that can be supported via Notes or the Web don't encompass all possible situations. These technologies work well for broad knowledge domains when there is no right answer to a problem or when there are many different answers scattered around the organization. The use of these tools requires substantial user time (to search the database and read the retrieved knowledge) and intelligence (to synthesize and interpret the retrieved knowledge). Not all knowledge management environments, needless to say, are blessed with these conditions.

Many firms have adopted both Notes and the Web for knowledge management. We have already mentioned both technologies, for example, at Hewlett-Packard. At National Semiconductor, employees in the marketing and sales functions gravitated to Notes for knowledge management, largely because they traveled frequently in their jobs and used the replication feature of Notes. Engineers, however, were drawn to the Web for their knowledge repositories, because they were comfortable with the Unix tools often employed with the Web

There's generally no rush to settle on a single technology strategy.

and because they were already heavy users of the Internet. The firm's managers decided that there was no reason—for the moment at least—to move to a single standard for knowledge tools. Early on in the life of knowledge management initiatives, a "let a thousand flowers bloom" technology strategy may be helpful in encouraging learning and exploration. Later on, however, the sharing of knowledge across organizational boundaries will be easier with a single, broadly employed toolset.

Focused Knowledge Environments

Some organizations have concentrated knowledge domains rather than a community of expert users. This is the best situation for expert systems, which can enable the knowledge of one or a few experts to be used by a much broader group of workers who need the knowledge—say, a group of insurance salespeople who need to be able to do financial planning for their customers but who don't know much about financial planning. The user normally needs to engage in a dialogue with the system, entering information about the problem or situation, a process that takes time. Expert systems, which are typically structured in a set of rules, can perform very complex reasoning, such as that required in detailed financial planning. However, it can be difficult to extract knowledge from an expert in the first place—either because the expert doesn't know what he or she knows, or because he or she doesn't want to surrender the knowledge. For this reason the rules governing the expert system must be carefully specified in a tight structure, and must not contain overlapping knowledge.

Expert systems have one other related requirement: because these highly structured systems are difficult to maintain or add knowledge to, the knowledge domain needs to be fairly stable. American Express, for example, still uses its Authorizer's Assistant expert system for credit authorization because the factors that make for good credit risks (or deadbeats) have remained fairly constant. On the other hand, Digital Equipment stopped using the XCON configuration system because its product line changed constantly, and the system was too difficult to maintain. One recent research study found that only a third of the expert systems developed in the 1980s were still in use by 1992. The systems were abandoned less for technical reasons than for organizational ones—their sponsor moved on, there were difficult politics in extracting knowledge from experts (or representing users as less than expert), or the systems were viewed as too expensive to update and maintain.[6]

Another option for companies with focused knowledge environments are constraint-based systems, which are suited for situations with high levels of data but normally less quantitative data than that required by neural networks. Like expert systems, they are suited for relatively narrow problem domains, such as product configuration or pricing. Constraint-based systems capture and model the constraints that govern complex decision making (determining, for example, what kind of memory, hard disk, modem, and video board work with a computer having a particular processor and operating system). Because constraint-based systems are usually object-oriented underneath (rather than rule-based), they are easier to modify than expert systems; there are no complex interactions to understand and modify.

Constraint-based systems from Trilogy Development Group are currently being employed in the configuration of complex products—from Boeing airplanes to Digital and Hewlett-Packard computers to office furniture layouts. At Boeing, for example, there are literally millions of possible configurations of airplane models, numbers of seats, galley and lavatory options and placements, and engine choices. Keeping track of valid configurations across multiple functional departments throughout multiple design changes has proven to be too difficult for either humans or ordinary computer systems. While Boeing has not yet completed the implementation of its configuration system, it expects to ultimately reduce its time-to-market for a configured airplane by 50 percent, and to reduce its production costs by 25 percent.[7] Trilogy technology is also behind a recently introduced application that allows you to "configure" custom-made Italian shoes quickly and at a reasonable cost. Similar constraint-based tools are being developed by other software manufacturers and will be embedded within broad "enterprise resource planning" packages that combine configuration with manufacturing, inventory management, and financial systems.

Real-Time Knowledge Systems

If you have little time and smarter users, the knowledge management tools described above will be less appropriate. Take customer support or "help desk" applications, for example. These processes are usually performed by bright analysts (especially in IT vendor firms), but time is usually of the essence because the customer is on the telephone in real time. In this situation there are a couple of options. If your users are only somewhat expert—capable of understanding problems, but not normally of solving them or classifying their symptoms—then case-based reasoning is your best bet. CBR applications require someone to input a series of "cases," which represent knowledge about a particular domain expressed as a series of problem characteristics and solutions. Then when a customer analyst is presented with a problem, its characteristics can be compared against the set of cases in the application, and the closest match is selected. CBR is a branch of artificial intelligence that is most commonly found in the customer service and support process in firms.

Inference Corporation is the leading vendor of CBR tools, which are used in a number of customer support environments, including Hewlett-Packard, Compaq, PeopleSoft, Reuters, Xerox, and Broderbund.[8] Broderbund offers its customers Web access to a version of the Inference tools: called the "Gizmo Tapper 586 LC," the site mimics a dialogue with detectives in the Carmen Sandiego computer game. Xerox uses a simple version of CBR to allow service dispatchers to solve some copier repair problems over the phone, rather than sending a service technician. Compaq built an application it calls SMART (Support Management Automated Reasoning Technology), created and managed by expert "knowledge engineers." Since implementing, SMART Compaq support processes involve a faster learning curve, are less affected by turnover, employ a less expert support worker, and resolve 95 percent of customer problems within ten minutes.[9]

CBR works best when you have one or a few experts construct the cases and maintain them over time. There must also be a domain expert—someone knowledgeable about the area supported by the system—who can decide when a new case is worth creating, when an old case has become obsolete, and whether a newly submitted case is actually correct. Case construction and modification is somewhat complex (though getting simpler with new tools) and requires knowledge of the CBR approach. If you have a large group of knowledge workers—expert not in CBR, but in the relevant knowledge domain—whose expertise you want to tap, you must either create a case administrator as intermediary or explore other real-time knowledge options.

One such option is a tool called SolutionBuilder developed by Primus Corporation for the Customer Support Consortium, a group of more than sixty high-tech firms working together to solve problems of knowledge management in customer support. Primus has developed an approach to managing customer support knowledge (and eventually other types) based on breaking down a problem or situation into its knowledge components (they haven't given it a name, but we'd call it "knowledge component analysis"). The support analyst can classify knowledge about the problem received from the customer, or add new knowledge about the problem, as one of the following seven components or statements:

1. The *goal* or task that the customer is trying to accomplish but cannot perform

2. A *fact* about the customer's technology environment

3. A *symptom* of the customer's problem

4. A recent *change* in the customer technology environment

5. A likely *cause* of the problem

6. A *negation* or a fact that is clearly irrelevant to the current problem

7. The *fix* for the problem

While the analyst classifies the components of the problem, Solution-Builder searches the database for solutions with similarities to the components of the customer's problem. An object-oriented database is employed to create dynamic relationships among the components to yield a solution to the problem. It's an empowered, democratic approach to knowledge management, but it requires an ability to classify knowledge components that not all users may possess. While a number of companies are conducting pilot programs with SolutionBuilder, it's not really a viable production tool yet.

Longer-Term Analysis Systems

If you have a lot of time and a user with a Ph.D. in statistics, neural networks are just the ticket for turning data into knowledge. A neural network is a statistically oriented tool that excels at using data to classify cases into one category or another—say, whether a loan customer is likely to default on a loan, or pay it back. Because of its statistical nature, one might question its fit with the concept of knowledge management. However, since one aspect of these systems is that they "learn"—which is to say, their classification becomes more accurate with more cases— they are often discussed in the realm of artificial intelligence and knowledge. Neural nets require a lot of (normally quantitative) data and a high-powered computer. They can yield very accurate classifications of cases even with many interrelated variables—an aspect of data that can create problems with conventional statistical analysis. Because setting up the analysis and interpreting results can be very tricky, these systems require a very knowledgeable user, at least to set up the initial model. Subsequent data (for example, a month's new scanner data in a consumer products firm) may be analyzed with the same model, so converting the data into knowledge can happen faster and with less expertise. Still, in order to make decisions based on the recommendations of neural networks, it's very helpful to know how they work.

However, neural networks are something of a "black box"; it's not easy to explain why they did what they did. A particular case will be classified in a particular fashion according to nodes and variable weightings, and is therefore difficult to interpret. Some new neural networking tools, such as those from a company called Trajecta, hide the complexity from the user and are able to explain to some degree why the system did what it did. Smart businesspeople, as opposed to smart statisticians, nevertheless may not like them for their difficulty of interpretation. This is one of the reasons why Fidelity Investments, which generally hires smart users as fund managers, is no longer using neural networks to select stocks in the Disciplined Equity fund, but has converted to a more algorithmic approach that is presumably easier to interpret in the context of fund management.

Neural networks and other artificial intelligence tools, as well as more conventional statistical analysis, are also used for what is known as "data mining." This approach also falls into the category of turning vast amounts of data into knowledge. Some advocates of this approach maintain that the pattern identification and matching capabilities of software can eliminate human intervention. They argue, for example, that a data mining system could by itself discover that a certain group of customers purchases more of a certain product on a certain day of the month. This may be true, but an intelligent human is still required to (a) structure the data in the first place; (b) interpret the data to understand the identified pattern; and (c) make a decision based on the knowledge. And in practice, most of the organizations we have come across have also used humans to generate the hypothesis for analysis. As a practical matter, then, data mining is essentially a new term for a relatively conventional and well-understood practice.

What Technologies Can't Do

While these technologies are exciting and clearly improving, it is important to bear in mind their limitations in any program of knowledge management. As we have noted throughout this book, effective knowledge management cannot take place without extensive behavioral, cultural, and organizational change. The installation of Notes or the Web or case-based reasoning software will not in itself bring about that change. Technology alone won't make a person with expertise share it with others. Technology alone won't get an employee

Technology alone won't make you a knowledge-creating company.

who is uninterested in seeking knowledge to hop onto a keyboard and start searching or browsing. The mere presence of technology won't create a learning organization, a meritocracy, or a knowledge-creating company.

Technology is common in the domain of knowledge distribution, but it rarely enhances the process of knowledge use. Distribution delivers knowledge to the potential user's desktop but cannot dictate what he or she does with it thereafter. It would be interesting to envision technologies that help to manage personal knowledge as it applies to decisions and actions, but beyond the very rudimentary "personal information managers" that allow searching of unrelated bits of information, little progress has been made toward "personal knowledge managers." On the group level, an interesting but unpopular tool attempted to capture graphically the process of applying knowledge to policy decisions. This "Graphical Issue-Based Information System" was developed in the late 1980s and early 1990s at the Microelectronics and Computer Corporation, a research consortium in Austin, and later marketed by Corporate Memory Systems as the CM1 product. However, perhaps because of its complexity and conceptual strangeness, the product never took off.[10]

Information technology is also relatively less helpful when it comes to knowledge creation, which remains largely an act of individuals or groups and their brains. There are technologies that purport to enhance these activities, but at best they operate on the margins of the problem. Group decision support systems, for example, involve a relatively small group of people, usually in the same location, attempting to employ technology to create some form of group knowledge out of their beliefs and experiences. Outlining tools, frequently used by writers, might be viewed as a means of converting unstructured tacit knowledge into structured and explicit knowledge. Systems for analyzing clinical data could be said to help create medical or pharmaceutical knowledge, just as systems for analyzing market data attempt to turn it into market knowledge. Recently, some systems have begun to address the problem of creativity and invention, suggesting prospective inventions based on a set of rules of thumb. The technological support for knowledge creation may improve in the future, but it is negligible today.

However, if the appetite, the skills, and the attention to knowledge are already present in an organization, technology can expand access and ease the problem of getting the right knowledge to the right person at the right time. The presence of knowledge management technologies may even have a positive effect on the knowledge culture of the organization. Workers who see their company investing time and money on its Web site, for example, may gain added incentive to take knowledge management seriously.

Here in the early days of knowledge management, what is most important in a knowledge technology strategy is to get a few toes into the water. You may not even know how willing people are to share knowledge through systems until you build a system and see how the organization responds. It will be difficult to determine which types of applications provide the best fit with an organization until you experiment. Right now, there is no right technology for knowledge management. We're all finding our way, and as long as technology isn't the only aspect of your knowledge management effort, the most essential thing is just to get started with something.

There is the world of ideas
and the world of practice.
—Mathew Arnold

8

Knowledge Management Projects in Practice

W H E N P E O P L E talk about knowledge management, the conversation often devolves into highly abstract and philosophical statements. But there is a real world of knowledge management—a world of budgets, deadlines, office politics, and organizational leadership. This is the area that we will explore in this chapter, which focuses on the knowledge management project. Such projects are attempts to make practical use of knowledge, to accomplish some organizational objective through the structuring of people, technology, and knowledge content. These projects are appearing throughout the business world, and in 1996 we undertook an effort to examine a number of them.[1]

By selecting the knowledge management project as the unit of analysis, we gain some illuminating perspectives on the topic. After all, it is through structured projects, however imperfect, that anything in companies actually gets done. Through the study of practices and practitioners at the vanguard of knowledge management, we hope to provide background for the uninitiated as well as practical guidelines for those more familiar with the subject. As we will see, however, none of these projects is an optimal model. Some beg the question of whether it is really "knowledge" that is being managed, and most fall short of knowledge-based organizational transformation. It is far easier to talk about such transformations than to achieve them.

In order to understand how knowledge is really being managed in companies today, we studied thirty-one different knowledge management projects in twenty different firms. In most companies we addressed only one project, but to get an in-depth look at knowledge management in a single organization, we also observed ten projects in one firm (Hewlett-Packard). We made site visits to four of the firms and interviewed the rest by telephone. Our sources were typically the managers of the knowledge projects, or of the knowledge management function across the organization. In addition, many of these firms were participants in a research program on multiple aspects of knowledge management, sponsored by Ernst & Young.[2] We refined our ideas in two review sessions with the program participants.

In the first section of the chapter, we briefly discuss the range of approaches we observed before presenting a high-level typology of knowledge management projects. We then attempt to shed some light on what makes for a successful knowledge project. Success and failure are ambiguous terms when applied to so nascent a field as knowledge management, but we discuss the characteristics of projects that were thriving when we observed them.

We conclude the chapter by going over some differences between success factors for knowledge management projects and those for other types of initiatives, such as information or data management efforts. One indication that knowledge management differs from these other areas is that the projects address different factors. Of course, it can be a fine line to distinguish between projects geared toward information and knowledge. When we asked our respondents about how they viewed the difference between those two terms, several admitted overlaps. Many noted that while their efforts to manage knowledge sometimes included information (but rarely data), they were always attempting to add value to the information and hence turn it into knowledge. Their projects also tended to devote substantial attention to human contributions, which is one characteristic that generally distinguishes knowledge from information or data.

Types of Knowledge Management Projects

Knowledge management is an evolving practice. Even the most developed and mature knowledge management projects we studied were unfinished works in progress. Most of their managers, however, were able to articulate specific business and knowledge management objectives, and some had already achieved some of their goals.

We found great variation among these thirty-one projects. Some were self-funding, using a market-based approach that charged users for knowledge services. Companies funded others out of overhead. Some took a hybrid approach: for example, relying on corporate funding during roll-out but requiring a transition to self-funding after some period of time. A centralized knowledge management function managed or coordinated some projects, while others occurred in a more bottom-up and decentralized fashion. Where some initiatives were fundamental to the very purpose and existence of a firm, others were peripheral; some defied economic justification and others actually generated revenue from external customers.

In many ways, however, these projects were alike. In addition to defined objectives, each had someone in charge of the effort, some specific commitment of financial and human resources, and, of course, a focus on knowledge as distinct from information or data. The projects also shared in common three very broad types of knowledge management objectives: attempts to create knowledge repositories, attempts to improve knowledge access, and attempts to improve knowledge cultures and environments.

Knowledge Repositories

Much of the energy in knowledge management has been spent on treating knowledge as an "it," an entity separate from the people who create and use it. Abstracting knowledge like this is not new; in fact it is as old as the book. The typical goal of this type of project is to take knowledge embodied in documents—memos, reports, presentations, articles, and so forth—and put it into a repository where it can be easily stored and retrieved. A somewhat less structured form of accumulated knowledge is the discussion database, in which participants record their own experiences on an issue and react to others' comments. In our research, we came across three basic types of knowledge repositories:

1. *External knowledge* (example: competitive intelligence)

2. *Structured internal knowledge* (example: research reports, product-oriented marketing materials and methods)

3. *Informal internal knowledge* (example: discussion databases full of know-how, sometimes referred to as "lessons learned")

We found no current examples of rule-based expert systems in our research, though these might also be classified as repositories of narrow knowledge domains. Contrary to expectations, as we discussed in Chapter 7, there are few commercial examples of this technology in business today.

An automobile company in our study, for example, compiled an external repository of competitive-intelligence knowledge. It encompassed analyst reports, trade journal articles, and external market research on competitors in the automobile industry. Using a tool called GrapeVINE (discussed in Chapter 7), the "knowledge managers" for this project could route information or knowledge on different topics to managers with a specified interest in that topic. Items of particular importance could be prioritized and sent to everyone, thus making the information or knowledge in the system more accessible and useful.

In the examples of internal knowledge repository projects, we observed the storage of both knowledge and information. If the distinction between knowledge and information is seen as more of a continuum than a sharp dichotomy, most projects that focus on internal knowledge deal with the middle of the continuum—information that represents knowledge to certain users. We've already mentioned, for example, Hewlett-Packard's Electronic Sales Partner, a system that provides technical product information, sales presentations, sales and marketing tactics, customer account information, and anything else that might benefit field personnel in the sales process. The leaders of this project had "knowledge manager" on their business cards, and although some of the content in the system felt more like information than knowledge, the HP managers tried to add value to their repository through careful categorization and pruning. We've also described Sequent Computer's system; Sun Microsystems and Silicon Graphics have similar repositories in place.

Finally, there is the tacit knowledge that resides within the minds of people in an organization but is not in structured, document-based form. We've already described different codification approaches for tacit and explicit knowledge earlier in this book, and other authors have done so elsewhere.[3] In the projects we studied, when firms wanted to extract tacit knowledge from employees for a repository, they opted for some sort of community-based electronic discussion. For example, in the Corporate Education Division at Hewlett-Packard, a project called "Trainer's Trading Post" attempts to capture tips, tricks, insights, experiences, and observations onto a Lotus Notes database shared by all the company's trainers and educators. One out of every fifty employees at HP hold such positions,

Knowledge repositories can help reinforce an organization's cultural rituals and routines.

but they are scattered across many different sites and previously could not easily share their knowledge. This type of knowledge repository attempts to accelerate and broaden the traditional knowledge sharing that happens with socialization of newcomers, the generation of organizational myths and stories, and the general transmission of cultural rituals and routines.[4]

Knowledge Access and Transfer

Another type of project we found was predicated on providing access to knowledge or facilitating its transfer among individuals. Where knowledge repositories aim at capturing knowledge itself, knowledge access projects focus on the possessors and prospective users of knowledge. These types of projects acknowledge that finding the person with the knowledge one needs, and then successfully transferring it from one person to another, can be a daunting process. If the metaphor of a library is useful for conceptualizing knowledge repository projects, then that of a "knowledge Yellow Pages" might best symbolize the purpose of knowledge access projects. Managers involved in knowledge access projects commonly used phrases like, "getting at the knowledge we know we have," "sharing our knowledge," and so forth, phrases that connote a need for connectivity, access, and transfer.

Like the knowledge repository projects, knowledge access projects vary in their technological orientation. For example, we came across several instances of companies who were building and managing expert networks (or, to use one of our own terms, maps of knowledge sources). At one company, the expert network was not an improvement targeted at some segment of the operation but was actually the primary business. The company, Teltech Resource Network Corporation, provides a technical expert referral service by maintaining a comprehensive database of external technical experts. Teltech provides these referrals to engineers, researchers, and scientists, in companies who have an occasional need for expert knowledge. The company motivates experts to participate in the network by paying them to answer client questions after being contacted through the database. The firm markets its services to technical managers and professionals within their client companies, constantly trying to remind potential customers that they are an available resource. Apparently it's not natural for engineers to ask for help, so Teltech works hard to overcome this predisposition.

We have already described several projects that fall into this category of knowledge access and transfer. Microsoft's SPUD project, which consolidates the knowledge of its system developers, is a vehicle for enhancing access to personal knowledge. BP's Virtual Teamwork project addresses the transfer of tacit knowledge. Sematech's knowledge transfer efforts focus largely on human communication, but also include information systems.

Knowledge Environment

The last type of project attempts to establish an environment conducive to knowledge management. Within this category we saw examples of projects intended to measure or improve the value of knowledge capital, efforts to build awareness and cultural receptivity, initiatives attempting to change behavior as it relates to knowledge, and attempts to improve the knowledge management process.

Some firms we studied were making concerted attempts to treat knowledge as an asset just as real as any other that appears on its balance sheet. Skandia undertakes an internal audit of the company's intellectual capital every year and issues a report to stockholders and the investment community. One goal of this analysis is to per-

Some firms now treat knowledge as another kind of capital asset.

suade investors of the value of Skandia's knowledge capital. Other firms focus on managing the value of the asset more than measuring it, through such activities as patent management or licensing.

Several firms have adopted higher-level and less focused efforts to change the general organizational attitude toward knowledge. At one large computer firm, there have been a series of ongoing efforts to encourage the re-use of a particular knowledge type: component designs. Over the years we have also seen a gradual shift in the attitudes of engineers to valuing time to market more than (or at least as much as) originality of design. At a direct-marketing firm we surveyed, the goal of knowledge management efforts is to increase awareness and re-use the knowledge embedded in client relationships. The firm appointed a chief knowledge officer who had no staff; he worked through the education and exhortation of others.

Some companies make knowledge-related employee behavior a specific target of their projects. A large consulting firm, for example, revamped its performance appraisal system to include contributions to the firm's knowledge base as an important part of compensation decisions.

The firm was making significant inroads toward changing employee perceptions of their jobs—encouraging consultants to think of themselves as creators and distributors of management knowledge.

Finally, some companies concentrate on the processes for creating, sharing, and using knowledge. At a simple level, a process orientation means developing methods of measuring of the speed, cost, impact, and customer satisfaction of the knowledge management activities. Teltech, for example, calls each customer after a referral to assess the quality of the expert and the expertise. We also observed process improvement and reengineering being applied directly to knowledge management in some projects. These approaches involved describing—at least at a high level—the desired steps in the process of knowledge management.

Projects with Multiple Characteristics

We view the projects just discussed as examples of conceptually pure or "ideal" types. In real life, of course, such ideals are rarely attained. Almost all the projects we studied were combinations of different types of projects. At Young & Rubicam, for example, divisional CKO Nick Rudd was striving to inculcate a knowledge-friendly culture, while at the same time setting up formal face-to-face knowledge transfer programs. The consulting firm we researched adopted almost all of the project types described above, including:

- Development of an expert network
- Development of internal document repositories
- Efforts to create new knowledge
- Development of "lessons learned" knowledge bases
- A high-level description of the knowledge management process
- The use of evaluation and compensation systems to change behavior

While it is too early to tell for sure, one would expect that knowledge management projects that work along multiple fronts would be more effective than those that employ only one type of initiative. This is consistent with the "ecological" approach to information and knowledge management that we have advocated elsewhere.[5]

One drawback to their approach is that the absence of clear demarcations of project types may cause measurement problems. The fuzziness of project objectives also defies easy quantification. How does one prioritize the different aspects of a project, that comprises, for example, 20 percent culture, 45 percent transfer, and 35 percent repository? Further, how does one measure cultural change and apportion the results to the investments? Finally, firms do not ask shareholders to pay money for ownership in order to have a knowledge-sharing culture or a knowledgeable sales force. Shareholders expect firms to make money, and establishing the link between knowledge and financial performance is, at best, tricky.[6] Let us turn, then, to the question of how one measures success in knowledge management projects.

Success in Knowledge Management Projects

What constitutes success in knowledge management? Since economic returns from knowledge have always been difficult to quantify, we must rely on more general indications of success. And because we observed these projects only for a finite period, we cannot know for sure whether current indications of success will persist over time. Still, the indications of success in knowledge management projects are not that different from the criteria companies use to measure success in other types of business change projects. Here are the primary attributes we use to define success in knowledge management:

- Growth in the resources attached to the project, including staffing and budgets.
- Growth in the volume of knowledge content and usage (for example, the number of documents or accesses for repositories, or participants for discussion database projects).
- The likelihood that the project will be sustaining beyond a particular individual or two, that is, the project is an organizational initiative, not an individual project.
- Comfort throughout the organization with the concepts of "knowledge" and "knowledge management."
- Some evidence of financial return, either for the knowledge management activity itself (if it is seen as a profit center) or for the larger organization. This linkage need not be rigorously specified and may be only perceptual.

In interviewing the managers of knowledge projects, we didn't ask if they felt their projects were successful. We did, however, ask about these particular indicators of success. The presence or absence of these indicators made it relatively easy to classify projects as successful, likely to fail, or not yet successful. About half the projects fit into the "successful" category. For two of the projects we felt that it was too early to characterize their degree of success.

The projects we defined as successful had most or all of these indicators present. Several lacked financial benefits today, but they had plans to develop them in the future. In contrast, the unsuccessful or not yet successful projects had few or none of these characteristics. Managers had to scrounge for resources. They struggled to get members of the organizations to contribute to repositories or use discussion databases. A few visionary—but lonely—individuals championed these projects. And any sense that the projects would make money for their firms was either not under consideration or a long way off. While conditions might change in the future, these projects were clearly failing to thrive in the present.

In evaluating these projects we observed two degrees of success. The most impressive type involved the fundamental transformation of a company. This was quite rare—just three cases—and debatable even in the firms where we felt it was present. The other type of success involved operational improvement limited to a bounded process or function. Managers intended knowledge management projects to bring about specific improvements in new product development, customer support, education and training, software development, patent management, and many other functions and processes. This was the primary form of success we found, but it is difficult to speculate how improvement in these relatively narrow areas might translate into broader organizational success.

At the large consulting firm we studied, knowledge was arguably responsible for a major transformation of the firm. The transformation was extensive in both depth and breadth of impact, and financial results improved markedly during the period of knowledge management. Line consultants drew heavily from the firm's centralized knowledge centers, accessing previous presentations to other clients, process and system design specifications, work plans, and other project-oriented collateral and artifacts. The firm increased its "win rate" in client proposals.

At the Sematech R&D consortium, knowledge creation and sharing has been critical to the organization's existence. Since it has employed approaches to knowledge management from its beginning, it is difficult to argue that these tactics led to transformation, but survival is an equally important form of success. Another firm where knowledge management has been critical to survival is Teltech. The knowledge management approaches it had adopted seemed to be working, as the company was growing when we studied them.

Factors Leading to Knowledge Project Success

The indicators described above tell us whether a project is successful or not, but not what makes it that way. After we had classified the projects, we next tried to identify the most telling variables, and found nine factors that were common throughout the successful projects. This was a highly exploratory effort and the causal factors we've identified should be viewed only as hypotheses about what makes a project successful. With this provision, we will describe each of the nine factors below:

- A knowledge-oriented culture
- Technical and organizational infrastructure
- Senior management support
- A link to economics or industry value
- A modicum of process orientation
- Clarity of vision and language
- Nontrivial motivational aids
- Some level of knowledge structure
- Multiple channels for knowledge transfer

Knowledge-Oriented Culture

A knowledge-friendly culture was clearly one of the most important conditions leading to the success of a project in our survey. It is perhaps the hardest factor to build from scratch, and has several different components:

- A positive orientation to knowledge: employees are bright and intellectually curious, are willing and free to explore, and their knowledge-creating activities are given credence by executives.
- The absence of knowledge inhibitors in the culture: people are not

resentful of the company and do not fear that sharing knowledge will cost them their jobs.

- The knowledge management project type fits the culture.

While we believe that all firms in business should have a positive orientation toward knowledge in their cultures, many do not. In our view, the most important factor in establishing a positive knowledge culture is the type of people that a firm attracts and hires. Employees who sought and applied knowledge in school and in early jobs will probably continue to do so. Unfor-

Building a positive knowledge culture is critical.

tunately, the U.S. educational system does not turn out a high proportion of such knowledge-oriented employees. It is possible, of course, to pursue knowledge at the expense of other job objectives, and this might be a downside of an excessively knowledge-oriented culture. We found this type of positive culture in several of the firms we studied—from consulting organizations to high-technology manufacturers to small knowledge-driven organizations like Teltech.

Given the downsizings in many American firms over the past decade, it wouldn't be surprising to find negative attitudes toward knowledge sharing in certain organizational cultures. For example, employees may feel that their knowledge is critical to their unique value as an employee, and thus their continued tenure in the organization. Under these circumstances they may be reluctant to share that knowledge. We found little evidence of this in our sample, perhaps because companies with such cultures might not even attempt a knowledge management project. Still, it would seem to be a factor that could easily lead to the failure of a project.

However, we noted other aspects of culture that did interfere with a project's objectives. At Young & Rubicam, the chief knowledge officer told us that on the creative side of the business, there was great pressure to be dynamic and original. The dominant attitude of "derogating the derivative" thus perpetuated an aversion to sharing and using already-created knowledge. In the advertising industry, trade journals and industry awards reinforce the value of creativity, giving less prestige to work based on campaign efficacy—getting a consumer to buy your client's product or service. In order to get the creative people to share their knowledge with their peers, the firm needed to change its incentive and reward systems.[7] While the CKO is gratified by some of the behavior changes he has observed, it is too early to call this program a success. It remains to be seen if and how internal systems can be changed to overcome the norms and expectations that exist at an institutional level. High-technology firms also struggle mightily with this problem; at a large telecommunications firm we studied, engineers had the "hero" mentality, respecting only individual design achievements. Top engineers viewed it as a sign of weakness to use an existing design, an admission that they couldn't do it themselves.

A third issue is the fit between an organization's culture and its knowledge management initiatives. Projects that don't mesh well with the culture probably won't thrive. At Hewlett-Packard, for example, knowledge management projects are popping up all around the firm, but they are highly decentralized. The firm's culture of highly autonomous business units would not easily support a coordinated, top-down project at the corporate level, or even a corporate-level senior knowledge executive.

Technical and Organizational Infrastructure

Knowledge projects are more likely to succeed when they can take advantage of a broader infrastructure of both technology and organization. Technological infrastructure is the easier of the two to put in place. As Chapter 7 describes in detail, it consists partially of technologies that are knowledge-oriented, such as Lotus Notes and the World Wide Web. If these tools and the skills to use them are already present, a particular initiative will have an easier time getting off the ground. Most of the companies we interviewed employ multiple tools, which we feel is appropriate at this early stage of knowledge management.

Another aspect of technology infrastructure for knowledge management projects is a uniform set of technologies for desktop computing and communications. At the simplest level, this means a capable, networked PC on every desk or in every briefcase, with standardized personal productivity tools (word processing, presentation software) so that documents can be exchanged easily throughout a company. More complex and functional desktop infrastructures can also be the basis of some types of knowledge management projects, as seen in BP's use of videoconferencing technology.

Building an organizational infrastructure for knowledge management means establishing a set of roles, organizational structures, and skills from which individual projects can benefit. The companies we interviewed generally found this difficult to do, perhaps because it involves spending money on new roles. Some firms, however, had been able to establish multiple levels of new roles, from chief knowledge officers to knowledge project managers to knowledge reporters, editors, and knowledge network facilitators. In Ernst & Young's consulting business, for example, there are facilitators of twenty-two different knowledge networks, managers of several new knowledge-oriented organizations that create or distribute knowledge, a CKO, and several new committees to prioritize knowledge projects and set knowledge strategy. Although these new roles and structures are expensive, they mean that any new project can take advantage of them for support and get up and running quickly. We described these organizational roles in detail in Chapter 6.

Senior Management Support

Like almost every other type of change program, knowledge management projects benefit from senior management support. We found that strong support from executives was critical for transformational knowledge projects but less necessary in efforts to use knowledge for improving individual functions or processes. The types of support that were helpful included the following:

- Sending out messages to the organization that knowledge management and organizational learning are critical to the organization's success

- Clearing the way and providing funding for infrastructure

- Clarifying what type of knowledge is most important to the company

We found that the executives who championed knowledge initiatives were themselves relatively cerebral and conceptual. They were well read and well educated, and set the tone for a knowledge-oriented culture.

A Link to Economics or Industry Value

Knowledge management can be expensive and therefore must somehow be linked to economic benefit or industry success. Buckman Laboratories, a specialty chemicals firm, estimates that it spends 2.5 percent of its revenues on knowledge management. Ernst & Young calculates 6 percent of its revenues, and McKinsey & Co., 10 percent. In "knowledge businesses" like these, in which knowledge is

Knowledge management can be linked to economic value.

clearly the key to success with customers, the payoff from projects may indeed be quantifiable. In more conventional businesses, however, the calculation of benefit may need to be made more explicit.

The most impressive benefits of good knowledge management involve money saved or earned. Dow Chemical's focus on better management of company patents produced results that showed up on its balance sheets. Texas Instruments had similar success when it pursued a strategy of increasing revenues through licensing of patents and intellectual property.

Benefit calculations may also be indirect, perhaps through process measures like cycle time, customer satisfaction, or even phone calls avoided. One pharmaceuticals firm we studied was attempting to manage drug development knowledge in order to reduce the cycle time for the process. Several knowledge management projects in the customer support process were attempting to improve customer satisfaction by reducing waiting time for phone support or by providing on-line knowledge. At Hewlett-Packard, for example, a knowledge management system for computer resellers has substantially reduced the number of calls for human support, and hence the number of people necessary to provide it.

A Modicum of Process Orientation

As we mentioned above, the primary objective of some projects we observed was to design a new knowledge management process. Even for other types of projects, however, we feel that adopting aspects of a process perspective is usually advisable. The knowledge project manager should have a good sense of his or her customer, the customer's satisfaction, and the productivity and quality of services offered. However, the project managers in our study did not find it useful in most cases to describe the detailed process steps used in knowledge management. This is consistent with previous findings on improving knowledge work processes (it is perhaps safe to conclude that "knowledge management" is "knowledge work").[8] One firm did take the process approach to a very detailed level, describing one "organizational learning" process, four subprocesses, fifteen sub-subprocesses, and fifty-three sub-sub-subprocesses. One might argue that this is excessive, particularly given that only about 5 percent of the redesigned processes had actually been implemented.

Clarity of Vision and Language

Clarity of purpose and terminology is a critical factor with any type of organizational change project, but it's a particularly important element of good knowledge management. The terms used in this realm—"knowledge," "information," "learning"—are subject to wide interpretation. The concept of "organizational learning," for example, can include everything from the most prosaic training to broad changes in culture.

The successful knowledge management projects we observed had all addressed this issue in some fashion, often by excluding particular terms and concepts from their charters. As noted above, some were careful to exclude the idea of "data." Chrysler, for example, tried to ensure that raw data was not added to its repositories of knowledge about engineering and design of key automobile components by drawing this kind of clear semantic distinction. Other firms excluded the expressions "education and training" or "cultural change" from their project guidelines.

Nontrivial Motivational Aids

Knowledge, being intimately bound up with people's egos and occupations, does not emerge or flow easily. Employees must therefore be motivated to create, share, and use knowledge. These motivational aids or incentives cannot be trivial, as some of our project managers learned. One gave out airline frequent-flyer mileage for browsing or contributing to a discussion database. He found that the free miles were enough to prompt an initial use of the system but insufficient to drive ongoing activity. Another manager of an expert network offered chocolate-covered ice cream bars—admittedly a premium brand—to any expert who contributed a biography to the system. Perhaps needless to say, this incentive was insufficiently motivating.

Motivational approaches for knowledge behaviors should be long-term incentives tied in with the rest of the evaluation and compensation structure. Both Ernst & Young and McKinsey and Co., for example, evaluate consultants partially on the knowledge they contribute to repositories and human networks. If incentives are short-term, they should be highly visible. At

The success of a project may hinge on the long-term incentives a company provides to its employees.

Buckman Laboratories, managers identify the top fifty "knowledge sharers" annually in on-line networks and repositories and reward them with a celebration conference at a resort location.

Some Level of Knowledge Structure

Successful knowledge management projects benefit from some degree—though not too much—of a knowledge structure. Because knowledge is naturally fluid and closely linked to the people who hold it, its categories and meanings change frequently. This means that knowledge will usually be resistant to engineering.

However, if a knowledge repository has no structure at all, it won't be able to serve its purpose. One professional services firm attempted to create a wholly unstructured knowledge repository, searchable on all words in the database. It was virtually unusable, always yielding either too many or too few items. Firms building a knowledge base or expert network must therefore create categories and key terms. It is often useful to devise a thesaurus to assist users as well. At Teltech, for example, a thesaurus of technical terms allows users to browse and search its expert network through terms that are familiar to them. Teltech employees update the system by recording the terms users employ in searches and adding them to the thesaurus daily. Therefore, the structure of the knowledge always reflects the pattern of use. Any knowledge manager should be prepared to redefine the structure of a company's knowledge base frequently.

Multiple Channels for Knowledge Transfer

Successful knowledge managers realize that knowledge is transferred through multiple channels that reinforce each other. Some of the firms that had knowledge repositories realized that they had to get contributors together in a face-to-face setting on a regular basis. In that "high bandwidth" situation, trust can be established, structures for knowledge can be developed, and difficult issues can be resolved. MIT researcher Tom Allen has found in many studies that scientists and engineers exchange knowledge in direct proportion to their level of personal contact.[9] In this day of the Web, Lotus Notes, and systems that cover the world, it is easy to forget the need for a common location. There is still a strong need for what the U.S. Army calls "face time."

Building a Knowledge Foundation

There are doubtless other factors that affect the success of knowledge projects, but firms that address these nine steps are clearly well on their way to succeeding. While it is impossible to prioritize among these nine based on our qualitative observations of the research sites, we do have an intuitive feel for the factors that matter most. Unfortunately, they also tend to be the factors that are most difficult to develop: a knowledge-oriented culture, human infrastructure, and senior management support (particularly for transformational objectives). Obviously, these circumstances are related. A senior management team that is committed to knowledge management will probably already have created some aspects of a knowledge-oriented culture, and is likely to be open to the idea of establishing an organizational infrastructure for knowledge management. Lacking all three of these conditions, a firm should only begin knowledge management on a small scale, with objectives involving efficiency or effectiveness of a single knowledge-oriented function or process.

Knowledge managers should also consider carefully the sequence in which they take on these objectives. There may be a life cycle to building effective knowledge management practices and processes. As with physical construction, a firm must first build a foundation. While not value-adding in and of itself—no one ever lived in a foundation—a certain amount of infrastructure helps to create value later. Knowledge environment projects establish the conditions necessary for subsequent knowledge-leveraging projects to thrive.

How Are Knowledge Projects Different?

Managers are becoming increasingly familiar with change programs of various types, and certainly some of the success factors described above are similar to those of information systems projects, reengineering projects, empowerment programs, and so forth. As a concluding topic we focus on how knowledge management projects differ from other familiar types.

All projects benefit from senior management support, but the attributes of senior managers who support knowledge projects vary in our research. In general, though, they are more given to conceptual thinking and have an implicit faith that knowledge management will benefit their organizations (although they usually also want to see measurements of the benefit where possible). Several of the CEOs in the firms we studied made public comments such as, "We're in the knowledge business."

All projects benefit from a sympathetic organizational culture, but they do not require the intensively knowledge-oriented culture we found in successful knowledge projects. All projects may profit from a process orientation, but the limits to the value of process in knowledge projects tend to be more pronounced. Information systems projects in particular have in common with knowledge projects the need for a combination of technical and human elements. However, in the knowledge management initiatives we observed, the level of human issues and problems was much higher than for most data or information management projects. Because of the prominent human element in knowledge, a flexible, evolving structure for knowledge is desirable. Furthermore, the motivational factors in creating, sharing, and using knowledge are critical. Data and information are constantly transferred electronically, but knowledge seems to travel most efficiently through a human network.

As we have noted throughout this book, successful knowledge management requires an unusual combination of human, technical, and economic skills. These attributes must be present not only in a firm's overall knowledge management effort but also in individual projects. It's often difficult to round up or inculcate them all into a project team, but it can be done. One of the encouraging aspects of the knowledge management projects we studied is that half of them appeared to be successful already, and perhaps an even higher proportion will ultimately succeed. That so many projects are going well at such an early stage in the history of knowledge management bodes well for the long-term prospects of the movement.

The great end of knowledge
is not knowledge but action.
    —Thomas Henry Huxley

9

The Pragmatics of Knowledge
Management

AFTER ENDURING many pages of our pontifications about
knowledge management, you're probably more than ready to get started.
If your knowledge management efforts have been underway for a while,
perhaps something we've said has helped to renew or refocus your
commitment. In any case, you're undoubtedly ready for some strictly
pragmatic advice about knowledge management—where to start, how
to get help, mistakes to avoid. In this concluding chapter we'll discuss
several entry points into knowledge management, "anchors" in existing
management approaches, and a few common pitfalls.

Common Sense about Knowledge Management

The good news about knowledge management is that good sense goes
a long way. If you sit down and think carefully about it, you'll probably
deduce such wisdom as:

- The place to start is with high-value knowledge.

- Start with a focused pilot project and let demand drive additional initiatives.

- Work along multiple fronts at once (technology, organization, culture).

- Don't put off what gives you the most trouble until it's too late.

- Get help throughout the organization as quickly as possible.

We will resist the tendency in management books to tell you that
knowledge management is totally new, that you must drop everything
else and adopt our nostrum, and that you can't possibly do it without

lots of high-priced help. First of all, it's not totally new. Knowledge management draws from existing resources that your organization may already have in place—good information systems management, organizational change management, and human resources management practices. If you've got a good library, a textual database system, or even effective education programs, your company is probably already doing something that might be called knowledge management. All you may need to do is expand or improve those practices to call yourself a knowledge manager.

You may recall some other managerial enthusiasms that required devotees to drop everything else. "Forget quality, it's time to reengineer." "Forget reengineering, it's time to think about competing for the future." Well, forget that. Knowledge management coexists well with business strategy, with process management, with staying close to your customers, and so forth. It can help you do a variety of things you're already doing better. Ultimately, knowledge management work needs to be blended in with these other activities or it's unlikely to be effective.

And, although both of us consult for some part of our livings, we wouldn't say that it's impossible to do a good job of managing knowledge without help from consultants. In general, a company has to make its own decisions about what knowledge is most important to manage, how to motivate people to share and use knowledge, and what will make a project succeed in its own specific environment. Consultants can help with designing and building big knowledge systems, mapping knowledge in some detail, assessing the current state of knowledge, and educating managers and workers about the fundamentals. While many people hire consultants because of the ideas they bring to a project, our view is that ideas are cheap (you've just bought a bunch in this book at about a dime each). It's the actual implementation of knowledge management projects that's the hard part, and we'd argue that it may make more sense to turn outside for help in implementation of a project than in its design.

It also is sensible to look broadly for help inside the organization. As we pointed out in Chapter 6, it's useful to have some dedicated roles within the organization, but for knowledge management to prosper everyone has to help out. Even if your firm has established a formal knowledge function, there will be many other sources of potential assistance from other functions. Information Systems can help with the technology infrastructure. Human Resources can help to motivate workers to share and use knowledge, and to identify knowledge nodes—individuals, teams, and networks. Finance and Accounting can help figure out how to value knowledge and the efforts to manage it. Other functions can help in mastering particular knowledge domains: Marketing and Sales with customer knowledge, Engineering and R&D with product knowledge, and Customer Service with service knowledge. When you're trying to manage knowledge, it's no time to be exclusionary; the more people and groups that buy into the effort, the more likely you'll be successful.

Getting Started in Knowledge Management

We subscribe to the belief that it's better to accomplish something first and then talk about it than the reverse. Many reengineering initiatives we've observed, for example, were sidetracked when the hype about what they were going to accomplish raised expectations well beyond what was actually possible. So in knowledge management, it's important to start small, actually accomplish something, and

Don't talk up your project until you have something worth talking about.

then trumpet what's been achieved.[1] Don't publish a newsletter, produce a video, or angle for your project's inclusion in the annual report until you have actually done something worth talking about.

Knowledge management should start with a recognized business problem that relates to knowledge. Customer defections, poorly designed products, losses of key personnel, or a lower "win rate" for service engagements are all business problems that might be traced to poor knowledge management.[2] Attacking these problems, identifying their knowledge component, and using the business value of solving them as justification for knowledge efforts are all good ways to get around in managing knowledge.

The most important factors in deciding where to start are the importance of the specific knowledge domain to the firm and the feasibility of the project. For example, customer knowledge is obviously central to most organizations, and offers obvious and high potential payoffs. If this is a weak link in your firm, perhaps it's a good starting point. But if you feel that it's so sensitive or difficult a problem that you'll never succeed, break off a piece of it. Try to manage the knowledge about "national accounts" or customers of a particular product or business unit. Then you can expand later to add knowledge of other types of customers. Perhaps needless to say, don't pick a knowledge domain just because it's handy or under your control. If you're the head of IT as well as a knowledge management enthusiast, don't try to manage, for example, IT support knowledge as your first project (unless that's the business of your company, as might be the case in an IT outsourcing firm). Even if you succeeded, no one would pay much attention.

Knowledge management can also involve a lot of abstract activity that may not ultimately pay off in terms of changed behaviors and tangible results. Knowledge mapping, for example, can consume substantial time and money, particularly when it is carried out with a high level of detail. Just as many elaborate "enterprise data models" were never applied in the development of information systems, highly detailed and complex knowledge maps may exceed the ability of the organization to use them. Here it is extremely important to start small—create a knowledge map with minimal detail in a fairly circumscribed knowledge domain. In other words, do just enough to test the concept. If individuals find it useful and begin to refer to it regularly, you can create more detail and expand the scope later.

To make headway with knowledge management, it's generally advisable to do a number of things along multiple fronts—technical, organizational, cultural—rather than to focus on a single topic. Knowledge is too complex a phenomenon to entrust to narrowly targeted change programs. The drawback to adopting multifaceted programs, however, is that seeing change will take longer, and results may be less obvious than they would with a single-focus initiative.

Leveraging Existing Approaches

We mentioned a few paragraphs back that knowledge management had its roots in other areas, and that it is folly to pretend that it's new. Whenever possible, firms should try to use existing management approaches and tactics as levers to assist in getting going with knowledge management. Existing initiatives and programs can jump-start knowledge management because many of them have better management of what the organization knows as an important component. Virtually every large or medium-sized organization will have one of the types of programs described below already underway.

Leading with Technology

Most firms make their first move with knowledge management in the domain of technology. They install Notes or an intranet Web, and then start searching for content to distribute with these tools. Throughout this book we've cautioned against a technology-centered knowledge management approach, but we've also argued that a technology infrastructure is a necessary ingredient for successful knowledge projects. It's also true that most firms implement knowledge-oriented software to serve other purposes as well (e-mail, data or information display, and so forth). So it's not that starting knowledge management with technology is a waste of time; you'll have to do it eventually.

However, if you're implementing new technology just for the purpose of knowledge management, it may be a waste of money. The knowledge behaviors you're seeking from users of knowledge systems may be slow to emerge. Getting content into those systems can also take a while. Setting up an organizational infrastructure for knowledge management—a necessary step if you want to build up your knowledge capital—may require hiring new people, training them in new skills, and creating new processes and procedures. Since the market value of, say, a powerful server for a knowledge repository decreases at about 7 percent a month, you may be better off buying the computers and software after you've gotten the other things in place. Unfortunately, it's usually much harder to get organizational consensus for behavior change and new roles than it is for technology—and if you start with technology, the other necessary factors may never materialize.

Implementing knowledge management through new technology can be a risky proposition.

One example of a firm that led its knowledge management efforts with technology is Andersen Consulting. Despite the cautions above, the firm has been largely successful with this approach, which still centers on its "Knowledge Xchange" (KX) system. In the late 1980s Andersen began to lay the technological foundations for knowledge management. It adopted Lotus Notes and the Microsoft Office tools so that consultants could share and use documents around the world. Starting with senior partners, consultants were given laptops and the training to use them. In addition to the KX system, more and more applications were added to the Notes platform, including a time and expense reporting system and a personnel evaluation system.

After putting the technology in place, Andersen began to create more knowledge manager roles, to develop new knowledge navigation tools, and to modify reward and compensation structures to motivate knowledge sharing and use by individual consultants. The firm already had a culture oriented to sharing, so that wasn't a problem. However, as one partner put it, "When you're already asking someone to work an eighty-hour week, it takes more than a sharing culture to motivate him to hop onto the KX at 11 P.M. in a hotel room and share what he learned that day." Andersen Consulting is a technology-oriented firm, of course, and a technology-first approach would work better there than in most organizations. What's most important, however, is that Andersen didn't stop at technology but also addressed the other issues that count.

Leading with Quality/Reengineering/Best Practices

Perhaps the second most popular approach to getting started with knowledge management is to build on a company's quality or reengineering efforts. A common objective of such process change programs is to compile and leverage "best practices," or effective ways to perform a process or subprocess that have been identified inside or outside the company. These best practices are often stored in electronic repositories for sharing around the organization, and thus can become the nucleus of a knowledge management initiative.

At Texas Instruments, for example, sharing best practices became a strong focus after the concept was strongly endorsed by Jerry Junkins, then the firm's CEO. "We cannot tolerate having world-class performance right next to mediocre performance simply because we don't have a method to implement best practices," he noted in a 1994 address.[3] In response to Junkins's exhortation, the company developed a common set of terms and methods around best practices sharing called the TI Business Excellence Standard (TI-BEST). Early best practices sharing across the firm's thirteen semiconductor fabrication plants (known as "fabs") had substantially reduced cycle time and performance variability, leading to capacity improvements equal to building a new fab.

To extend best practices sharing across the entire firm, Texas Instruments formed an Office of Best Practices staffed by employees with backgrounds in IT management, reengineering, and quality. The office focused initially on building the supply of best practices, contacting those with expertise and documenting their knowledge in a "card catalogue" of best practices information. The cards—originally on paper, later computerized—included a brief description of the practice and the problem it solved, improvement measures, and information about which TI employees to contact for more details. Each card was referenced by its key words, the business process it involved, and TI's internal criteria for "world-class" status. The goal was not to specify all the needed knowledge about a best practice but rather to provide enough information to allow an interested TI employee to "qualify" the practice and contact the expert for more details.

The Office of Best Practices realized that their efforts alone would not be sufficient to facilitate the identification and transfer of best practices, so they took other steps to build an organizational and technical infrastructure. They identified 138 TI employees around the world as part-time Best Practices Sharing Facilitators to find and document best practices in their areas, to communicate them in personal interactions, and to promote the use of sharing tools. TI gave each facilitator a day of training on such "knowledge broker" skills as interviewing, categorizing, documenting, and searching. TI also created a "Best Practices Knowledgebase" on Lotus Notes that contained the catalogue, a discussion database, and external best practices and benchmarks. The Office of Best Practices also developed an intranet Web site for broader access within TI. As mentioned in Chapter 3, the firm held a "ShareFair" in 1996 at which the first annual "Not Invented Here, But I Did It Anyway" award was presented. Fifty-two nominations were submitted, with savings cited of over a billion dollars. (We are waiting for a company to create an award named after the Spanish proverb "Well stolen is half done.")

Despite the success at Texas Instruments (and at other firms starting knowledge management with best practices, including Chevron and Citicorp), we believe that too strong a focus on best practices knowledge can be limiting. There are many other types of knowledge that can be shared in organizations: customer, product, and technical knowledge come to mind immediately. It's a great idea to use best practices as a springboard to other forms of knowledge management, but this can be problematic if they are viewed as the only form of knowledge worth collecting and sharing. Moreover, firms should not underestimate the difficulties of importing best practices from one part of the organization to another—or even more so, from another company. Best practices may be so contextual and specific to an organization that they don't "take" in their new environment. Finally, best practices–oriented knowledge management programs deal only with articulated and documented practices. More tacit knowledge about how work is done is not easily summarized into a best practice, and broader knowledge management initiatives are usually required to incorporate certain kinds of complex expertise into organizational knowledge.

Leading with Organizational Learning

To begin knowledge management with a focus on organizational learning would be a good idea, but firms rarely do so. Depending on what school of organizational learning to which an organization subscribes, the concepts and approaches involved may include:

- Thinking about the organization as a "system."
- Building and facilitating communities of learning and practice.
- Focusing on issues of personal development and "mastery."
- Creating less hierarchical, more "self-organizing" organizational structures.
- Planning with the use of scenarios.

Each of these concepts has value as a means of advancing knowledge management. Since they largely address cultural and behavioral issues, which are often the hardest to change, they may be a more appropriate initial focus than relatively easy-to-fix problems like technology. But it is rare for organizational learning initiatives to lead to knowledge management because many learning-oriented organizations ignore the possibilities for structuring and leveraging knowledge. Only a few firms, such as Coca-Cola and Monsanto, are working simultaneously on organizational learning issues and the more tangible knowledge management problems.

Peter Senge, the influential author of *The Fifth Discipline*, has argued recently that organizations seeking to manage knowledge have placed too much emphasis on information technology and information management.[4] We agree. However, the world of organizational learning places too little emphasis on structured knowledge and the use of technology to capture and leverage it. In fact, the word "knowledge" may appear somewhere in Senge's thoughtful book, but it is not in the index. We believe that without an approach to managing structured knowledge, organizational learning is too conceptual and abstract to make a long-term difference to organizations.

Therefore, we can say that taking the organizational learning route to knowledge management is similar in one respect to the other starting points. It's an important component of knowledge management success—maybe even more so than others. But by itself it's insufficient.

Leading with Decision Making

What makes knowledge valuable to organizations is ultimately the ability to make better the decisions and actions taken on the basis of the knowledge. If knowledge doesn't improve decision making, then what's the point of managing it? For this reason, a few organizations are taking a decision-oriented approach to knowledge management. They are attempting to monitor and track "who knows what when" to determine how knowledge is reflected in specific decisions.

While we admire the effort to link knowledge to decisions, it's a tricky business for at least two reasons. First, it's just very difficult to link specific knowledge or even information to specific decision outcomes. As James March, the eminent scholar of organizational decision making, has pointed out, this "rational" view of knowledge and decisions means that the analyst needs very good information indeed: "Determining the optimal information strategy, code, investment, or structure requires complete information about information options, quality, processing, and comprehension requirements. It requires a precise specification of preferences that resolve complicated tradeoffs over time and space."[5] Such circumstances are, of course, rarely present in real life.

Even if we are aware of all that was going on in the decision maker's head, there's another problem with linking knowledge to decisions— politics. We've often mused, for example, that one way to determine the value of knowledge would be the same way organizations measure the value of quality—by calculating what it costs when it's absent. Just as the value of quality is really the cost of poor quality, the value of knowledge equals the cost of stupidity. Just think of all the poor decisions managers have made in our organization, and how much richer the firm would be if the right knowledge had been applied to those decisions! Then think of how short your career would be in the organization if you attempted to measure the cost of stupidity! Senior managers, in particular, might balk at the idea of examining their decisions in detail to understand what knowledge they applied and how the decision turned out.

There are exceptions, however. The U.S. Army examines the relationship between knowledge and decisions in the context of its "After Action Reviews" (AAR). Both enlisted soldiers and officers are asked what they knew about a situation and how they decided to act based on their knowledge. The army considers the link between knowledge and decision making to be a critical aspect of learning from experience. However, as we discussed in Chapter 1, the army has developed an admirable culture that allows for this type of discussion without blame or recrimination. A key assumption of the AAR is that the highest level of learning results when mistakes are made and acknowledged. The army is also scrupulous about separating anything that happens in an AAR from career-evaluation processes. If your organization has this type of culture, then tying knowledge to decision making makes a lot of sense. If it doesn't, watch out for politics.

General Motors is the largest corporation that is attempting to link knowledge and decisions (of course, it's also the largest corporation, period). Due largely to the efforts of market researcher and information manager Vince Barabba, GM is actually interviewing managers to learn what knowledge they used when making key decisions. Barabba also established a process several years ago specifying the types of information and knowledge that engineers should use in making new car development decisions.[6] Although GM is still in the early stages of linking knowledge and decisions, Barabba reports no political problems yet from managers objecting to having their decisions examined.

Leading with Accounting

It's no secret that accounting systems are a poor reflection of the intangible and intellectual assets of corporations. A few firms have grown sufficiently impatient with this situation to create their own internal accounting for knowledge and intellectual capital. As we've mentioned, the insurance company Skandia has been the most aggressive adopter of this approach. Leif Edvinsson, the firm's Director of Intellectual Capital, has become a strong advocate of changing accounting systems to reflect intellectual capital. He has even written a book on the subject.[7] He has also convened other firms with the purpose of beginning to change the accounting system in Western economies.

While we agree with Edvinsson and others that the accounting system needs work, we don't recommend this area as a place to start managing knowledge. We don't see much evidence that accounting systems and practices are going to change anytime soon, and for an individual company to adopt such change as a cause would be a Sisyphian exercise. Even firms such as Microsoft that clearly have substantially more knowledge capital than physical capital are not advocates of overhauling the system.[8]

Selecting the Right Anchor

In deciding where to anchor your knowledge management approach, it's important to lead with a style that is consistent with the firm's culture. Some firms are strongly technology-based (for example, IBM or Andersen Consulting), and hence it's reasonable for them to build knowledge management on top of technology initiatives and plans. Other

Take a hard look at your culture before launching a knowledge initiative.

firms will be more oriented to finance and accounting, to quality, or to organizational change programs. What may be appealing conceptually as an anchor for knowledge management may not in reality fit the culture. Therefore, knowledge managers should spend some time assessing their organization's culture before deciding the foundation on which to base a knowledge management effort.[9]

If you want knowledge management to thrive and become institutionalized, your organization must ultimately adopt multiple "anchors" for knowledge management. Any of the approaches described above may be sufficient to get a knowledge initiative off the ground, but keeping it in the air will require the support and skills of many different groups around the company. No single approach will give it the institutional base that it needs to prosper over time.

Knowledge Management Pitfalls

Despite the value of good management sense in knowledge management, we see many organizations that have gone astray. We will devote the rest of the chapter, then, to describing the most common pitfalls firms encounter in the knowledge management business. We usually know that a company has lost its way when we hear a concise sentence or two that sums up an entire knowledge management problem syndrome. Since these catchphrases often take the form of "conventional wisdom," we'd like to rebut them one by one, and point out why you shouldn't fall for them. We've referred to some of these misconceptions elsewhere in the book, but having all our caveats listed in one place may be useful. Like all myths, the fact that each expression has some element of truth makes them even more seductive.

If We Build It . . .

They won't come. At least, your building it has little to do with whether they will come or not. "It," of course, is an information-based system for storing and distributing knowledge. You can buy as many Notes or Netscape licenses as you want; you can create a very attractive Web page; you can even put some Java-based interactive applications on your system—but it doesn't mean anyone will use or get value out of your investments in technology and sophisticated programming.

Remember our $33\frac{1}{3}$ rule: if you're spending more than a third of your time, effort, and money on technology, you're neglecting the other factors that will help them to come—the content, the organizational culture, the motivational approaches, and so forth. Almost every day we see implementations of Lotus Notes that can't get beyond e-mail, or intranet-based knowledge repositories to which no one will contribute their knowledge. We've made this point often, and that's because an excessive focus on technology is the most common pitfall in knowledge management. When firms take their eyes off knowledge, they default to technology because it's easier to buy, implement, and measure.

Let's Put the Personnel Manual On-line!

This failure syndrome sounds something like the following: "Now that we've got our Intranet up and running, we've got to populate it with knowledge. Gee, how about the personnel manual, the procedures manual, our cafeteria menus, and the campus shuttle bus schedule?" We cringe. The Web and Notes are exciting technologies. Were they developed for this?

We'll grudgingly admit that digitizing this boring content has some efficiency advantages, and we're as much in favor of saving trees as anyone. But don't call it knowledge, and don't call the system on which you install these yawn-inducing tomes a knowledge management system. Simply putting your paper documents on-line will weaken your terminological currency, and should you later decide to put some real knowledge into this repository, no one will notice. Let's use the technologies that have sparked the rise of knowledge management to store and disseminate real value-added, insight-laden, wisdom-inducing knowledge. Be aggressive and vehement in arguing for worthwhile content. Your knowledge base will grow more slowly, but no one will chuckle when you call it that.

None Dare Call It Knowledge

As most of us learn quickly enough in grade school, we live in an anti-intellectual society. In companies where a few lonely individuals are pursuing knowledge management, the concession to know-nothingism often sounds something like this: "We're afraid to use the term "knowledge" because everyone in the company is so pragmatic. So we call it 'best practices.'" There is a certain logic in trying to adapt to the dominant culture, but we think it's self-defeating to try to conceal what you're doing by calling it something else. If the word "knowledge" is suspect in your organization, your knowledge management program probably won't succeed anyway.

Here's why it's a bad idea to refer to knowledge as "best practices," "benchmarks," "information resources," or whatever pragmatic euphemism your boss happens to prefer. First of all, none of these terms do justice to the entire domain of knowledge. If you call it "best practices," for example, how about the knowledge of a customer's business situation and needs that involve no "practice" at all? If you call it something related to information, you'll be dragged back into the corporate information systems morass that really involves data.

More importantly, the inability to use the word "knowledge" suggests that the senior management of your firm doesn't buy into the big idea behind knowledge management—that what people know and can learn more valuable than any other business resource. Eventually these philistines will cut back the funding for your Information Resource Center or your Best Practices Database when they find out what you're really up to.

So we say call it what it is, and false down-to-earth American pragmatism be damned. Spend your time arguing about the worth of knowledge up front, rather than fighting rearguard skirmishes later. And if your company doesn't like the word "knowledge," put "knowledge manager" proudly on your resume and look for one that does.

Don't be afraid to put "knowledge manager" on your resume.

Every Man a Knowledge Manager

This problem relates to the last. The telling remark here goes something like, "We think knowledge management is everybody's job. So we're not going to build up some big staff organization of knowledge managers to do the work everyone should be doing." Obviously this misconception has more than a grain of truth in it, or we wouldn't have said something similar to it in Chapter 6. It should be everyone's job to create, share, and use knowledge—to some degree.

Let's face reality here. Every engineer in your organization should be creating and using new product development knowledge. But not every engineer can or will do a good job at writing down what he or she knows. Every person should reflect on life, but not everyone can write poems or novels about their musings. Knowledge management will not succeed if there are no workers and managers whose primary jobs involve extracting and editing knowledge from those who have it, facilitating knowledge networks, and setting up and managing knowledge technology infrastructures.

The next time someone says this to us, we plan to retort: "So since it's also everybody's job to monitor costs and enhance revenues, you've also eliminated the finance and accounting organizations?"

Justification by Faith

This one's a little less common than the others, but just as false. We know it's in effect when we hear, "Our CEO is a big believer in knowledge management. So we don't feel the need to justify our knowledge management work with numbers or anecdotes—we've got faith!" Well, faith may propel us into Heaven, but it won't help us keep our knowledge manager jobs for long. Every week or two we run into a former manager of reengineering, whose boss previously had faith in that concept—and these people are looking for jobs today.

Even if your senior management team is gung-ho about knowledge, the crunch will eventually come. A new CEO will come in, the company will have a bad quarter, some hot new fad will come along. And a powerful person will utter the fateful words, "Exactly what are all these knowledge managers doing for us?"

So even if no one is interested today, start trying to measure the worth of what you do. If possible, convert the knowledge you manage into cold, hard figures, cash that the company has made or saved because they were fortunate enough to have you as a knowledge manager. If this seems impossible (though remember, even accountants get creative these days), do some serious "anecdote management," with sworn testimony from the regional sales manager that, "This sale would not have gone through without the knowledge in your Xpert Xchange." Consider reprinting these remarks in your monthly newsletter. If your company frowns on internal boosterism, keep these numbers and anecdotes in your drawer until you need them.

Restricted Access

Here is another fateful catchphrase: "Our focus is on creating better access to our knowledge." The authors of this book are perhaps alone in the world in their distaste for the term "access." We feel that access is oversold, overblown, overdone. Do you really think that the reason no one ever looked at the market research reports was because they had to walk up a flight of stairs to get to them? That the sales force didn't consult white papers on product performance because they had to make a phone call to get a copy?

Try not to get mesmerized by the mantra of "access."

Sure, it's amazing how lazy we all can be, and we've seen the research suggesting that certain types of workers (engineers are the most notorious) will travel only a few furlongs to seek needed knowledge. Better access does increase the likelihood that knowledge sources will be consulted. But it's just the first step, and often the easiest one.

The next time someone on your project team uses the A-word, speak up with some substitutes. How about "attention"—as in how do we get anybody to pay attention to what we're doing? How about "appetite"—is anyone really hungry for our knowledge? Why not "affiliation"—a bit of a circumlocution, but how can we get people to feel sufficiently loyal and trustful to share their knowledge with the rest of their co-workers?

Bottoms Up!

In some organizations, one hears this sort of spiel: "Knowledge management isn't a hierarchical thing in our company. We don't need senior management approval; they're not the ones with the knowledge anyway. Knowledge is flattening the organization chart, making our organization more democratic." These are often the companies where we read later that the CEO in this supposedly flat company has engineered himself a very large number of stock options.

For thousands of years knowledge has been strongly associated with hierarchy, and we see no evidence that things are any different today. Those who know have power; those who have power will have control over who knows what. Knowledge management is a highly political undertaking. You'll have to tread lightly in giving access (there's that word again) to knowledge to those who formerly lacked it. Or you will almost certainly run afoul of someone powerful to whom your knowledge management activities are threatening.

A slight variation on this syndrome is the false notion that knowledge management can thrive without support from senior executives. True, you might be able to build a small knowledge repository in some out-of-the-way domain like purchasing or the research lab without senior management's support. But it's impossible to "transform our company through knowledge management" unless the CEO and his or her management team is standing on the front lines of knowledge management with you.

A Last Word

There are undoubtedly other problem syndromes we could discuss, but we believe it's important to keep the list fairly short. Then it will be a bit easier to catch yourself before falling into these relatively few common pitfalls. We also don't want to imply that knowledge management is fraught with peril. This is not rocket science (in fact, an executive at the Jet Propulsion Laboratory once told us that even rocket science isn't that hard anymore). It's good sense and managerial basics. As long as you work along multiple fronts and don't believe that any one tool or approach is the answer to knowledge management success, your knowledge management effort has a good chance of thriving. Then your organization will be able to say truthfully that it really is managing its most valuable asset.

Just as balance is necessary in using different approaches to knowledge management, balance is required in trading off knowledge management with other change approaches and with simply getting the day-to-day work done in an organization. If success in business is a mix of learning and doing, we must be careful not to spend too much time acquiring and managing knowledge for its own sake. Knowledge and learning must always serve the broader aims of the organization. Otherwise it becomes at worst a liability and at best a distraction. Just as we shouldn't undertake any action without examining what can be learned from it, we shouldn't learn anything without relating it to practice. A healthy tension between knowledge and action is the key to organizational (and probably individual) success.

Notes

Introduction

1. See, for example, Richard Rumelt, ed., *Fundamental Issues in Strategy* (Boston: Harvard Business School Press, 1993); Giovanni Dosi and Franco Materba, eds., *Organization and Strategy in the Evolution of the Enterprise* (London: Macmillan, 1996); and Cynthia Montgomery, ed., *Resource-based and Evolutionary Theories of the Firm* (Boston: Kluwer, 1995).

2. The first modern economist to analyze these and related knowledge issues was Fritz Machlup. See his three-volume *Knowledge: Its Creation, Distribution, and Economic Significance* (Princeton, N.J.: Princeton University Press, 1980–84). A book edited by Machlup, *The Study of Information: Interdisciplinary Messages* (New York: Wiley, 1983), is a fine and still useful collection of expert essays on information and knowledge.

3. The best summarizations of the fad problem are in Robert Eccles and Nitin Nohria, with James Berkeley, *Beyond the Hype: Rediscovering the Essence of Management* (Boston: Harvard Business School Press, 1992), and in Eileen Shapiro, *Fad Surfing in the Boardroom* (Reading, Mass.: Addison-Wesley, 1995).

4. The results of that work can be read about in James McGee and Laurence Prusak, *Managing Information Strategically* (New York: Wiley, 1992); Thomas H. Davenport, *Process Innovation* (Boston: Harvard Business School Press, 1993); and Thomas H. Davenport with Larry Prusak, *Information Ecology* (New York, Oxford University Press, 1997).

5. Sidney G. Winter, "On Coase, Competence, and the Corporation," in *The Nature of the Firm,* ed. Oliver Williamson and Sidney Winter (Oxford University Press, 1994), 189.

6. See, for example, books published in 1997 by Tom Stewart (Doubleday Currency) and Leif Edvinsson and Michael Malone (HarperCollins), both entitled *Intellectual Capital.* For a more academic collection of essays on the subject, see Georg von Krogh and Johan Roos, eds., *Managing Knowledge* (London: Sage, 1996). For a collection of articles on knowledge management tools, see Rudy L. Ruggles III, ed., *Knowledge Management Tools* (Boston: Butterworth-Heinemann, 1996). Similar collections on knowledge management and organizational design are Paul Myers, ed., *Knowledge Management and Organizational Design*

(Boston: Butterworth-Heinemann, 1996) and Larry Prusak, *Knowledge in Organizations* (Boston: Butterworth-Heinemann, 1997).

Chapter 1

1. Alan M. Webber, "What's So New About the New Economy?" *Harvard Business Review* (January–February 1993): 27.

2. If you're interested in pursuing the idea of wisdom, see Robert J. Sternberg, ed., *Wisdom: Its Nature, Origins, and Development* (New York: Cambridge University Press, 1989).

3. We know that data is a plural noun, but we've chosen to use the more popular singular usage.

4. Information about CALL comes from a study by Lloyd Baird, John Henderson, and Stephanie Watts of the Boston University School of Management and from a book by Gordon R. Sullivan and Michael Harper, *Hope Is Not a Method* (New York: Random House, 1996).

5. Witness, for example, the contrast between how Richard Pascale (no Tolstoy, but an astute observer of people and organizations) described Honda's entry into the U.S. market and how it was described by consultants and other strategists. This debate is chronicled in "CMR Forum: The 'Honda Effect' Revisited," *California Management Review* (Summer 1996): 78–117.

6. Karl E. Weick, *Sensemaking in Organizations* (Thousand Oaks, Calif.: Sage Publications, 1995), 34–35.

7. Karl Weick, "Cosmos vs. Chaos: Sense and Nonsense in Electronic Contexts," *Organizational Dynamics* (Autumn 1985): 57.

8. Ikujiro Nonaka and Hirotaka Takeuchi, *The Knowledge-Creating Company* (New York: Oxford University Press, 1995), 58.

9. Thomas H. Davenport, "Saving IT's Soul: Human-Centered Information Management," *Harvard Business Review* (March–April 1994): 121.

10. Three recent volumes make these points with extensive evidence and analysis. Organization for Economic Cooperation and Development, *Employment and Growth in the Knowledge-Based Economy* (Paris: OECD, 1996); Peter Howitt, ed., *The Implications of Knowledge-Based Growth for Micro-Economic Policies* (Calgary: University of Calgary Press, 1996); Gunnar Eliasson, ed., *The Knowledge-Based Information Economy* (Stockholm: Industrial Institute for Economic and Social Research, 1996).

11. Webber, "What's So New About the New Economy?" 26.

12. Quoted in Nonaka and Takeuchi, *The Knowledge-Creating Company,* 7.

13. Emily Thornton, "Japan Lays Off Its Robots," *Far Eastern Economic Review* (Hong Kong, March 21, 1996). Reprinted in *World Press Review* (July 1996): 31–32.

14. Lee Berton, "Many Firms Cut Staff in Accounts Payable and Pay a Steep Price," *Wall Street Journal,* September 5, 1996, 1, 6.

15. Quoted in Richard Tanner Pascale, *Managing on the Edge* (New York: Touchstone, 1990).

16. Webber, "What's So New About the New Economy?" 26–27.

17. Liz Seymour, "Custom Tailored for Service: VF Corporation," *Hemispheres* (March 1996): 26–27.

18. Debra M. Amidon Rogers, "Analog Devices Invests in Intellectual Assets," *Knowledge Inc.,* June 1996, 3.

19. Paul M. Romer, "Two Strategies for Economic Development: Using Ideas and Producing Ideas," Proceedings of the World Bank Annual Conference on Development Economics, The World Bank, 1993, 64.

20. This has been illustrated with respect to a knowledge-oriented system in M. Lynne Markus and Mark Keil, "If We Build It, They Will Come: Designing Information Systems that Users Want to Use," *Sloan Management Review* (Summer 1994): 11–25.

21. This issue is well illustrated in Wanda Orlikowski, "Learning from Notes: Organizational Issues in Groupware Implementation," in *Knowledge Management Tools,* ed. Rudy L. Ruggles III (Boston: Butterworth-Heinemann, 1996), 231–246.

22. Nonaka and Takeuchi, *The Knowledge-Creating Company,* 115.

Chapter 2

1. It is actually what economists call a "quasi market," since its transactions cannot be enforced by formal contracts.

2. See White's comments in Richard Swedborg, ed., *Economics and Sociology* (Princeton, N.J.: Princeton University Press, 1994).

3. This concept of search is slightly modified from James March and Herbert Simon's *Organizations* (Oxford: Blackwell, 1993) and many subsequent works based on their insights.

4. See Thomas H. Davenport, Robert G. Eccles, and Larry Prusak, "Information Politics," *Sloan Management Review* (Fall 1992): 53–65.

5. Michael L. Tushman and Thomas Scanlan, "Characteristics and External Orientations of Boundary Spanning Individuals," *Academy of Management Journal* 24, no. 1 (1981): 83–98.

6. For the importance of gossip to organizations, see James March, "Gossip, Information, and Decision-Making," in his collection *Decisions and Organizations* (Oxford: Blackwell, 1988).

7. See Jim Matarazzo, *Closing the Corporate Library* (Washington, D.C.: Special Libraries Association, 1987).

8. An interesting analysis of trust as an economic and social value is Francis Fukayama's *Trust* (New York: Free Press, 1995).

9. John Seely Brown and Paul Duguid, "Organizational Learning and Communities-of-Practice: Toward a Unified View of Working, Learning, and Innovation," *Organization Science*, no. 1 (February 1991): 40–57.

10. March and Simon, *Organizations*.

11. Ikujiro Nonaka and Hirotaka Takeuchi, *The Knowledge-Creating Company* (New York: Oxford University Press, 1995), 81.

12. See Carlos Cipolla, *Guns, Sails, and Empire* (Lawrence, Kansas: Sunflower Books, 1984).

13. For a full description of this concept, see David J. Teece, Richard Rumelt, Giovanni Dosi, and Sidney Winter, "Understanding Corporate Coherence," *Journal of Economic Behavior and Organization* 23 (1994): 1–30.

14. Quoted by Karl Weick, *Sensemaking in Organizations* (Thousand Oaks, Calif.: Sage Publications, 1995), 38.

15. Nonaka and Takeuchi, *The Knowledge-Creating Company*, 75.

16. Nonaka and Takeuchi, *The Knowledge-Creating Company*, 173.

Chapter 3

1. Thomas H. Davenport, Sirkka L. Jarvenpaa, and Michael C. Beers, "Improving Knowledge Work Processes," *Sloan Management Review* (Summer 1996): 53–65.

2. Ikujiro Nonaka and Hirotaka Takeuchi, *The Knowledge-Creating Company* (New York: Oxford University Press, 1995); Dorothy Leonard-Barton, *Wellsprings of Knowledge*, (Boston: Harvard Business School Press, 1995).

3. A thorough analysis of this type of acquisition is provided in Joseph Badaracco, Jr., *The Knowledge Link* (Boston: Harvard Business School Press, 1991).

4. These institutions are beginning to look seriously at this issue, however. See, for example, Real Miller's OECD booklet and Organization for Economic Cooperation and Development, *Employment and Growth in the Knowledge-Based Economy* (Paris: OECD, 1996).

5. Leonard-Barton, *Wellsprings of Knowledge*, 171.

6. See, for example, D.J. Teece, *The Multinational Corporation and the Resource Cost of International Technology Transfer* (Cambridge, Mass.: Ballinger Publishing Co., 1976).

7. Joseph Badaracco, Jr., *The Knowledge Link*, 5.

8. See M. Gibbons et. al., *The New Production of Knowledge* (London: Sage, 1996) for recent thinking in this field.

9. Doug Smith and Robert C. Alexander, *Fumbling the Future* (New York: William Morrow, 1988).

10. Nonaka and Takeuchi, *The Knowledge-Creating Company,* 181.

11. Leonard-Barton, *Wellsprings of Knowledge,* 63–64.

12. Ibid., 59.

13. Nonaka and Takeuchi, *The Knowledge-Creating Company,* 99.

14. Information about IDEO comes from Robert Sutton and Andrew Hardagon, "Brainstorming Groups in Context: Effectiveness in a Product Design Firm," *Administrative Science Quarterly* 41, no. 4 (1996): 685–718 and conversations with the authors.

15. Stuart Kaufman's *At Home in the Universe* (New York: Oxford University Press, 1996) and John Holland's *Hidden Order* (Reading, Mass.: Addison-Wesley, 1966) are good places to pursue these ideas.

16. Richard H. Thaler, *The Winner's Curse* (Princeton, N.J.: Princeton University Press, 1997).

17. Quoted in Leonard-Barton, *Wellsprings of Knowledge,* 29.

18. Leonard-Barton, *Wellsprings of Knowledge,* 31, 260.

19. Quoted in Nonaka and Takeuchi, *The Knowledge-Creating Company,* 79.

20. A school of strategic thinking often called the resource-based theory of the firm provides much of the strategic and economic focus for what we are saying here. See, for example, Edith Penrose, *The Theory of the Growth of the Firm,* 2d. ed. (New York: Oxford University Press, 1995) and Cynthia Montgomery, ed., *The Resource-Based Theory of the Firm* (Boston: Kluwer, 1995).

21. See Nitin Nohria and Robert Eccles, *Networks and Organizations* (Boston: Harvard Business School Press, 1994) for an excellent summary of recent thinking regarding networks in organizations.

22. David Krackhardt and Jeffrey Hanson, "Informal Networks: The Company behind the Chart," *Harvard Business Review* (July–August, 1993): 104–111, and Erik von Hippel, *The Sources of Innovation* (New York: Oxford University Press, 1988).

Chapter 4

1. Sidney G. Winter, "Knowledge and Competence as Strategic Assets," in *The Competitive Challenge* ed. D.J. Teece (Cambridge, Mass.: Ballinger, 1987), 170.

2. The classic works on this subject are Michael Polanyi's *The Tacit Dimension* (New York: Doubleday, 1957) and *Personal Knowledge* (Chicago: University of Chicago Press, 1984).

3. There is a voluminous and somewhat vituperative literature on the subject of whether tacit knowledge can be effectively captured, since it is at the heart of the debate about artificial intelligence. We are ill equipped technically to enter this fray. For some representative arguments pro and con, see Peter Baumgartner and Sabine Payr, eds., *Speaking Minds* (Princeton, N.J.: Princeton University

Press, 1995) and Stephen Graubard, ed., *The AI Debate* (Cambridge, Mass.: MIT Press, 1988).

4. Carol Hildebrand, "Guiding Principles," *CIO,* July 1995.

5. There is specific software available for mapping knowledge routes and flows. IBM's network analyzer, Aegis, and Blue Marble are examples.

6. Thomas H. Davenport, "Some Principles of Knowledge Management," *Strategy and Business* (Winter 1996), reprint no. 96105.

7. Hildebrand, "Guiding Principles," 6.

8. *The Economist,* April 20, 1996. Reprinted in *World Press Review* (July 1996).

9. Karl E. Weick, *Sensemaking in Organizations* (Thousand Oaks, Calif.: Sage Publications, 1995), 127.

10. See his *Dynamic Memory* (Cambridge University Press, 1982) and, with R. Abelson, *Scripts, Plans, Goals, and Understanding* (Hillsdale, N.J.: Lawrence Erlbaum, Inc., 1977).

11. D. McLoskey, *Rhetoric and Explanation in Economics* (Cambridge University Press, 1993); Robert Eccles and Nitin Nohria, with James Berkley, *Beyond the Hype: Rediscovering the Essence of Management* (Boston: Harvard Business School Press, 1992).

12. Weick, *Sensemaking in Organizations,* 60–61.

13. Cited in Dorothy Leonard-Barton, *Wellsprings of Knowledge* (Boston: Harvard Business School Press, 1995), 171.

14. Interview with Gordon Petrash and Thomas Stewart, "Your Company's Most Valuable Asset: Intellectual Capital," *Fortune,* October 3, 1994.

15. For a discussion of this issue, see Thomas H. Davenport, "Saving IT's Soul: Human-Centered Information Management," *Harvard Business Review* (March–April 1994): 122–123.

16. In *Speaking Minds,* 307.

Chapter 5

1. David V. Gibson and Everett M. Rogers, *R&D Collaboration on Trial* (Boston: Harvard Business School Press, 1994). The subject of technology transfer at MCC is described in Chapter 5; technology transfer at Sematech is described on pages 521–527.

2. Memorandum from Jeff Conklin to Craig Fields cited in Gibson and Rogers, *R&D Collaboration on Trial,* 326.

3. Marilyn Redmond, interview with authors, Sematech, Austin, Tex., May 1996.

4. Alan M. Webber, "What's So New About the New Economy?" *Harvard Business Review* (January–February 1993): 28.

5. An interesting study on this subject comes from Ronald Purser, William Passmore, and Ramakrishnan Tenkasi, "The Influence of Deliberations on

Learning in New Product Development Teams," *Journal of Engineering and Technology Management* 9, no. 2 (1992): 1–28.

6. "How Japan Remembers," *The Economist,* April 20, 1996, 52.

7. Britton Monasco and Lewis Perelman, "Booz Allen's Global Knowledge Strategy," *Knowledge Inc.* 1, no. 1 (1996): 4.

8. IBM Consulting Group, "The Learning Organization: Managing Knowledge for Business Success" (The Economist Intelligence Unit, New York, 1996), 108–109.

9. Gerald T. O'Conner et al., "A Regional Intervention to Improve the Hospital Mortality Associated with Coronary Artery Bypass Graff Surgery," *Journal of the American Medical Association* (March 20, 1996): 841–845.

10. David Kanouse and Itzhak Jacoby, "When Does Information Change Practitioners' Behavior?" *International Journal of Technology Assessment in Health Care* 7, no. 2 (1988): 30.

11. Thomas Allen, "People and Technology Transfer," The International Center for Research on the Management of Technology, August 1990, 5.

12. Information about 3M's culture is drawn from interviews with 3M managers in Austin, Texas, and "The Learning Organization," 41–44.

Chapter 6

1. Christopher Bartlett, "Managing Knowledge and Learning at McKinsey & Company" (Harvard Business School case study, 1996).

2. Tom Peters, *Liberation Management* (New York: Knopf, 1992), 408.

3. Dorothy Leonard-Barton, *Wellsprings of Knowledge* (Boston: Harvard Business School Press, 1995).

4. We learned about the Owens-Corning situation through interviews with the firm's managers and in Nancy Lemon, "Climbing the Value Chain," *Online* 20, no. 6 (November–December 1996): 1–3.

5. We have argued this before in an article called "Blow Up the Corporate Library," *International Journal of Information Management* (Winter 1993): 405–412.

6. Homa Bahrami, "The Emerging Flexible Organization: Perspectives from Silicon Valley," in *Knowledge Management and Organizational Design,* ed. Paul S. Myers (Boston: Butterworth-Heinemann, 1996), 64–65.

Chapter 7

1. On expert systems in business, see Edward Feigenbaum, Pamela McCorduck, and H.P. Nii, *The Rise of the Expert Company* (New York: Times Books, 1988); on case-based reasoning, see Janet Kolodner, *Case-Based Reasoning* (San Mateo, Calif.: Morgan Kaufman Publishers, 1993).

2. Robert L. Sproull, "Foreword," in Paul Harmon and David King, *Expert Systems: Artificial Intelligence in Business* (New York: Wiley, 1985), ix.

3. Harmon and King, *Expert Systems,* 1–2.

4. Quoted by Theodore Roszak in "The Virtual Duck and the Endangered Nightingale," *Digital Media,* June 5, 1995, 68–74.

5. Kolodner, *Case-Based Reasoning,* 563.

6. Grandon Gill, "Early Expert Systems: Where Are They Now?" *MIS Quarterly* 19, no. 1 (March 1995): 51–81.

7. M. Mehler, "Boeing Leaves Past Behind with Production Redesign," *Investors Business Daily,* May 23, 1995, A8.

8. In the interest of full disclosure, Thomas H. Davenport is a director of Inference Corporation.

9. Bruce Arnold, "Expert System Tools Optimizing Help Desks," *Software Magazine* 13, no. 1 (January 1993).

10. For a discussion of these tools, see J. Conklin and M.L. Begelman, "gIBIS: A Hypertext Tool for Exploratory Policy and Discussion," *Proceedings of the 1988 Conference on Computer-Supported Cooperative Work* (Portland, Or., 1988), n.p.

Chapter 8

1. Dave DeLong and Michael Beers participated in this research project as well. Both of them wrote drafts of working papers from which we draw in this chapter.

2. The broader project was called "Managing the Knowledge of the Organization" and is managed by Ernst & Young's Center for Business Innovation in Boston. Fifteen companies sponsored this program in 1996.

3. The information about Texas Instruments is from Ikujiro Nonaka and Hirotaka Takeuchi, *The Knowledge-Creating Company* (New York: Oxford University Press, 1995).

4. Lynne Zucker, "The Role of Institutionalism in Cultural Persistence," in *The New Institutionalism in Organizational Analysis,* ed. Walter W. Powell and Paul J. Dimaggio (University of Chicago Press, 1991), 83–107. See also Cyert and March, *A Behavioral Theory of the Firm,* 2d ed. (Cambridge, Mass.: Blackwell, 1992) for a discussion of organizational learning.

5. Thomas H. Davenport with Larry Prusak, *Information Ecology: Mastering the Information and Knowledge Environments* (New York: Oxford University Press, 1997).

6. For an attempt to relate learning and financial performance, see Robert Kaplan and David Norton, *The Balanced Scorecard* (Boston: Harvard Business School Press, 1996).

7. Randy Russell, "Providing Access: The Difference between Sharing Infor-

mation or Just Reporting," *Information Strategy: The Executive Journal* 12, no. 2 (Winter 1996): 28–33.

8. Thomas H. Davenport, Sirkka Jarvenpaa, and Michael C. Beers, "Improving Knowledge Work Processes," *Sloan Management Review* (Summer 1996): 53–65.

9. Many of these studies are reported in Thomas J. Allen, *Managing the Flow of Technology* (Cambridge, Mass.: MIT Press, 1977).

Chapter 9

1. In operations research circles, this is known as a "seed, select, and amplify" approach.

2. For an example of what can happen when knowledge is lacking in financial services, see Chris Marshall, Larry Prusak, and David Shpilberg, "Financial Risk and the Need for Superior Knowledge Management," *California Management Review* 38, no. 3 (Spring 1996): 77–102.

3. Information about the Texas Instruments example came from discussions with company managers and from the firm's "Information Technology Award Nomination Information Document" (ComputerWorld Smithsonian Awards, TI Office of Best Practices, January 1997).

4. Peter Senge, *The Fifth Discipline: The Art and Practice of the Learning Organization* (New York: Doubleday/Currency, 1990). Senge's arguments about knowledge management are also available in a videotape, *Creating Transformational Knowledge* (Cambridge, Mass.: Pegasus Communications, 1996).

5. James G. March, *A Primer on Decision Making* (New York: Free Press, 1997), 27.

6. This "dialogue/decision process" is described in detail in Barabba's book *Meeting of the Minds* (Boston: Harvard Business School Press, 1995).

7. Leif Edvinsson and Michael Malone, *Intellectual Capital* (New York: HarperCollins, 1997).

8. Microsoft's Chief Financial Officer, Mike Brown, argued against such changes in an address to the "Knowledge Imperative" conference, Ernst & Young–Strategic Issues Forum, San Diego, California, December 10, 1996.

9. For a useful categorization of cultural types, see Edgar Schein, "Three Cultures of Management: The Key to Organizational Learning," *Sloan Management Review* (Fall 1996): 9–21.

Index

Accounting, as focus for beginning knowledge management, 171–172
Acquisition of knowledge, 53–56
"Action," and knowledge, 2
Adaptation, knowledge generated through, 62–65
Aeschylus, 5
Akers, John, 90–91
Allen, Thomas, 98, 159
Altruism, and price of knowledge, 33–34
American Airlines, xii
American Express, 137
Analog Devices, 16
Andersen Consulting, 58, 121, 132, 133, 167, 171
  and knowledge management jobs, 110
  and Knowledge Xchange repository, 7, 121, 132, 166
Apple Computer, 50, 59
Aristotle, ix
Artificial intelligence, 125–128, 140–141
Artificial scarcity, and knowledge markets, 43–44
Assignees, 89–90, 100–101
AT&T, xii
  and purchase of NCR, 54

Badaracco, Joseph, Jr., 56
Barabba, Vince, 171
Beliefs and values, and knowledge, 11–12
Best practices, as focus for beginning knowledge management, 167–169
Boeing, 63, 127, 138
Bold Beranek & Newman, 133
Bonfire of the Vanities, 32
Booz, Allen & Hamilton, 96, 119
Boston Harbor tunnel project, and New Zealand tunnelers, 99

Boundary spanners, 98–99. *See also* Brokers
British Petroleum, 64, 99
  Andrew Project of, 22
  knowledge management principles reflected by Virtual Teamwork Program, 24
  lessons learned through Virtual Teamwork Program, 23–24
  and "Thief of the Year" award, 53
  Virtual Teamwork Program of, 19–24, 35, 39, 45, 72, 77, 128, 149, 155
Broad knowledge repositories, 130–137
Broderbund, and Gizmo Tapper 586 LC, 139
Brokers, 98–99, 168
  and knowledge markets, 29–30
Brown and Root, 22
Browne, John, 19, 23
Brownian motion theory of knowledge exchange, 91
Buckman Laboratories, 114, 116, 121, 130, 156, 158
Business firm, definition of, 13
Buyers, and knowledge markets, 28

Canon, 64
Case examples
  British Petroleum Virtual Teamwork Program, 19–24
  Hewlett-Packard, 123–125
  Javelin Development Corporation, 41–42
  Microsoft's knowledge map, 74–77
  Monsanto's Knowledge Management Architecture, 85–87
  3M, 104–106
Case-based reasoning (CBR), xiv

189

Case-based reasoning (CBR) *(continued)*
   applications of, 138–139
   technology of, 127–128
Chaparral Steel, 109
ChaseManhattan Bank, 77
   and ATMs, 16
Chemical Bank. *See* Chase Manhattan
   Bank
Chevron, 168
Chief knowledge officer (CKO), 114–122
   personal characteristics of, 116–117
   reporting relationships of, 117–118
   tasks and responsibilities of, 114–116
Chief learning officer, 114, 118
Chrysler Corporation, and "Engineering
   Books of Knowledge," 7, 18, 34,
   132, 158
Citibank, 39
   and ATMs, 16
Citicorp, 168
Clarity of vision and language, as factor
   for success, 158
Clough, Arthur Hugh, 25
Coca-Cola, 16, 119, 169
   and knowledge management jobs, 110
Common ground, and knowledge trans-
   fer, 97–100
Common sense about knowledge man-
   agement, 162–164
Communities of practice, and knowledge
   markets, 38–39
Company Watch, 133
Compaq, 139
Comparison, and knowledge, 6
CompuServe, 130
Computer networks and knowledge
   exchange, 18–19
Connections, and knowledge, 6
Consequences, and knowledge, 6
Constraint-based systems, 137–138
Consultants
   and knowledge management, 163
   as rented knowledge, 7
Consumer Reports, 40
Conversation, and knowledge, 6
Coopers & Lybrand, 119, 132
Core competencies, ix, 64
"Core rigidities," 64

Corporate asset, knowledge as, 12–19
Corporate coherence, and knowledge
   markets, 49
Corporate knowledge, ix
Corporate librarians, as knowledge
   brokers, 29
Corporate Memory Systems, 142
Corporate size, and knowledge manage-
   ment, 17–18
Creative abrasion, 61
"Creative chaos," 60
Cross, John, 20
CSIRO, 57, 94
Cultural mismatch, as barrier to technol-
   ogy transfer, 98
Customer Support Consortium, 139

Dai-Ichi Pharmaceuticals, 46, 92
Data, definition of, 2–3
Data management, evaluating, 2
Data mining, 141
Decision makers, and politics, 170
Decision making, as focus for beginning
   knowledge management, 170–
   171
Dedicated resources, knowledge genera-
   tion through, 58–59
Demerest, Mark, 118
DeSimone, Livio, 105
Dialog, 130
Digital Equipment Corporation, 44, 50,
   63, 137, 138
Dow Chemical, xiii, 85, 114, 116, 119,
   157
Downsizing
   and knowledge scarcity, 43–44
   and sharing knowledge, 154
Drew, Dick, and Scotch tape, 105
Drucker, Peter, xiii, 2, 4
Dun & Bradstreet, 133

EC, 55
Eccles, Bob, 81
Economics, as lens to see organizations,
   27
Economics or industry value, link to, as
   factor for success, 156–157
EDS, 119

Education and position, and knowledge
    markets, 36–37
Edvinsson, Leif, 116, 119, 171
EL Products, 55, 83
Electronic knowledge "yellow pages,"
    45, 77, 148
Embedded knowledge, 83
Emerson, Ralph Waldo, 52
Erikson, Erik, 34
Ernst & Young, xiii, 77, 94, 111, 116,
    119–120, 132, 145, 156, 158
    and Center for Business Innovation,
    58,
    and Center for Business Knowledge,
    111
    and knowledge management jobs, 110
Executives, questioning own knowledge,
    61–62
Experience, and knowledge, 78
Expert systems, ix, 120, 125–128, 137
Experts, 7–8, 136, 148
Explicit knowledge, evaluating, 84–85
External knowledge, as type of knowl-
    edge repository, 146

Face time, and U.S. Army, 35, 100, 159
Face-to-face meetings, and knowledge
    transfer, 94–95, 159
FASB, 55
Fast Company magazine, 16
Federal Drug Administration, xiv
Fidelity Investments, 141
Fifth Discipline, The, 169
Focused knowledge environments, 137–
    138
Ford, x, 14, 133
Fortune magazine, xiii, 14
France, 16
Franklin, Benjamin, ix
Frictions, most common, 96–97
Fry, Art, and Post-It Notes, 105
Fusion, knowledge generated through,
    59–62

Gatekeepers, 98–99. See also Brokers
GATT, 55
General Electric, 118
General Motors, 121, 171

Gibson, David V., 89
GrapeVINE, 125, 133, 147
Grapevine Technologies, 133
Graphical Issue-Based Information Sys-
    tem, 142
Greek Agora, 46
Grimes, 55, 83
Ground truth, 82
    and knowledge, 8–9
Guare, John, 74

Haiti, 8
Hewlett-Packard, xii, xiv, 27, 82–83, 120,
    121, 123–125, 133, 136, 138, 139,
    144, 155, 157
    and Connex, 124
    and Electronic Sales Partner (ESP) sys-
    tem, 123–124, 147
    and knowledge management jobs, 110,
    113
    and Trainer's Trading Post, 147
Hirshberg, Gerald, 60, 62
Hoeschst, 57
Hoeschst-Celanese, 66–67
Hoffmann-LaRoche, xiv, 113
    and knowledge map, 73
    Right First Time knowledge project of,
    69
Honda, 69
Hoover, 133
Hughes Aerospace, 28
Hughes Communications Knowledge
    Highway, 73
Hughes Space and Communications, 71
Huxley, Thomas Henry, 162
Hypertext Markup Language (HTML),
    134

IBM, xii, 14, 81, 90–91, 171
    and purchase of Lotus, 53
    and purchase of ROLM, 56
IBM Consulting, xiii, 58, 110, 119
IBM Global Services, 77
IBM's Deep Blue, 84
Ideas, and potential for growth, 17
IDEO, 61
Illusions of accuracy, 9–10
Individual Inc., 133

Industry-university consortia, 56–57

Inference Corporation, and CBR tools, 139

Informal internal knowledge, as type of knowledge repository, 146

Informal networks, and knowledge markets, 37–38

Information
definition of, 3–5
incompleteness of, 40

Information management, quantitative measures of, 4

Information technology, 4
using wisely, 45–46

Innovation, 60

Insights, xii
and knowledge, 2

International Harvester, x

Internet, x, 4, 18, 39, 47, 78, 130, 131

Intuition, and rules of thumb, 10–11

IRS, 3

Jacoby, Itzhak, 98, 102

Japan, corporate structure of, 92

Java, 173

Javelin Development Corporation, 41–42

Jet Propulsion Laboratory, 177

Jobs, Steve, 50, 59

Johnson, Jerry, 16

Judgment, 10

Junkins, Jerry, 167

Kaka, Ryuzaburo, 64

Kanouse, David, 98, 102

Kao, 49

Kerr, Steve, 118–119

Knowledge
in action, 6–12
and the anti-intellectual society, 174
asymmetry of, 40–41
codifying different types of, 70
compared to atomic particle, 5–6
and complexity, 9–10
as corporate asset, 12–19
definition of, 5
embedded, 83
and experience, 7–8
and ground truth, 8–9
how managed, xii
and judgment, 10
kinds of, 95–96
localness of, 41
mapping of, 72–80
modeling of, 80
and rules of thumb and intuition, 10–11
as sustainable competitive advantage, 15–17
and values and beliefs, 11–12
a working definition of, 1–6

Knowledge access and transfer, 148–149

Knowledge boom, ix

Knowledge brokers. See Brokers

Knowledge chart, 133

Knowledge codification
basic principles of, 68–72
and coordination, 68–87

Knowledge components, and Solution-Builder, 139–140

Knowledge consulting, ix

Knowledge-Creating Company, The, xiii, 19, 52, 60

Knowledge engineering, 128

Knowledge engineers, 111

Knowledge environment, 149–150

Knowledge exchange and computer networks, 18–19

Knowledge fairs and open forums, 93–95

Knowledge generation, 52–67
acquisition, 53–58
adaptation, 62–65
dedicated resources, 58–59
fusion, 59–62
networking, 65–67

Knowledge in systems, codifying, 84–87

Knowledge management, xiv
and consultants, 163
and corporate size, 17–18
common sense about, 162–164
a decision-oriented approach to, 169
five principles of, 62
getting started in, 164
leveraging existing approaches to, 165–172
leading with accounting, 171–172

leading with decision making, 170–171

leading with organizational learning, 169–170

leading with quality/reengineering/best practices efforts, 167–169

leading with technology, 166–167

selecting the right anchor, 172

pitfalls of, 172–177

pragmatics of, 162–178

technologies for, 123–143

artificial intelligence, 125–128

broad knowledge repositories, 130–137

case-based reasoning (CBR), 127–128

constraint-based systems, 137–138

expert systems, 125–128

focused knowledge environments, 137–138

implementing, 128–130

limitations of, 141–143

longer-term analysis systems, 140–141

real-time knowledge systems, 138–140

Knowledge management principles reflected by Virtual Teamwork Program of British Petroleum, 24

Knowledge management projects

in practice, 144–161

success in, 151–153

primary attributes used to define, 151

types of, 145–151

knowledge access and transfer, 148–149

knowledge environment, 149–150

knowledge repositories, 146–148

projects with multiple characteristics, 150–151

Knowledge management tools, key dimensions of, 129–130

Knowledge management workers, 109–112

Knowledge manager, 147, 163, 174

Knowledge map, 72–73, 165

assembling, 73–74

example of, 74

Knowledge markets, xii

developing, 45–48

inefficiencies of, 39–42

pathologies of, 43–45

artificial scarcity, 43–44

monopolies, 43

trade barriers, 44–45

payment scenario for, 31

peripheral benefits of, 48–50

political economy of, 27–30

brokers, 29–30

buyers, 28

sellers, 28–29

price system of, 30–36

promise and challenge of, 25–51

recognizing, 26

signals of, 36–39

trust as essential condition of, 35

value of, creating and defining, 47–48

Knowledge "movement," x

Knowledge-oriented culture, as factor for success, 153–155

Knowledge-oriented personnel, 108–109

Knowledge problem, not expecting software to solve, 26

Knowledge project manager, activities performed, 112–113

Knowledge projects

differences among, 160–161

factors leading to success with, 153–160

clarity of vision and language, 158

knowledge-oriented culture, 153–155

a link to economics or industry value, 156–157

a modicum of process orientation, 157

multiple channels for knowledge transfer, 159

nontrivial motivational aids, 158

senior management support, 156

some level of knowledge structure, 159

technical and organizational infrastructure, 155–156

194   **Index**

Knowledge repositories, 146–148
  market value of, 166
  types of, 146
Knowledge roles and skills, 107–122
  chief knowledge officer (CKO), 114–122
  knowledge management workers, 109–112
  knowledge-oriented personnel, 108–109
  managers of knowledge projects, 112–114
Knowledge sharing versus knowledge hoarding, 28–29
Knowledge stock, 49–50
Knowledge structure, as factor for success, 159
Knowledge technologies, implementing, 128–130
Knowledge transfer, 88–106
  and common ground, 97–100
  culture of, 96–104
  and face-to-face meetings, 94–95
  multiple channels for as factor for success, 159
  and organization size, 89
  and physical proximity, 100
  and shared language, 98–99
  strategies for, 89–97
    knowledge fairs and open forums, 93–95
    talk rooms, 92–93
    water coolers, 90–91
  and talk rooms, 92–93
  and trust, 97–100
  and velocity and viscosity, 102–104
  and water coolers, 90–91

Land, Edwin, 50
Latin America, 74
Learning organization, ix
Lee Jeans, 16
Leonard-Barton, Dorothy, xiii, 52, 55, 60, 61, 64, 102, 109
Lexis/Nexis, 130
Lincoln National Life, 120, 121
Loder Drew & Associates, 15
Loder, Richard, 15
Longer-term analysis systems, 140–141

Lotus Development, 81
Lotus Notes, xi, 4, 18, 53, 77, 86, 87, 92, 96, 109, 115, 123–126, 131, 132, 134136, 142, 147, 155, 159, 166, 168, 173
Lumley, Ted, 80, 103

Macintosh, 59
MacPherson, C.B., 34
Managers of knowledge projects, 112–114
  functions performed, 112–113
Mapping knowledge, 72–80
  politics of, 79–80
  technology of, 77–79
March, James, 27, 38, 41, 170
Marketplaces, building, 46–47
Marx, Karl, 27
Massachusetts General Hospital Molecular Biological Institute, 57
Matsushita Electric, Ltd., 15, 19
  and automatic breadmaking machine, 60–61
Matsushita, Konosuke, 15
McCloskey, Donald (Deidre), 81
McDonald's, 58
McDonnell Douglas Corporation, 63, 126–127
McDonnell, John F., 63
McKinsey & Company, xiii, 77, 108, 110, 156, 158
McLuhan, Marshall, 4
Medium Is the Message, The, 4
Merck, 58
Meritocracy of ideas, and knowledge markets, 49
Message, as "information," 3
Microelectronics and Computer Corporation (MCC), 89, 100–101, 142
Microsoft, 14, 54
  and SPUD project, 74–77, 149
Microsoft Office, 166
Mill, John Stuart, 27
Minsky, Marvin, 126
Mizukami, Tomiaki, 15
Mobil Exploration and Producing, 80
Mobil Oil, 27, 103–104
Modeling knowledge, and variables affected by management action, 80
Monopolies, and knowledge markets, 43

Monsanto, 65, 119, 169
  Knowledge Management Architecture
    project of, 85–87
Motorola, 58

Narratives, value of, 81–83
National Cooperative Research Act of
  1984, 57
National Semiconductor, 136
NationsBank, and "Project Agora," 46
NCR, and purchase by AT&T, 54, 56
NEC, 15
Netscape, 173
Networks, 3
  knowledge generated through, 65–67
Neural networks, 140–141
NewsPage, 133
Nietzsche, Friedrich, 88
Nissan Design International, 60
Nohria, Nitin, 81
Nonaka, Ikujiro, xiii, 12, 19, 43, 49, 52,
  60, 61, 98
Nontrivial motivational aids, as factor for
  success, 158
Northwestern University, 11
NYNEX, 29

OECD, 55
Olsen, Ken, 44, 50
On-line thesaurus, 134, 135, 159
On-line yellow pages, 45, 77, 148
OneSource Information Services, 133
Organization culture, and knowledge
  management initiatives, 155
Organization size, and knowledge trans-
  fer, 89
Organizational chart versus knowledge
  map, 72
Organizational knowledge, 12
  as focus for beginning knowledge man-
    agement, 171–172
  harmonizing, not homogenizing, 86
  studies of, xiii
Owens-Corning, and "Knowledge Re-
  source Center," 111

Peetz, John, 116, 119
People, roles of in knowledge technologies, 129

PeopleSoft, 77, 139
Personal Internet Newspaper, 133
Peters, Tom, 108
Petrash, Gordon, 85, 116, 119
Physical proximity, and knowledge trans-
  fer, 100
PIMS method, 55
Plato, ix
Platt, Lew, xii
Polanyi, Michael, 71
Polaroid, 50
Polavision, 50
Political science, as lens to see organiza-
  tions, 27
Position and education, and knowledge
  markets, 36–37
Post-It Notes, 105
Pragmatics of knowledge management,
  162–178
Price system of knowledge markets, 30–
  36
  altruism, 33–34
  reciprocity, 32
  repute, 32–33
  trust, 34–36
Price Waterhouse, 132
Primus corporation, 139
Process orientation, as factor for success,
  157
Product and service, convergence of, 13–
  15
Prusak, Larry, childhood story of, 71, 81

Quality movement, x
Quality program, as focus for beginning
  knowledge management, 167–169
Quinn, James Brian, 14

R&D departments, 58
Raychem, and Internal Information Inter-
  view Network, 96
Real-time knowledge systems, 138–140
Reciprocity, and price of knowledge, 32
Redundancy, 43
Reengineering, and knowledge market in-
  frastructure, 45
Reengineering program, as focus for be-
  ginning knowledge management,
  167–169

Rental of knowledge, 56–58
Repute, and price of knowledge, 32–33
"Requisite variety," 60
"Resolve," and knowledge, 2
Restrac, 77
Resumix, 77
Reuters, 139
Rodgers, Dave, 134
Rogers, Everett M., 89
ROLM, 56
Roman Forum, 46
Romer, Paul, xiii, 17
Rosenblum, Judith, 119
Rudd, Nick, 118, 121, 150
Rules of thumb and intuition, 10–11
Rwanda, 8

Sandia National Laboratories, 44
Sandpoint Systems, 133
SAP software package, 57, 77
Schank, Roger, 11, 81
Schoeffler, Sid, 55
Search-and-retrieval knowledge manage-
    ment, 134–135
Sears, 63
Seemann, Patricia, 69
Sellers, and knowledge markets, 28–
    29
Sematech, 89–90, 149, 152
Senco Products, 69
Senge, Peter, 169
Senior management support, as factor for
    success, 156
Sensemaking in Organizations, 9
Sequent Computer, 118, 120, 147
    and Knowledge Depot, 134
Sequent Corporate Electronic Library
    (SCEL), 134
Service and product, convergence of, 13–
    15
Shared language, as essential to knowl-
    edge transfer, 98–99
Sharing knowledge, and downsizing, 154
Sharp, 59
Silicon Graphics, 147
Simon, Herbert A., 41
Six Degrees of Separation, 74
Skandia, 114, 116, 119, 120, 149, 171

Skill sharing, and coronary-artery bypass
    surgery, 97–98
Skillview, 78
Slack time for learning and thinking, im-
    portance of, 93
SMART (Support Management Auto-
    mated Reasoning Technology), 139
"Snowball sample," 73–74
Social Security Administration, 3
Sociology, as lens to see organizations,
    27
SolutionBuilder, 139–140
Somalia, 8
Standard Life, 65
Stasey, Robert, 16
Status of the knower, 100–101
Steelcase, 14
Stewart, Tom, xiii
Strategy focus, ix
Structured internal knowledge, as type of
    knowledge repository, 146
Stupidity, cost of, 170
Sturgeon, Theodore, 62, 64
Success Factor Systems, 78
Success in knowledge management proj-
    ects, primary attributes used to
    define, 151
Sun Microsystem, 147
Sustainable competitive advantage, 15–17

Tacit knowledge
    capturing, 81–83
    and codification, 70–72
Takeuchi, Hirotaka, xiii, 12, 19, 43, 49,
    52, 60, 61, 98
Talk rooms, and knowledge transfer, 92–
    93
Talk, value of, 39
Taurus design team, x
"Techknowledgy," 123
Technical and organizational infrastruc-
    ture, as factor for success, 155–156
Technical communicators, 111
Technologies limitations, 141–143
Technology, as focus for beginning knowl-
    edge management, 167–169
Teltech Resource Network Corporation,
    136, 148, 150, 154, 159

Texas Instruments, 157
  and "Not Invented Here, but I Did It
    Anyway" award, 53, 168
  and Office of Best Practices, 167–168
  and "Share Fair," 46, 168
  and TI Business Excellence Standard
    (TI-BEST), 167
3M, 14, 104–106
Time, 74
Time Life Information Center, 74, 79
Timex, 27
Tolstoy, Leo, 9
Trade barriers, and knowledge markets,
  44–45
Trafalgar House, 22
Trajecta, 141
Transfer = transmission + absorption
  (and use), 101–102
Trilogy Development Group, 138
Trust
  and knowledge transfer, 97–100
  and price of knowledge, 34–36
TWA Flight 800, 131

Ungson, Geraldo, 49
U.S. Army
  and After Action Review (AAR) pro-
    gram, 8, 171
  and Center for Army Lessons Learned
    (CALL), 8, 100
  and face time, 35, 100, 159
U.S. GDP, and changing global economy,
  13

Values and beliefs, and knowledge, 11–12
Veblen, Thorstein, 27
Velocity and viscosity, and knowledge
  transfer, 102–104
Verifone, 82–83
VF, 16
Vietnam War, 8
Virtual offices, 91

Virtual Teamwork Program of British
  Petroleum, 19–24

Wal-Mart, 63, 64–65
Walsh, James, 49
Wang, An, 50
Wang Labortories, 50, 63
War and Peace, 9
"War stories," 82
Ward, Arian, 28, 71–72, 73
Water coolers and knowledge transfer,
  90–91
Webber, Alan, 14, 16, 90–91
Weick, Karl, 9, 11, 81, 82
"Well stolen is half done," 53, 168
Wellsprings of Knowledge, xiii, 52, 102
White, Harrison, 27
Williams, Ted, 71, 81
Winter, Sidney, xiii, 13, 70
"Wisdom," and knowledge, 2
Wolfe, Tom, 32
Work environment, changes in, 56
Workforce diversity, 60
Workforce morale, and knowledge mar-
  kets, 49
World Bank, 101
World Wide Web, x, 86, 109, 115, 123–
  126, 130–133, 135, 136, 142, 143,
  155, 159, 166, 168, 173
Wunderman Cato Johnson, 118, 121

Xerox, 14, 139
Xerox Palo Alto Research Center
  (PARC), 58, 59
  and graphical interface computer,
    59

Young & Rubicam, 118, 119, 121, 150,
  154

Zadeh, Lofti, 87
Zildjian cymbal company, 16

Other Books by Thomas H. Davenport and Laurence Prusak

THOMAS H. DAVENPORT

Cyrus F. Gibson and Barbara Bund Jackson, with contributions by Thomas H. Davenport, *The Information Imperative: Managing the Impact of Technology on Businesses and People* (1987)

Thomas H. Davenport, *Process Innovation: Reengineering Work through Information Technology* (1993)

Thomas H. Davenport, *Mission Critical: Realizing the Promise of Enterprise Systems* (2000)

Donald A. Marchand, Thomas H. Davenport, and Tim Dickson, Editors, *Mastering Information Management* (2000)

LAURENCE PRUSAK

Laurence Prusak with James McGee, *Managing Information Strategically* (1994)

Knowledge in Organizations, Editor (1997)

THOMAS H. DAVENPORT AND LAURENCE PRUSAK

Thomas H. Davenport with Laurence Prusak, *Information Ecology: Mastering the Information and Knowledge Environment* (1997)

About the Authors

THOMAS H. DAVENPORT is Director of the Accenture Institute for Strategic Change, a research center in Cambridge, Massachusetts. He is also a Distinguished Scholar in Residence at Babson College. His most recent book, *The Attention Economy: Understanding the New Currency of Business* (coauthored with John C. Beck) was published in 2001. The hardcover edition of *Working Knowledge* and his book, *Process Innovation: Reengineering Work through Information Technology*, were bestsellers. He is also the author of *Mission Critical: Realizing the Promise of Enterprise Systems, Information Ecology: Mastering the Information and Knowledge Environment*, and coauthor of *Reengineering the Organization: Transforming to Compete in the Information Economy*.

LAURENCE PRUSAK is a Managing Principal with IBM Global Services and is the Founder and Executive Director of the IBM Institute for Knowledge Management. He has taught in several leading universities on the topic of knowledge management and is frequently quoted in such periodicals as *Fortune, Business Week,* and *CIO.* Prusak is the coauthor of *In Good Company: How Social Capital Makes Organizations Work* (with Don Cohen) and *Managing Information Strategically* (with James McGee), and editor of *Knowledge in Organizations.* He is also published in several journals, including the *Sloan Management Review, International Journal of Information Management,* and *California Management Review.*